"THE ORIGINAL CONSUMER PRICE AUTHORITY"

Publisher: Peter Steinlauf

IMPORT CAR PRICES

TABLE OF CONTENTS

APRIL 1994　　　　　　　**VOL I2703 - 9404**

Published by:
Edmund Publications Corp.
300 N Sepulveda Suite 2050
Los Angeles, CA 90245

SBN: 87759-433-3
ISSN: 1048-9738
Library of Congress Catalog No:
78-80098

Creative
/Design Director:
Julie Finger

Copy Editor:
William Badnow

Production:
Rachel Abrash
Kevin McMillan
John Ward

Advertising Manager:
Barbara Abramson

Printed in the United States

Understanding the Language of Auto Buying

Buying a new vehicle is an expensive, confusing and sometimes frustrating experience. If you feel confused, you are not alone! The problem is that the language and terms used by dealers and manufacturers are often unclear. To assist you, here are some helpful definitions:

Dealer Cost The amount that dealers pay for a car and/or its optional accessories.

Suggested List Price The manufacturer's recommended selling price.

Destination Charge The amount charged to cover the cost of delivery from the Port of Entry or manufacturer to the dealer. This charge is passed on to the buyer without any mark-up.

Advertising Fee The amount you are charged to cover the cost of national and local advertising. This fee should be no more than 1-1½% of the suggested list price.

Dealer Charges These are highly profitable "extras" that dealers try to sell in addition to the vehicle. Items such as rustproofing, undercoating and extended warranties fall into this category. Most consumer experts do not recommend purchasing these "extras".

Manufacturer's Rebates/Dealer Incentives Programs offered by the manufacturers to increase the sales of slow-selling models or to reduce excess inventories. While manufacturer's rebates are passed directly on to the buyer, dealer incentives are passed on only to the dealer —who may or may not elect to pass the savings on to the customer.

Note: Occasionally there wll appear in the "Dealer Cost" and "Sgst'd List" columns, prices enclosed in brackets. —Example: (90). This indicates a credit or refunded amount is involved.

08594.3690 TV

ABS	—Anti-lock Braking System	
ADJ	—Adjustable or Adjuster	
AC or AIR		
COND	—Air Conditioning	
AH	—Ampere Hours	
ALT	—Alternator	
ALUM	—Aluminum	
AMP	—Amperes	
ANT	—Antenna	
APP	—Appearance	
AT	—Automatic Transmission	
AUTO	—Automatic	
AUX	—Auxiliary	
AVAIL	—Available	
BLK	—Black	
BSW or BW		
(tires)	—Black Sidewall	
CAP	—Capacity	
CASS	—Cassette	
CD	—Compact Disc	
CID	—Cubic Inch Displacement	
COL	—Column	
COMP	—Compartment	
CONV	—Convertible	
CPE	—Coupe	
CTRL	—Control	
CUST	—Custom	
CU IN	—Cubic Inches	
CYL	—Cylinder	
DFRS	—Dual Facing Rear Seats	
DIAM	—Diameter	
DK	—Dark	
DLX	—Deluxe	
DOHC	—Dual Overhead Camshaft	
DR	—Door	
DRW	—Dual Rear Wheels	
EFI	—Electronic Fuel Injection	
ELEC	—Electronic or Electronically	
ENG	—Engine	
EQUAL	—Equalizer	
EQUIP	—Equipment	
ETR	—Electronically Tuned Radio	
EX	—Except	
EXT	—Exterior	
EXTD	—Extended	
F (tires)	—Fiberglass	
F & R	—Front & Rear	
FB	—Fastback	
FI	—Fuel Injection	
FRT	—Front	
FWD	—Front Wheel Drive	
GAL	—Gallon	
GRP	—Group	
HB	—Hatchback	
HD	—Heavy Duty	
HO	—High Output	

HP	—Horsepower	
HSC	—High Swirl Combustion	
HT	—Hardtop	
HUD	—Head Up Display	
HVY	—Heavy	
ILLUM	—Illuminated or Illumination	
INC	—Includes	
INCLD	—Included	
INJ	—Injection	
INT	—Interior	
L (eng)	—Liter	
L & R	—Left & Right	
LB	—Liftback or Long Bed	
LBS	—Pounds	
LD	—Light Duty	
LH	—Left Hand	
LT	—Light	
LTD	—Limited	
LUX	—Luxury	
LWB	—Long Wheelbase	
LWR	—Lower	
MAN	—Manual	
MAX	—Maximum	
MDLS	—Models	
MED	—Medium	
MH	—Must Have	
MIN	—Minimum	
MLDGS	—Moldings	
MPI or		
MPFI	—Multi Port Fuel Injection	
MPG	—Miles Per Gallon	
MSR	—Minimum Size Required	
MT	—Manual Transmission	
NA or		
N/A	—Not Available	
NB	—Notchback	
NC	—No Charge	
NL	—Not Listed	
OD	—Overdrive	
OHC	—Overhead Camshaft	
OHV	—Overhead Valves	
OPT	—Optional	
OS	—Outside	
OWL		
(tires)	—Outline White Letter	
OZ	—Ounce	
PASS	—Passenger	
PEG	—Preferred Equipment Group	
PEP	—Preferred Equipment Package	
PERF	—Performance	
PGM FI	—Programmed Fuel Injection	
PKG	—Package	
PR	—Pair	
PREM	—Premium	
PU	—Pickup	
PWR	—Power	

QTR	—Quarter	
QTS	—Quarts	
RBL		
(tires)	—Raised Black Letters	
RDSTR	—Roadster	
REQ	—Requires	
REV	—Reverse	
RH	—Right Hand	
R or RR	—Rear	
RPM	—Revolution Per Minute	
RWD	—Rear Wheel Drive	
RWL		
(tires)	—Raised White Letters	
SB	—Short Bed	
SBR (tires)		
	—Steel Belted Radial	
SDN	—Sedan	
SEFI or		
SFI	—Sequential Electronic Fuel	
Injection		
SRS	—Supplemental Restraint System	
SOHC	—Single Overhead Camshaft	
SP or		
SPD	—Speed	
SPFI	—Sequential Port Fuel Injection	
SPKRS	—Speakers	
SPT	—Sport	
S/R	—Sunroof	
SRW	—Single Rear Wheels	
STD	—Standard	
SWB	—Short Wheelbase	
SYNC	—Synchromesh or Synchronized	
TACH	—Tachometer	
TBI	—Throttle Body Injection	
TEMP	—Temperature	
TPI	—Tuned Port Injection	
TRANS	—Transmission	
TRU	—Truck	
TW or		
T/W	—Together With	
VOL	—Volume	
W/	—With	
WB	—Wheelbase	
WGN	—Wagon	
W/O	—Without	
WSW or WW		
(tires)	—White Side Wall	
W/T	—Work Truck	
2WD	—Two Wheel Drive	
4WD	—Four Wheel Drive	
4WS	—Four Wheel Steering	
3A/4A	—3-Speed Automatic /4-Speed Automatic	
4M/5M	—4-Speed Manua /5-Speed Manual.	

To Lease or Not To Lease

by Burke Leon, Ph.D.

If Shakespeare's Hamlet was in the market for a new vehicle today, he might say: "TO LEASE OR NOT TO LEASE, THAT IS THE QUESTION !"

Even experts don't seem to be able to come up with a definitive answer as to whether it's better to lease a new vehicle or to buy (and finance) one. There are certainly advantages in leasing for the automobile dealer: and there are both pros and cons in leasing for the consumer. The fact that experts can't come up with an unequivocal answer indicates that the decision to lease or to buy/finance is either too close to call, or depends in each case on individual circumstances.

Leasing Is Good For The Dealers

Leases were introduced not to give consumers a choice about the way to pay for a vehicle but rather as a sales tool. Salespeople love leasing, because the thought of lower down payments and lower costs per month may induce you, the consumer, to close a deal today, when otherwise you might just decide to wait another year or so.

From a psychological point of view, the lease is a great sales and marketing tool. Many consumers will negotiate strongly for a vehicle when they are paying cash or buying on credit. However, when people lease a vehicle and the down payment and monthly payments are much lower than when buying, they usually will not argue as much about the price; often, they will just pay what is asked in the leasing arrangement.

Leasing suddenly becomes a way to avoid the haggling about price that we all hate. The net result is that a lease may cost you considerably more than a buy because you do not fight for the best price for your trade in, you do not get the lowest payment schedule for your leased vehicle, and you may accept a couple of high priced extras such as an upgraded radio or a theft-deterrent system simply because your payments seem so low. Thus, leasing makes it easy to surrender control of your vehicle selection; and you could get it over your head on a "better" vehicle than you could normally afford.

Leasing is also good for Detroit and Tokyo because the leasing transaction and agreement are more complicated to complete. For example, negotiation is required so that you don't get unduly penalized for the condition of the vehicle when you turn it in. If you drive a lot, you will need to work out some sort of higher mileage allowance. Furthermore, leases come in several different forms, both the open-end and closed-end variety — so many choices, so little knowledge. Most people, including experts do not understand all the aspects of leasing, and the complexity works primarily to the dealer's favor. The lease also assures dealers that you will most likely come back into the automobile market when the lease expires, which might not be the case when your car loan is payed up. Thus, when you lease you may ignore the fact that at the end of the lease term, you do not really own the vehicle...but you decide to worry about this problem later.

Your Advantages of Leasing versus Buying

In spite of the fact that leasing was "invented" as an auto industry marketihg tool, it does offer some real advantages to consumers, including the following:

1) Leasing requires a lower down payment. If you're not able to come up with the needed down payment to buy, the lower down payment on a lease may make an immediate acquisition of a new vehicle easier for you.

2) Leasing requires a lower monthly payment than buying, which may be an absolute must for you if your monthly expense budget is limited.

3) Leasing generally makes it possible for you to get a better, higher-priced vehicle than you could obtain by paying cash or by buying with short-term financing.

4) Leasing instead of buying makes it easier for you to get a new vehicle every few years.

5) Leasing can cut down on your repair worries, especially since you can usually maintaln a newer versus older vehicle by leasing rather than buying.

6) When you lease, you do not have to worry about selling the vehicle when the lease is terminated — you just give it back to the leasing company and wave goodbye.

7) If you lease, many of the costs are deferred to the tail-end of the lease, and you do not have to face them until later, when you may be more financially prepared to do so.

8) You may enjoy some benefits to leasing over buying based on the tax laws associated with your business, but the degree of any tax advantage may change from year to year with the whims of the IRS.

Your Disadvantages of Leasing versus Buying

As expected, leasing also carries some significant disadvantages when compared to buying, for example:

1) Since you don't really own a leased vehicle (unless you buy it at the end of the lease period), you can't, at any time, transfer the title by selling it, passing it on to a friend or relative, donating it to a worthy organizaton, etc.

2) Unlike when you buy a car and all the costs are incurred up front, you might be surprised by unforseen payouts at the end of the lease due to extra mileage, poor vehicle condition,a turn-in fee, etc.

3) If you drive heavy miles each year, you may find it economically better to buy a vehicle rather than to pay leasing mileage penalties at the end of your lease. (If you expect excessive mileage and still decide to lease, try to negotiate a higher mileage allowance, which may result in higher monthly payments but probably lower overall costs.)

4) Leases are not easy to get out of early . If you take a four-year lease on a sports car, and subsequently get married and have triplets, you may want to trade in the sports car for a minivan, but you may find it prohibitively expensive to do so.

Negotiating Strategy When Leasing

The single biggest problem with leasing from a negotiation point of view is that people do not fight for the best price. To get the lease, they just take whatever price is offered for the vehicle. The best way to lease a vehicle is to shop for the lowest possible payments. Do this as if you were buying the vehicle, and then lease it based on this best "sales" price. Do not give up bargaining on price }ust because you are intending to lease.

Leasing is interesting, because the salesperson often will not quote you a price for the vehicle, but only a down and monthly payment. It is your job as a consumer to shop for the lowest payments and the best set of leasing parameters. If you drive a lot, ask for a higher mileage allowance. If you are hard on a vehicle, get a relaxation on the physical condition the vehicle must have when it is turned in.

In conclusion, to get lower down payments and lower monthly payments, it may be better for you to lease than to buy but be careful not to give way on the final price of a new vehicle just to get good leasing terms.

Burke Leon, Ph.D., a noted expert in automobile buying/selling and a special contributor to Edmund's Vehicle Price Guides is the author with Stephanie Leon of the highly acclaimed book, The Insider's Guide to Buying a New or Used Car (hundreds of tips in easy to use checklist format from a veteran insider), publlshed by Betterway Books (Cincinnati, Ohio), 1993.

Suzuki 2-Door Sidekick

CODE	DESCRIPTION	DEALER	LIST

ACURA

INTEGRA

DC434R	RS 2-Dr Sport Coupe (5-spd)	12594	14670
DC444R	RS 2-Dr Sport Coupe (auto)	13238	15420
DB754R	RS 4-Dr Sedan (5-spd)	13375	15580
DB764R	RS 4-Dr Sedan (auto)	14019	16330
DC435R	LS 2-Dr Sport Coupe (5-spd)	14775	17210
DC445R	LS 2-Dr Sport Coupe (auto)	15419	17960
DB755R	LS 4-Dr Sedan (auto)	14981	17450
DB765R	LS 4-Dr Sedan (auto)	15625	18200
DC238R	GS-R 2-Dr Sport Coupe (5-spd)	16689	19440
DB858R	GS-R 4-Dr Sedan (5-spd)	17153	19980
Destination Charge: Alaska		645	645
Hawaii		215	215
Other States		365	365

Standard Equipment

INTEGRA RS COUPE: 1.8L 16-valve DOHC inline 4-cylinder engine, programmed fuel injection (PGM-FI), 5-speed manual transmission, 4-wheel independent double-wishbone suspension, front and rear stabilizer bars, variable power assisted rotary-valve rack-and-pinion steering, 4-wheel disc brakes with ventilated front discs, P195/60R1485H M & S tires, driver and front passenger air bag supplemental restraint system (SRS), side-impact door beams, side-intrusion hip pads, 3-point outboard rear seat belts, 5 mph front/rear bumpers, front and rear crumple zones, projector beam headlights (low beams), body-colored front and rear bumpers, dual-power operated door mirrors, protective body-side moldings, rear window defroster with timer, rear window wiper/washer, body-colored door handles, galvanized body panels, 3-coat/3-bake paint, driver's seat lumbar adjustment, passenger-side walk-in seat, center console with armrest, 50/50 fold-down rear seatback, rear seat divider, rear seat headrests, tilt steering wheel, power windows, AM/FM stereo cassette with 4 speakers, power-operated antenna, intermittent front wipers with mist, remote trunk/fuel-filler door releases.

LS COUPE (also has in addition to or instead of RS COUPE equipment): Michelin XGT-H4 P195/60R1485H M & S tires, anti-lock braking system (ABS), air conditioning, cruise control, power door locks, power moonroof, map light.

ACURA

GS-R COUPE (also has in addition to or instead of LS COUPE equipment): 1.8L 16-valve DOHC inline 4-cylinder engine with VTEC, knock sensor, 5-speed manual transmission with close ratios, cast aluminum alloy wheels, Michelin XGT-V4 P195/55R15 84V M & S tires, rear spoiler with integral brakelight, AM/FM stereo cassette with 6 speakers.

INTEGRA RS SEDAN: 1.8L 16-valve DOHC inline 4-cylinder engine, programmed fuel injection (PGM-FI), 5-speed manual transmission, 4-wheel independent double-wishbone suspension, front and rear stabilizer bars, variable power assisted rotary-valve rack-and-pinion steering, 4-wheel disc brakes with ventilated front discs, P195/60R14 85H M & S tires, driver and front passenger airbag supplemental restraint system (SRS), side-impact door beams, side-intrusion hip pads, side-intrusion shoulder pads, 3-point outboard seat belts (rear), 5 mph front/rear bumpers, front and rear crumple zones, child-proof rear door locks, projector beam headlights (low beams), body-colored front and rear bumpers, dual power-operated door mirrors, protective bodyside molding, rear window defroster with timer, body-colored door handles, sashless door glass, galvanized body panels, 3-coat/3-bake paint, driver seat lumbar adjustment, center console with armrest, one-piece fold-down rear seatback, rear seat headrests, seat belt height adjustment, tilt steering wheel, power windows, power door locks, AM/FM stereo cassette w/4 speakers, power-operated antenna, intermittent front wipers w/mist, remote trunk/fuel-filler door releases.

LS SEDAN (also has in addition to or instead of RS SEDAN equipment): Michelin XGT-H4 P195/60R14 85H M & S tires, anti-lock braking system (ABS), air conditioning, cruise control.

GS-R SEDAN (also has in addition to or instead of LS SEDAN equipment): 1.8L 16-valve DOHC inline 4-cylinder engine with VTEC, knock sensor, 5-speed manual transmission with close ratio, cast-aluminum alloy wheels, Michelin XGT-V4 P195/55R15 84V M & S tires, power moonroof, AM/FM stereo cassette with 6 speakers, map light.

NOTE: Acura accessories are dealer installed. Contact an Acura dealer for accessory availability.

LEGEND COUPE

		DEALER	LIST
KA816R	L 2-Dr Coupe (6-spd)	31604	37700
KA826R	L 2-Dr Coupe (auto)	31604	37700
KA817R	LS 2-Dr Coupe (6-spd)	34789	41500
KA827R	LS 2-Dr Coupe (auto)	34789	41500
Destination Charge:		385	385

CODE	DESCRIPTION	DEALER	LIST

Standard Equipment

LEGEND L COUPE: 3.2L 24-valve SOHC 90 degree V-6 inline longitudinally mounted engine, programmed fuel injection (PGM-FI) with variable induction system, 6-speed manual transmission, 4-wheel independent double-wishbone suspension, variable power-assisted rack-and-pinion steering, anti-lock braking system, driver and front passenger airbag supplemental restraint system (SRS), front seat belts with automatic tensioners, variable diameter door beams, 3-point outboard rear seat belts, 5 mph front/rear bumpers, front/rear impact-absorption zones, flush-mounted high efficiency dual lens halogen headlights, tinted glass, dual power-operated body-colored door mirrors, protective body colored bodyside moldings, rear window defroster with timer, heated door mirrors, anti-soiling bottom door guards, galvanized body panels, 4-coat/4-bake paint, leather-trimmed interior and steering wheel, simulated wood-trimmed console and power window controls, driver's 8-way power seat with adjustable lumbar support and memory, folding rear center armrest, passenger's 4-way power seat, height and tilt adjustable front headrests, rear headrests, air conditioning, Acura/Bose music system, steering wheel-mounted remote control audio system, pre-wiring for CD changer, power windows with key-off feature, power door locks with driver's side dual unlocking feature, theft deterrent system, electronic tilt and telescopic steering column with automatic tilt-up, seat and steering wheel memory system, center console with armrest/covered storage compartment, power operated moonroof w/sliding shade.

LS COUPE (in addition to or instead of L equipment): Traction control system (TCS), burled walnut-trimmed console and power window controls, heated front seats, automatic climate control, Acura/Bose premium music system with 8 speakers/AM/FM stereo cassette/Dolby/Dynamic Noise Reduction (DNR)/FM diversity antenna system/anti-theft feature, illuminated entry system.

NOTE: *Acura accessories are dealer installed. Contact an Acura dealer for accessory availability.*

LEGEND SEDAN

	DEALER	LIST
KA755RL 4-Dr Sedan w/Cloth Interior (5-spd)	28335	33800
KA765RL 4-Dr Sedan w/Cloth Interior (auto)...	29005	34600
KA756RL 4-Dr Sedan w/Leather Interior (5-spd)	29592	35300

CODE	DESCRIPTION	DEALER	LIST
KA766RL	4-Dr Sedan w/Leather Interior (auto)	30263	36100
KA767R	LS 4-Dr Sedan (auto)	32358	38600
KA758R	GS 4-Dr Sedan (6-spd)	34119	40700
KA768R	GS 4-Dr Sedan (auto)	34119	40700
	Destination Charge:	385	385

Standard Equipment

LEGEND L SEDAN 3.2L 24-valve SOHC 90 degree V-6 inline longitudinally mounted engine, programmed fuel injection (PGM-FI) with variable induction system, 5-speed manual transmission, 4-wheel independent double-wishbone suspension, variable power assisted rack-and-pinion steering, anti-lock braking system (ABS), driver and front passenger airbag supplemental restraint system (SRS), front seat belts with automatic tensioners, variable diameter door beams, 3-point outboard seat belts (rear), 5 mph front/rear bumpers, impact-absorption zones (front/rear), flush mounted high efficiency dual lens halogen headlights, tinted glass, dual power-operated body colored door mirrors, protective body side body-colored moldings, rear window defroster with timer, heated door mirrors, anti-soiling bottom door guards, galvanized body panels, 4-coat/4-brake paint, full moquette upholstery, simulated wood-trimmed console and power window controls, driver's 8-way power seat with adjustable lumbar support and memory, folding rear center armrest, passenger's 4-way power seat, height/tilt adjustable front/rear headrests, air conditioning, Acura/Bose music system, steering wheel mounted remote control audio system, pre-wiring for CD changer, power-operated moonroof with sliding shade, power windows with key-off feature, power door locks with driver's side dual unlocking feature, theft-deterrent system, electronic tilt and telescopic steering column with automatic tilt-up, seat and steering wheel memory system, centered console with armrest/covered storage compartment.

LS SEDAN (also has in addition to or instead of L equipment): Electronically controlled 4-speed automatic transmission, leather-trimmed interior and steering wheel, burled walnut-trimmed console and power window controls, heated front seats, automatic climate control, Acura/Bose Premium music system w/8 speakers, AM/FM stereo cassette, Dolby Dynamic Noise Reduction (DNR), FM diversity antenna system, anti-theft feature, illuminated entry system.

GS SEDAN (also has in addition to or instead of LS equipment): 6-speed manual transmission, traction control system (TCS).

NOTE: Acura accessories are dealer installed. Contact an Acura dealer for accessory availability.

VIGOR

CODE	DESCRIPTION	DEALER	LIST
CC254R	LS 4-Dr Sedan (5-spd)	22355	26350
CC264R	LS 4-Dr Sedan (auto)	22992	27100
CC256R	GS 4-Dr Sedan (5-spd)	24052	28350
CC266R	GS 4-Dr Sedan (auto)	24688	29100
Destination Charge:		385	385

Standard Equipment

VIGOR - LS 2.5L 20-valve SOHC inline 5-cylinder longitudinally mounted engine, programmed fuel injection (PGM-FI) with dual-stage induction system, 5-speed manual transmission, 4-wheel independent double-wishbone suspension, speed-sensitive variable power-assisted rack-and-pinion steering, dual diagonal power assisted 4-wheel disc brakes, 205/60R15 91H M & S all season tires, 6.0 JJ x 15 cast-aluminum alloy wheels, anti-lock braking system (ABS), driver and front passenger airbag supplemental restraint system (SRS), front seat belts with direct-clamping mechanism, 3-point outboard rear seat belts, 5 mph front/rear bumpers, front and rear impact-absorption zones, side-impact door beams, flush-mounted halogen headlights, integral fog lights, tinted glass, dual power-operated door mirrors, protective body-side moldings, rear window defroster with timer, galvanized body panels, 3-coat/3-bake paint, full moquette upholstery, leather-wrapped steering wheel, wood-trimmed dash and doors, height adjustable front headrests, air conditioning, Acura Music System/AM/FM stereo cassette with Dolby/8 speakers/anti-theft feature, automatic power antenna, pre-wiring for CD changer, power windows, power door locks, cruise control, theft-deterrent system, tilt-adjustable steering column, variable intermittent windshield wipers, side window defoggers.

GS (also has in addition to or instead of LS equipment): Leather-trimmed interior, driver's 4-way power seat, in-dash CD player, power operated moonroof with sliding shade.

NOTE: Acura accessories are dealer installed. Contact an Acura dealer for accessory availability.

CODE	DESCRIPTION	DEALER	LIST

164

	DEALER	LIST
LS 4-Dr Sedan (5-spd)	28610	34890
Q 4-Dr Sedan (5-spd)	30905	37690
Destination Charge:	425	425

Standard Equipment

164 LS: 3.0 liter V6 engine, electronic fuel injection, 5-speed manual transmission with overdrive, cruise control, power steering, electric rear window defroster, tinted glass, power windows, P195/65VR15 steel belted radial BW tires, cast alloy wheels, air conditioning with auto temp control, power sunroof, leather-wrapped steering wheel, leather seats and trim, power 4-wheel disc brakes with anti-lock brake system, front and rear fog lights, headlight washers, dual heated outside mirrors, driver side air bag, center and overhead consoles, heated power bucket seats, digital clock, power door locks with central locking system, premium sound system with cassette.

164 Q (in addition to or instead of 164 LS equipment): Sport alloy wheels, body ground effects, dual color-keyed heated power outside mirrors, power sport buckets seats, electronic sport suspension.

Accessories

		DEALER	LIST
—	**California Emission System**	48	48
—	**Compact Disc Player**	520	625
—	**Automatic Transmission** — 4-speed - LS	655	800
—	**Metallic Paint** — LS	345	420

ALFA ROMEO

CODE	DESCRIPTION	DEALER	LIST

90 (1993)

NOTE: 1994 Audi 90 models were unavailable at time of publication.

		DEALER	LIST
8C24Y4	S 4-Dr Sedan (5-spd)	22631	26650
8C25Y4	CS 4-Dr Sedan (5-spd)	25025	29500
8C25Y5	CS Quattro Sport AWD 4-Dr Sedan (5-spd)	28007	33050
	Destination Charge:	445	445

Standard Equipment

90 S: Air conditioning, power steering, 5-speed manual transmission, cruise control, power 4-wheel disc brakes with anti-lock system, alloy wheels, anti-theft alarm system, digital clock, tachometer, headlight washers, AM/FM ETR stereo radio with cassette and six speakers, dual diversity antenna, 195/65HR15 SBR tires, electric rear window defroster, leather-wrapped steering wheel, assist grips, trip odometer, fog lights, driver's side air bag, center console, 2.8 liter V6 EFI engine, bodyside molding, power windows with driver side express-down feature, retained accessory power, power door locks with central locking including trunk and fuel filler door, tinted glass, map pockets, velour upholstery, front and rear floor mats, color-keyed bumpers, dual color-keyed power heated mirrors, intermittent windshield wipers, 60/40 split fold-down rear seat, courtesy lights.

CS (in addition to or instead of S equipment): Leather upholstery, power sunroof, air conditioning with auto temp control, 8-way power driver's seat, infrared remote entry/locking system, dual illuminated visor vanity mirrors.

CS QUATTRO SPORT (in addition to or instead of CS equipment): 205/60VR15 SBR performance tires, 4-wheel drive, sport-tuned suspension, spoke alloy wheels, color-keyed rear spoiler, engine oil cooler, front and rear stabilizer bars.

Accessories

—	**California Emissions**	140	140
—	**Automatic Transmission** — 4-speed - NA on CS Quattro Sport Sedan	750	800
3X1	**Ski Sack** — CS Quattro Sport Sedan	120	150
—	**Paint** — metallic pearlescent	400	500
H5B	**Tires** — 195/65R15 SBR all-season - CS Quattro Sport Sedan	NC	NC

CODE	DESCRIPTION	DEALER	LIST
3FD	**Power Sunroof** — tilt/slide - S..	728	910
PA3	**All-Weather Pkg** — S	336	420
	incls heated front seats, heated windshield washer nozzles and heated front door locks		
PA5	**All-Weather Pkg** — CS, CS Quattro Sport Sedan	256	320
	incls heated front seats and heated windshield washer nozzles		

100 (1993)

NOTE: 1994 Audi 100 models were unavailable at time of publication.

4A22Y4	Base 4-Dr Sedan (5-spd)	26224	31300
4A23Y4	S 4-Dr Sedan (5-spd)..	28590	34150
4A24Y4	CS 4-Dr Sedan (5-spd)	32325	38650
4A24Y5	CS Quattro 4-Dr Sedan (5-spd)...	34981	41850
4A54Y6	CS Quattro 4-Dr Wagon w/o Bose Sound System (auto)..............	37720	45150
4A54B6	CS Quattro 4-Dr Wagon w/Bose Sound System (auto).................	38218	45750
	Destination Charge:...	445	445

Standard Equipment

100 BASE: 2.8 liter 6 cylinder EFI engine, 5-speed manual transmission, tinted glass, cruise control, air conditioning, tachometer, power steering, full wheel covers, engine oil cooler, anti-theft alarm system, bodyside moldings, front and rear stabilizer bars, AM/FM ETR radio with cassette and eight speakers, dual diversity antenna, analog clock, leather-wrapped steering wheel, trip odometer, intermittent windshield wipers, electric rear window defroster, velour upholstery, rear fog lights, auto check system, retained accessory power for windows, tilt/telescopic steering wheel, power decklid release, power 4-wheel disc brakes with anti-lock brake system, 195/65HR15 SBR all-season tires, power door locks with central locking, outside temperature display, driver and passenger air bags, reclining front bucket seats, center console, power fuel filler door release, front and rear mats, front and rear center fold-down armrests, map pockets, passenger assist handles, courtesy lights, carpeting, dual power heated OS mirrors, dual illuminated visor vanity mirrors.

S (in addition to or instead of BASE equipment): Alloy wheels, retained accessory power for sunroof, speed-sensitive power steering, dual 8-way power front seats, ski sack.

CODE	DESCRIPTION	DEALER	LIST

CS (in addition to or instead of S equipment): 4WD (Quattro), power glass moonroof, front /rear fog lights, air cond w/auto temp control, all-weather package (Wagon), 4-position driver seat w/memory, power OS mirrors, AM/FM ETR radio with cassette and Bose sound system, infrared remote door locks, leather seats.

Accessories

Code	Description	Dealer	List
—	**California Emissions**..	165	165
—	**Automatic Transmission** — 4-speed (std on CS Quattro Wagon)	750	800
—	**Paint** — metallic pearlescent (NA on Base)................................	400	500
—	**Leather Seats** — S	1150	1385
CD2	**CD Changer** — CS Sedan	632	790
9W1	**Cellular Telephone** — NA on Base......................................	792	990
WP2	**All-Weather Pkg** — CS Sedan	296	370
	incls heated front seats, heated windshield washer nozzles, headlight washers		
WP3	**All-Weather Pkg** — S	376	470
	incls heated front seats, heated windshield washer nozzles, heated front door locks, headlight washers		

S4 (1993)

NOTE: 1994 Audi S4 models were unavailable at time of publication.

4A2555	4-Dr 4WD Turbo Sedan (5-spd)	39878	47750
	Destination Charge:...	445	445

Standard Equipment

S4: 2.2 liter 5 cylinder EFI turbocharged engine with intercooler, 5-speed manual transmission, air conditioning with auto temp control, leather-wrapped steering wheel, tachometer, leather upholstery, tinted glass, cruise control, bodyside moldings, auto check system, electric rear window defroster, front and rear stabilizer bars, trip odometer, intermittent windshield wipers, engine oil cooler, clearcoat metallic paint, anti-theft alarm system, analog clock, ski sack, sport suspension, headlight washers, color-keyed bumpers, driver and passenger air bags, AM/FM ETR stereo radio with cassette, Bose music system, dual diversity antenna, power glass moonroof, power 4-wheel disc brakes with anti-lock feature, front fender flares, cellular telephone, front and rear fog lights, P225/50ZR16 performance BW tires, alloy wheels, passenger assist grips, front and rear mats, power door locks with central locking system including trunk and fuel filler door, speed-sensitive power steering, power windows with driver side express-down feature, sport instrumentation, courtesy lights, map pockets, 8-way power sport reclining bucket seats with memory, heated front and rear seats, dual power heated OS mirrors with memory feature, dual illuminated visor vanity mirrors, carpeting, infrared remote locking system, tilt/telescopic steering wheel, heated windshield washer nozzles, front and rear center fold-down armrests, retained accessory power.

Accessories

Code	Description	Dealer	List
—	**California Emissions**	165	165
CD2	**CD Changer**	632	790
HR4	**Tire/Wheel Pkg**	NC	NC
	incls 215/60VR15 all-weather BW tires and 6-spoke sport alloy wheels		
—	**Paint** — metallic pearlescent	400	500

V8 QUATTRO (1993)

NOTE: 1994 Audi V8 Quattro models were unavailable at time of publication.

		Dealer	List
4C2276	4-Dr 4WD Sedan (auto)	47763	57250
Destination Charge:		445	445
Gas Guzzler Tax:		2100	2100

Standard Equipment

V8 QUATTRO: 4.2 liter V8 EFI engine, engine oil cooler, 4-speed auto transmission, power windows with driver express-down feature, front and rear fog lights, tachometer, electric rear window defroster, speed-sensitive power steering, cruise control, auto check system, bodyside moldings, air cond w/auto temp control, ski sack, leather-wrapped steering wheel, tinted glass, driver and passenger air bags, power sunroof, tilt/telescopic steering wheel, headlight washer system, analog clock, anti-theft alarm system, AM/FM ETR stereo radio with cassette, CD changer and Bose music system; front stabilizer bar, center console, cellular telephone, leather upholstery, power decklid release, dual diversity antenna, power door locks with central locking system, assist handles, 215/60HR15 SBR all-season tires, courtesy lights, intermittent windshield wipers, trip computer, map pockets, trip odometer, heated windshield washer nozzles, front and rear center fold-down armrests, clearcoat metallic paint, dual power heated mirrors w/memory feature, dual illuminated visor vanity mirrors, retained accessory power, light alloy aero wheels.

Accessories

—	**California Emissions**..	165	165
—	**Paint** — metallic pearlescent...	400	500

BMW 318i SEDAN

318i 4-Dr Sedan (5-spd)	20680	24675
Destination Charge:	450	450

Standard Equipment

318i SEDAN: 1.8L dual overhead cam 16 valve 4 cylinder engine, electronic fuel injection, electronic breakerless direct ignition system, Digital Motor Electronics engine-management system with self-diagnosis capability, 5-speed manual transmission, exhaust system with stainless steel components, 4 wheel independent suspension, twin-tube gas-pressure shock absorbers, engine-speed-sensitive variable-assist power rack-and-pinion steering, anti-roll bars front and rear, 4 wheel disc brakes, ventilated front discs (vacuum assisted), anti-lock braking system (ABS), 15x6J steel wheels with full wheel covers, 185/65R15 87H SBR tires, undercoating and cavity seal, hydraulic impact bumpers with compressible mounting elements (damage control to 9 mph), halogen free form headlights (low beams), 2-speed windshield wipers with single-wipe control, dual power outside mirrors, illuminating master key, central locking system with double-lock anti-theft feature (includes trunk and fuel-filler door), driveaway protection (disables engine when double-lock feature is engaged), pre-wiring for BMW remote keyless entry security system, reclining front seats (height adjustable driver's seat, head restraints adjustable for height and inclination), storage nets on front seatbacks, automatic front seatbelt tensioners, dual airbag supplementary restraint system, cloth or leatherette upholstery, velour carpeting, time-delay courtesy lights, impact sensor (unlocks doors, switches on interior lights and 4-way hazard flashers in case of accident), tinted glass with dark upper windshield band, power windows with key-off operation (one-touch lowering and raising of front windows), electronic speedometer and tachometer, LCD main and trip odometers, Service Interval Indicator, energy control fuel-economy indicator, multi information display with alphanumeric LCD readout (including outside temperature display and freeze warning, multi-function digital clock), rear window defroster, air conditioning and heating with separate electronic temperature control for left and right sides (CFC-free refrigerant), microfiltered ventilation, power 2-way sunroof with wind deflector, anti-theft AM/FM stereo radio/cassette audio system, CD ready, six speakers, diversity antenna system, pre-wiring for BMW CD changer, locking illuminated glovebox with rechargeable flashlight, drop-down toolkit in trunklid, full-use spare wheel and tire.

Accessories

—	**Automatic Transmission**	740	900
—	**Metallic Paint**	390	475
—	**Limited Slip Differential**	430	530
—	**Cruise Control/Fog Lights**	570	695
—	**Heated Front Seats/Heated Mirrors**	370	450
—	**Fold-Down Rear Seats**	225	275

318is COUPE

318is 2-Dr Coupe (5-spd)	21625	25800
Destination Charge:	450	450

Standard Equipment

318is COUPE: 1.8L dual overhead cam 16 valve 4 cylinder engine, electronic fuel injection, electronic breakerless direct ignition system, Digital Motor Electronics engine-management system with self-diagnosis capability, 5-speed manual transmission, exhaust system with stainless steel components, 4 wheel independent suspension, twin-tube gas-pressure shock absorbers, engine-speed-sensitive variable-assist power rack and pinion steering, anti-roll bars front and rear, 4 wheel disc brakes, ventilated front discs (vacuum assisted), anti-lock breaking system (ABS), 15x7J cast alloy wheels, 205/60R15 91H SBR

CODE	DESCRIPTION	DEALER	LIST

all season tires, undercoating and cavity seal, hydraulic impact bumpers with compressible mounting elements (damage control to 9 mph), halogen free form headlights (low beams), 2-speed windshield wipers with single-wipe control, dual power outside mirrors, illuminating master key, central locking system with friction anti-theft feature (includes trunk and fuel-filler door), driveaway protection (disables engine when double-lock feature is engaged), pre-wiring for BMW remote keyless entry security system, reclining front seats, height-adjustable driver's seat, head restraints adjustable for height and inclination, storage nets on front seatbacks, automatic front seatbelt tensioners, dual-airbag supplementary restraint system, cloth or leatherette upholstery, velour carpeting, time-delay courtesy lights, impact sensor (unlocks doors, switches on interior lights and four-way hazard flashers in case of accident), tinted glass with dark upper windshield band, power front windows w/key-off operation/one-touch lowering and raising/automatic positioning of windows for positive sealing, electronic speedometer and tachometer, LCD main and trip odometers, Service Interval Indicator, energy control fuel-economy indicator, multi information display with alphanumeric LCD readout (including outside temperature display and freeze warning, multi-function digital clock), rear window defroster, air conditioning and heating with separate electronic temperature control for left and right sides (CFC-free refrigerant), microfiltered ventilation, power 2-way sunroof with wind deflector, conceal panel, key-off operation; anti-theft AM/FM stereo radio/cassette audio system, CD-ready, six speakers, diversity antenna system, pre-wiring for BMW CD changer, locking, illuminated glovebox with rechargeable flashlight, split fold-down rear seats, drop-down toolkit in trunklid, full-size spare wheel and tire.

Accessories

—	**Automatic Transmission**	740	900
—	**Metallic Paint**	390	475
—	**Limited Slip Differential**	430	530
—	**Cruise Control/Fog Lights**	570	695
—	**Heated Front Seats/Heated Mirrors**	370	450

325i SEDAN

325i 4-Dr Sedan (5-spd)	25855	30850
Destination Charge:	450	450

Standard Equipment

325i SEDAN: 2.5L dual overhead cam 24 valve 6 cylinder engine with variable valve timing, electronic fuel injection, electronic breakerless direct ignition system, Digital Motor Electronics engine-management system with self-diagnosis capability, 5-speed manual transmission, electronic cruise control, dual exhaust system with stainless steel components, 4-wheel independent suspension, twin-tube gas-pressure shock absorbers, engine-speed-sensitive variable-assist power rack and pinion steering, anti-roll bars front and rear, 4-wheel disc brakes, ventilated front discs (vacuum-assisted), anti-lock braking system (ABS), 15x7J cast alloy wheels, 205/60R15 91H all season SBR tires, undercoating and cavity seal, hydraulic impact bumpers with compressible mounting elements (damage control to 9 mph), halogen free form headlights (low beams), halogen free form foglights, 2-speed windshield wipers with single-wipe control, dual power outside mirrors, illuminating master key, central locking system with double-lock anti-theft feature (includes trunk and fuel-filler door), drivaway protection (disables engine when double-lock feature is engaged), pre-wiring for BMW remote keyless entry security system, 8-way power front seats with ergonomic controls, head restraints adjustable for height and inclination, storage nets on front seatbacks, automatic front seatbelt tensioners, dual airbag supplementary restraint system, leatherette upholstery, velour carpeting, front center armrest, time-delay courtesy lights, impact sensor (unlocks doors, switches on interior lights and 4-way hazard flashers in case of accident), tinted glass with dark upper windshield band, power windows (with key-off operation, one-touch lowering of all windows, one-touch lowering and raising of front windows), electronic speedometer and tachometer, LCD main and trip odometers, Service Interval Indicator, energy control fuel-economy indicator, multi-information display with alphanumeric LCD readout (including outside temperature display and freeze warning, multi-function digital clock, check control vehicle monitor system), rear window defroster, air conditioning and heating with separate electronic temperature control for left and right sides (CFC-free refrigerant), microfiltered ventilation, power 2-way sunroof with wind deflector, anti-theft AM/FM stereo radio/cassette audio system, CD-ready, 10x25-watt (250-watt peak power) amplification, 10 speakers, diversity antenna system, pre-wiring for BMW CD changer, locking illuminated glovebox with rechargeable flashlight, drop-down toolkit in trunklid, full-size spare wheel and tire.

Accessories

		DEALER	LIST
—	**Automatic Transmission**	740	900
—	**Metallic Paint**	390	475
—	**Leather Upholstery**	940	1150
—	**Limited Slip Differential**	430	530
—	**Heated Front Seats/Heated Mirrors**	370	450
—	**On-Board Computer**	355	430
—	**Fold-Down Rear Seats**	225	275
—	**Sport Pkg 1**	720	875
	incls sport seats, sport suspension cross-spoke wheels		
—	**All-Season Traction**	815	995

CODE	DESCRIPTION	DEALER	LIST

325is COUPE

325is 2-Dr Coupe (5-spd).. 26985   32200
Destination Charge:... 450   450

Standard Equipment

325is COUPE: 2.5L dual overhead cam 24 valve 6 cylinder engine with variable valve timing, electronic fuel injection, electronic breakerless direct ignition system, Digital Motor Electronics engine-management system with self-diagnosis capability, 5-speed manual transmission, electronic cruise control, dual exhaust system with stainless steel components, 4-wheel independent suspension, twin-tube gas-pressure shock absorbers, engine-speed-sensitive variable-assist power rack and pinion steering, anti-roll bars front and rear, 4-wheel disc brakes, ventilated front discs (vacuum-assisted), anti-lock braking system (ABS), 15x7J cast alloy wheels, 205/60R15 91H SBR all season tires, undercoating and cavity seal, hydraulic impact bumpers with compressible mounting elements (damage control to 9 mph), halogen free form headlights (low beams), halogen free form foglights, 2-speed windshield wipers with single-wipe control, dual power outside mirrors, illuminating master key, central locking system with double-lock anti-theft feature (includes trunk and fuel-filler door), driveaway protection (disables engine when double-lock feature is engaged), pre-wiring for BMW keyless remote entry security system, height adjustable steering wheel, 8-way power front seats with ergonomic controls (head restraints adjustable for height and incli-nation), storage nets on front seatbacks, automatic front seatbelt tensioners, dual airbag supplementary restraint system, leather seating upholstery, front center armrest, velour carpeting, time-delay courtesy lights, impact sensor (unlocks doors, switches on interior lights and 4-way hazard flashers in case of acci-dent), tinted glass with dark upper windshield band, power front windows (with key-off operation, one-touch lowering and raising, automatic positioning of windows for positive sealing), electronic speedome-ter and tachometer, LCD main and trip odometers, Service Interval Indicator, energy control fuel-econo-my indicator, multi information display with alphanumeric LCD readout (including outside temperature dis-play and freeze warning, multi-function digital clock, check control vehicle monitor system), rear window defroster, air cond and heating w/separate electronic temperature control for left /right sides (CFC-free refrigerant), microfiltered ventilation, power 2-way sunroof w/wind deflector, anti-theft AM/FM stereo

BMW

| CODE | DESCRIPTION | DEALER | LIST |

radio/cassette audio system, CD ready, 10x25-watt (250-watt peak power) amplification, 10 speakers, diversity antenna system, pre-wired for BMW CD changer, locking illuminated glovebox w/rechargeable flashlight, split fold-down rear seats, drop-down toolkit in trunklid, full size spare wheel and tire.

Accessories

		DEALER	LIST
—	**Automatic Transmission**	740	900
—	**Metallic Paint**	390	475
—	**Limited Slip Differential**	430	530
—	**Heated Front Seats/Heated Mirrors**	370	450
—	**On-Board Computer**	355	430
—	**Sport Pkg 1**	720	875
	incls sport seats, sport suspension, cross-spoke wheels		
—	**All-Season Traction**	815	995

325iC CONVERTIBLE

	DEALER	LIST
325iC 2-Dr Convertible (5-spd)	32520	38800
Destination Charge:	450	450

Standard Equipment

325iC CONVERTIBLE: 2.5L dual overhead cam 24-valve 6 cylinder engine w/variable valve timing, electronic fuel injection, electronic breakerless direct ignition system, Digital Motor Electronics (Motronic) engine-management system w/knock control and self-diagnosis capability, 5-speed manual transmission w/direct drive 5th gear, electronic cruise control, stainless steel exhaust system, 4-wheel independent suspension (strut-type front suspension, central-link rear suspension), twin tube gas pressure shock absorbers, engine speed-sensitive variable-assist power rack and pinion steering, front and rear anti-roll bars, 4-wheel disc brakes (ventilated front discs, vacuum-assisted), anti-lock braking system (ABS), 15x7J cast alloy wheels, 205/60R15 91H SBR tires, undercoating and cavity seal, hydraulic impact bumpers w/compressible mounting elements (damage control to 9 mph), halogen free form headlights

CODE	DESCRIPTION	DEALER	LIST

(low beam), halogen free form foglights, 2-speed windshield wipers w/single-wipe control (car-speed controlled intermittent operation), dual power outside mirrors, illuminating master key, central locking system w/double-lock anti-theft mechanism (glove box, trunk, fuel-filler), pre-wiring for BMW keyless remote entry security system, height-adjustable steering wheel, 8-way power front seats w/ergonomic controls, adjustable head restraints for height and inclination, automatic forward movement for access to rear seats, ergonomically optimized rear seatbelts w/outboard buckles, automatic front seatbelt tensioners, driver and passenger side airbags, leather seating upholstery/steering-wheel rim/manual shift knob/handbrake grip and boot, front center armrest, driver's door coinbox, velour carpeting, time-delay courtesy light, impact sensor (unlocks doors, switches on interior lights and 4-way hazard flashers in case of accident), tinted glass w/dark upper windshield band, power convertible top includes automatic opening and closing of top storage compartment, power windows with one up/down feature, electronic speedometer and tachometer, LCD main and trip odometers, service interval indicator, energy control fuel-economy indicator, multi information display w/alphanumeric LCD readout (includes outside temperature display and freeze warning, multi-function digital clock, check control vehicle monitor system), rear window blower-type defroster, CFC-free refrigerant air conditioning and heating w/separate electronic temperature control for left and right sides, microfiltered ventilation, anti-theft AM/FM stereo radio/cassette audio system (CD ready, 10x25-watt amplification [250-watt peak power], 10 speakers), pre-wiring for CD changer, illuminated locking glovebox, drop-down toolkit in trunklid, full-size spare wheel and tire.

Accessories

		DEALER	LIST
—	**Automatic Transmission**	740	900
—	**Metallic Paint**	390	475
—	**Limited Slip Differential**	430	530
—	**Heated Front Seats/Heated Mirrors**	370	450
—	**On-Board Computer**	355	430
—	**Sports Pkg 2**	495	600
	incls sports seats and cross-spoke wheels		
—	**Rollover Protection System**	1140	1390
—	**All-Season Traction**	815	995

CODE	DESCRIPTION	DEALER	LIST

525i SEDAN

525i 4-Dr Sedan (5-spd) 32200 38425

Destination Charge:.. 450 450

Standard Equipment

525i SEDAN: 2.5L dual overhead cam 24 valve 6 cylinder engine with variable valve timing, electronic fuel injection, electronic breakerless direct ignition system, Digital Motor Electronics engine-management system with self-diagnosis capability, 5-speed manual transmission with direct 5th gear, electronic cruise control, dual exhaust system with stainless steel components, 4-wheel independent suspension, twin-tube gas-pressure shock absorbers, engine-speed-sensitive variable-assist power steering, anti-roll bars front and rear, 4-wheel disc brakes (ventilated front discs), anti-lock braking system (ABS), 15x7J cast alloy wheels, 205/60R15 94H SBR tires, undercoating and cavity seal, hydraulic impact bumpers with front compressible elements (damage control to 9 mph), halogen ellipsoid headlights (low beams), halogen free form foglights, 2-speed plus intermittent windshield wipers with car-speed-controlled wiping speed, heated windshield washer jets, dual power/heated outside mirrors, heated driver's door lock, illuminating master key, central locking system with double-lock anti-theft feature, driveaway protection (disables engine when double-lock feature is engaged), pre-wiring for BMW remote keyless entry security system, metallic paint at no additional charge, telescopically adjustable, leather-covered steering wheel, 10-way power front seats including power adjustable head restraints, ergonomic controls, automatic front seatbelt tensioners, dual airbag supplementary restraint system, gathered leather seating upholstery, high-gloss walnut trim, velour carpeting, front center armrests, rear center armrest with storage compartment, seatback storage pockets, time-delay courtesy lights with actuation from driver's exterior door handle (automatic switch-on when engine is turned off at night), impact sensor (unlocks doors, switches on interior lights and hazard flashers in case of accident), map reading lights, tinted glass with dark upper windshield band, power windows (with key-off operation, one-touch lowering of all windows, one-touch lowering and raising of driver's window), electronic speedometer and tachometer, LCD main and trip odometers, Service Interval Indicator, energy control fuel-economy indicator, check control vehicle monitor system with alphanumeric LCD readout, 2-stage rear window defroster, air conditioning and heating with separate controls for left and right sides (CFC-free refrigerant), microfiltered ventilation, power 2-way sunroof with key-off and one-touch operation, anti-theft AM/FM stereo radio/cassette audio

CODE	DESCRIPTION	DEALER	LIST

system, CD-ready, 10x25-watt (250-watt peak power) amplification, 10 speakers, diversity antenna system, pre-wiring for BMW CD changer, pre-wiring for BMW cellular phone incl remote operation and audio muting, dual illuminated vanity mirrors, locking glovebox with rechargeable flashlight, fully finished trunk with luggage straps and drop-down toolkit, full-size spare wheel and tire.

Accessories

		DEALER	LIST
—	**Automatic Transmission**	740	900
—	**Heated Front Seats**	305	370
—	**On-Board Computer**	355	430
—	**All-Season Traction**	815	995

525iT TOURING WAGON

	DEALER	LIST
525iT 5-Dr Wagon (auto)	34025	40600
Destination Charge:	450	450

Standard Equipment

525i TOURING WAGON: 2.5L dual overhead cam 24 valve 6 cylinder engine with variable valve timing, electronic fuel injection, electronic breakerless direct ignition system, Digital Motor Electronics engine-management system with self-diagnosis capability, 4-speed electronically controlled automatic transmission with economy, sport & manual shift modes, shift interlock, electronic cruise control, dual exhaust system with stainless steel components, 4-wheel independent suspension, twin-tube gas-pressure shock absorbers, engine-speed-sensitive variable-assist power steering, anti-roll bars front and rear, 4-wheel disc brakes (ventilated front discs, vacuum-assisted), anti-lock braking system (ABS), 15x7J cast alloy wheels, 225/60R15 95V SBR tires, undercoating and cavity seal, hydraulic impact bumpers with front compressible elements (damage control to 9 mph), halogen ellipsoid headlights (low beams), halogen free form foglights, 2-speed + intermittent windshield wipers with car-speed-controlled wiping speed, heated windshield-washer jets, dual power/heated outside mirrors, heated driver's door lock, illuminating master key, central locking system with double-lock anti-theft feature, driveaway protection (disables engine when double-lock feature is engaged), pre-wiring for BMW remote keyless entry security system,

CODE	DESCRIPTION	DEALER	LIST

recessed tracks for multi-function roof-rack system, metallic paint at no additional charge, telescopically adjustable leather-covered steering wheel, 10-way power front seats including power-adjustable head restraints with ergonomic controls, automatic front seatbelt tensioners, dual airbag supplementary restraint system, gathered leather seating upholstery, high-gloss walnut trim, velour carpeting, front center armrests, rear center armrest, split fold-down rear seats, seatback storage pockets, time-delay courtesy lights with actuation from driver's exterior door handle (automatic switch-on when engine is turned off at night), impact sensor (unlocks doors, switches on interior lights and hazard flashers in case of accident), map reading lights, tinted glass with dark upper windshield band, power windows (with key-off operation, one-touch lowering of all windows, one-touch lowering and raising of driver's window), electronic speedometer and tachometer, LCD main and trip odometers, Service Interval Indicator, energy control fuel-economy indicator, check control vehicle monitor system with alphanumeric LCD readout, 2-stage rear-window defroster, air conditioning and heating with separate controls for left and right sides (CFC-free refrigerant), microfiltered ventilation, anti-theft AM/FM stereo radio/cassette audio system, CD-ready, 10x25-watt (250-watt peak power) amplification, 10 speakers, diversity antenna system, pre-wiring for BMW CD changer, pre-wiring for BMW cellular phone incl. remote operation and audio muting, dual illuminated vanity mirrors, locking glovebox with rechargeable flashlight, tailgate with separately openable window and drop-down toolkit, variable cargo area with velour carpeting, four tie-downs, cargo cover, full-use spare wheel and tire.

Accessories

		DEALER	LIST
—	**Heated Front Seats**	305	370
—	**On-Board Computer**	355	430
—	**All-Season Traction**	815	995
—	**Luggage Net**	215	260
—	**Double Electric Sunroof**	1090	1325

530i SEDAN

	DEALER	LIST
530i 4-Dr Sedan (5-spd)	34760	41500
Destination Charge:	450	450

Standard Equipment

530i SEDAN: 3.0L DOHC 4-cam 32 valve V-8 engine, electronic fuel injection w/hot-film air-mass measurement, electronic breakerless direct ignition system, Digital Motor Electronics (Motronic) engine-management system w/self-diagnosis capability, 5-speed manual transmission w/direct 5th gear, electronic cruise control, stainless steel exhaust system, 4-wheel independent suspension (double-pivot strut-type front suspension, track link rear suspension), twin-tube gas-pressure shock absorbers, front and rear anti-roll bars, 4-wheel disc brakes (ventilated front discs, vacuum assisted), anti-lock braking system (ABS), 15x7J cross-spoke cast alloy wheels, 225/60R15 95V SBR tires, under-coating and cavity seal, 5 mph hydraulic impact bumpers w/front compressible elements (damage control to 9 mph), halogen ellipsoid headlights (low beams), halogen free form foglights, 2-speed intermittent windshield wipers w/car-speed controlled wiping speed/single-wipe control/heated windshield washer jets, dual power/heated outside mirrors, heated driver's door lock, illuminating mater key, central locking system w/friction anti-theft feature (window and sunroof closing possible from driver's door lock), metallic paint, leather-covered telescopically adjustable steering wheel, 10-way power front seats including power-adjustable head restraints (ergonomic controls), ergonomic seatbelt system (automatic height adjustment for front seatbelts, inboard-anchored rear seatbelts), automatic front seatbelt tensioners, driver's side airbag, knee bolster, gathered leather seating/door panels/center console, high-gloss walnut trim, velour carpeting, front center armrests, rear center armrest w/storage compartment, seatback storage pockets, time-delay courtesy light with actuation from driver's exterior door handle (automatic switch-on when engine is turned off at night), impact sensor (unlocks doors, switches on interior lights and hazard flashers in case of accident), map reading lights, tinted glass with dark upper windshield band, power windows with key-off operation and one up/down feature, electronic speedometer and tachometer, LCD main and trip odometers, Service Interval Indicator, energy control fuel-economy indicator, check control vehicle monitor system w/alphanumeric LCD readout, two-stage rear-window defroster, CFC-free refrigerant air conditioning and heating w/separate controls for left and right sides, automatic ventilation system (can be programmed to switch on interior ventilation when car is standing), power two-way sunroof w/key-off and one-touch operation, anti-theft AM/FM stereo radio/cassette audio system with 4x25-watt amplification/10 speakers/diversity antenna system, pre-wired for BMW cellular telephone (includes remote operation and audio muting), pre-wired for BMW alarm system/CD changer/automatic-dimming inside rearview mirror, locking glovebox, trunk luggage straps and drop-down toolkit, full-size spare wheel and tire.

Accessories

—	Automatic Transmission	900	1100
—	Heated Front Seats	305	370
—	On-Board Computer	355	430
—	All-Season Traction	1110	1350

CODE	DESCRIPTION	DEALER	LIST

530iT TOURING WAGON

	DEALER	LIST
530iT 5-Dr Wagon (auto)..	38385	45800
Destination Charge:...	450	450

Standard Equipment

530i TOURING WAGON: 3.0L DOHC 4-cam 32 valve V-8 engine, electronic fuel injection, electronic breakerless ignition, Digital Motor Electronics (Motronic) engine-management system w/self-diagnosis capability, electronically controlled 5-speed automatic transmission with Economy/Sport/Winter shift modes and shift interlock, automatic stability control plus traction (ASC+T), electronic cruise control, dual exhaust system w/stainless-steel components, 4-wheel independent suspension (double-pivot strut-type front suspension, track link rear suspension), twin-tube gas-pressure shock absorbers, front and rear anti-roll bars, engine-speed-sensitive variable-assist power steering, 4-wheel disc brakes (ventilated front discs, vacuum-assisted anti-lock braking system [ABS]), 15x7J cross-spoke cast alloy wheels, 225/60R15 95V SBR tires, undercoating and cavity seal, 5 mph hydraulic impact bumpers w/front compressible mounting elements (damage control to 9 mph), halogen ellipsoid headlights (low beams), halogen free from foglights, 2-speed intermittent windshield wipers w/car-speed-controlled wiping speed and interval/single-wipe control/heated windshield-washer jets, dual power/heated outside mirrors, heated driver's door lock, illuminating master key, central locking system w/double-lock anti-theft feature (window and sunroof closing possible from driver's door lock), tracks for multi-function roof-rack system, metallic paint, telescopically adjustable steering wheel, 10-way power front seats (include power-adjustable head restraints/ergonomic controls, ergonomic seatbelt system (automatic height adjustment for front seatbelts, rear seatbelt w/outboard buckles, automatic front seatbelt tensioners, supplementary restraint system (driver's side airbag, knee bolster), leatherette upholstery, high-gloss walnut trim, velour carpeting, front center armrests, 2/3 - 1/3 split folding rear seas, time-delay courtesy light w/actuation from driver's exterior door handle (automatic switch-on when engine is turned off at night), impact sensor (unlocks doors, switches on interior lights, four-way hazard flashers in case of accident, map reading lights, tinted glass w/dark upper windshield band, power windows w/key-off operation and one up/down feature, electronic speedometer/tachometer/trip odometer, Service Interval Indicator, energy control fuel-economy indicator, check control vehicle monitor system w/alphanumeric LCD readout, 2-stage rear window defroster, CFC-free refrigerant air conditioning and heating w/separate controls for left and right sides, microfiltered ventilation, automatic ventilation system (can be programmed to switch on interior ventilation when car is standing), power twin-panel sunroof w/one-touch and key-off operation, anti-theft AM/FM stereo radio/cassette audio system/CD ready/4x25-watt amplification/10 speakers, pre-wired for BMW cellular telephone (includes audio muting/provision for remote control), pre-wired for BMW alarm system/CD changer/auto-dimming mirror, locking glovebox, variable cargo area w/velour carpeting and four tie-downs, roll-back cargo cover, tailgate w/separately openable rear window/drop-down toolkit, full-use spare wheel and tire.

Accessories

—	Heated Front Seats	305	370
—	On-Board Computer	355	430
—	Luggage Net	215	260

540i SEDAN

540i 4-Dr Sedan (auto)	39805	47500
Destination Charge:	450	450
Gas Guzzler Tax:	1000	1000

Standard Equipment

540i SEDAN: 4.0L DOHC 4-cam 32 valve V-8 engine, electronic fuel injection with hot-film air-mass measurement, electronic breakerless direct ignition system, Digital Motor Electronics (Motronic) engine-management system w/self-diagnosis capability, electronically controlled 5-speed automatic transmission with Economy/Sport/Winter shift modes, electronic cruise control, stainless steel exhaust system, 4-wheel independent suspension (double-pivot strut-type front suspension, track link rear suspension), twin-tube gas-pressure shock absorbers, front and rear anti-roll bars, four-wheel ventilated disc brakes (vacuum-assisted), anti-lock braking system (ABS), 15x7J Honeycomb design cast alloy wheels, 225/60R15 95V SBR tires, undercoating and cavity seal 5 mph hydraulic impact bumpers w/front compressible elements (damage control to 9 mph), halogen ellipsoid headlights (low beams), halogen free form foglights, two-speed intermittent windshield wipers w/car-speed-controlled wiping speed (single wipe control/heated windshield-washer jets), dual power/heated outside mirrors, heated driver's door lock, illuminating master key, remote-actuated central locking and alarm system (keyless entry) with friction anti-theft feature (window and sunroof closing possible from driver's door lock), metallic paint, power telescopically adjustable leather-covered steering wheel, 10-way power front seats (includes power-adjustable head restraints/ergonomic controls), memory system for driver's seat and seatbelt height/steering wheel/outside mirrors - 3 memory settings, ergonomic seatbelt system (automatic height adjustment for front seatbelts; inboard-anchored rear seatbelts), automatic front seatbelt tensioners, driver's side airbag/knee bolster, gathered leather seating/door panels and door pulls/center console, high-gloss walnut trim, velour carpeting, front center armrests, rear center armrest w/storage compartment, seatback storage pockets, time-delay courtesy light w/actuation from driver's exterior door handle (automatic switch-on when engine is turned off at night), impact sensor (unlocks doors/switches on interior lights/hazard flashers in case of accident), map reading lights, tinted glass w/dark upper windshield band, power windows with key-off operation and one up/down feature, electronic speedometer and tachometer, LCD main and trip odometers, Service Interval Indicator, energy control fuel-economy indicator, check control vehicle monitor system w/alphanumeric LCD readout, on-board computer, 2-stage rear-window defroster, CFC-free refrigerant air cond/heating w/separate controls for left and right sides, microfiltered ventilation, automatic ventilation system (can be programmed to switch on interior ventilation when car is standing), power 2-way sunroof w/key-off and one-touch operation, anti-theft AM/FM stereo radio/cassette audio system with 4x25-watt amplification/10 speakers/diversity antenna system, pre-wired for BMW cellular telephone includes remote operation/audio muting, pre-wired for CD changer and auto-dimming inside rearview mirror, locking glovebox, trunk luggage straps/drop-down toolkit, full-use spare wheel and tire.

Accessories

—	**Heated Front Seats**	305	370
—	**All-Season Traction**	1110	1350

740i/740iL SEDANS

	DEALER	LIST
740i 4-Dr Sedan (auto)	45745	55950
740iL 4-Dr Sedan (auto)	49015	59950
Destination Charge:	450	450
Gas Guzzler Tax:	1000	1000

CODE	DESCRIPTION	DEALER	LIST

Standard Equipment

740i/740iL SEDANS: 4.0L DOHC 4 cam 32 valve V8 engine, electronic fuel injection, electronic breakerless direct ignition system, Digital Motor Electronics engine-management system with self-diagnosis capability, electronically controlled 5-speed automatic transmission with economy, sport and winter shift modes, shift interlock, electronic cruise control, exhaust system with stainless-steel components, 4-wheel independent suspension, twin-tube gas-pressure shock absorbers (740iL: single-tube rear shock absorbers), anti-roll bars front and rear, vehicle-speed-sensitive variable-assist power steering, 4-wheel disc brakes (4-wheel ventilated discs, vacuum-assisted), anti-lock braking system (ABS), 15x7J cast alloy wheels, 225/60R15 95Z SBR tires, undercoating and cavity seal, 5 mph hydraulic impact bumpers with front compressible elements (damage control to 9 mph), halogen ellipsoid low-beam headlights, high-pressure headlight/foglight cleaning system (740iL), halogen free form foglights, 2-speed plus intermittent windshield wipers, heated windshield-washer jets, dual power/heated outside mirrors, automatic positioning of right outside mirror for visibility of curb when backing up, heated driver's door lock, illuminating master key, central locking system with double-lock anti-theft feature, remote keyless entry and security system, driveaway protection (disables engine when double-lock feature is engaged), metallic paint at no additional charge, power telescopically adjustable, leather-covered steering wheel, 10-way power front seats including power-adjustable head restraints with ergonomic controls, power driver's seat lumbar support, memory system for driver's seat/steering wheel/front seatbelt height/outside mirrors (three memory settings), automatic-dimming inside rearview mirror, automatic front seatbelt tensioners, dual airbag supplementary restraint system, adjustable rear head restraints, Nappa gathered leather upholstery seats/center console/door panels, high-gloss walnut interior trim with contrasting inlays, velour carpeting, front center armrests, rear center armrest with storage compartment, door storage compartments, time-delay courtesy light (with actuation from driver's exterior door handle, automatic switch-on when engine is turned off at night), impact sensor (unlocks doors, switches on interior lights and 4-way hazard flashers in case of accident), map reading lights, rear reading lights, tinted glass with dark upper windshield band, power windows (with key-off operation, one-touch lowering of all windows, one-touch lowering and raising of driver's window), electronic speedometer and tachometer, LCD main and trip odometers, Service Interval Indicator, energy control fuel-economy indicator, check control system with alphanumeric LCD readout, automatic dimming inside rearview mirror, onboard computer, 2-stage rear window defroster, automatic climate control with separate controls for left and right sides (CFC-free refrigerant), microfiltered ventilation, automatic ventilation system (can be programmed to switch on interior ventilation automatically when car is standing), power 2-way sunroof with key-off and one-touch operation, anti-theft AM/FM stereo radio/cassette audio system, CD-ready, 10x25-watt (250-watt peak power) amplification, 10 speakers, diversity antenna system, pre-wiring for BMW CD changer, pre-wiring for BMW cellular telephone incl. remote operation and audio muting, dual illuminated vanity mirrors, locking illuminated glovebox with rechargeable flashlight, fully finished trunk with luggage straps and drop-down toolkit, full-use spare wheel and tire.

Accessories

—	Heated Front Seats	305	370
—	All-Season Traction	1110	1350
—	Electronic Damping Control	1200	1500
—	Ski Sack	155	190
—	Electric Rear Sun Shade — 740iL	370	465

CODE	DESCRIPTION	DEALER	LIST

750iL SEDAN

	DEALER	LIST
750iL 4-Dr Sedan (auto)..	68640	83950
Destination Charge:...	450	450
Gas Guzzler Tax:	3000	3000

Standard Equipment

750iL SEDAN: 5.0L SOHC V12 engine, electronic fuel injection, electronic breakerless ignition system, dual Digital Motor Electronics engine-management systems with self-diagnosis capability, electronic throttle, electronically controlled 4-speed automatic transmission with economy, sport and manual shift modes, shift interlock, electronic cruise control, exhaust system with stainless steel components, 4-wheel independent suspension, gas-pressure shock absorbers (twin-tube front/single-tube rear), anti-roll bars front and rear, vehicle-speed-sensitive variable-assist power steering, all season traction, 4-wheel disc brakes (4-wheel ventilated discs, hydraulically assisted), anti-lock braking system (ABS), 15x7J cross-spoke cast alloy wheels, 225/60R15 95Z SBR tires, undercoating and cavity seal, 5 mph hydraulic impact bumpers with front compressible elements (damage control to 9 mph), Xenon ellipsoid low-beam headlights, high-pressure headlight/foglight cleaning system, halogen free form foglights, 2-speed + intermittent windshield wipers, heated windshield-washer jets, dual power/heated outside mirrors, automatic positioning of right outside mirror for visibility of curb when backing up, heated driver's door lock, illuminating master key, central locking system with double-lock anti-theft feature, remote keyless entry and security system, driveaway protection (disables engine when double-lock feature is engaged), metallic paint at no additional charge, power telescopically adjustable leather-covered steering wheel, 10-way power front seats including power-adjustable head restraints, ergonomic controls, power driver's seat lumbar support, memory system for driver's seat, steering wheel, front seatbelt height and outside mirrors (three memory settings), automatic-dimming inside rearview mirror, automatic front seatbelt tensioners, dual airbag supplementary restraint system, 2-stage heated front and rear seats, power individual rear seats, power-adjustable rear head restraints with automatic retraction when seat is unoccupied, Nappa gathered leather upholstery (seats, center console, door panels, lower instrument panel), high-gloss walnut interior trim with contrasting inlays, velour carpeting, front center armrests, rear center armrest with storage compartment, door storage compartments, time-delay courtesy light (with actuation from driver's exterior door handle, automatic switch-on when engine is turned off at night), impact sensor (unlocks doors, switches on interior lights and 4-way hazard flashers in case of accident), map reading lights, rear reading lights, tinted glass with dark upper windshield band, double-pane insulating side windows, power windows (with key-off operation, one-touch lowering of all windows, one-touch lowering and raising of driver's window), electronic speedometer and tachometer, LCD main and trip odometers, Service Interval Indicator, energy control fuel-economy indicator, check control system with alphanumeric LCD readout, automatic dimming inside rearview mirror, onboard computer, 2-stage rear window defroster, automatic climate control with separate controls for left and right sides (CFC-free refrigerant), microfiltered ventilation, automatic ventilation system (can be programmed to switch on interior ventilation automatically when car is standing), power 2-way sunroof with key-off and one-touch operation, anti-theft AM/FM stereo radio/cassette audio system, CD-ready, 10x25-watt (250-watt peak power) amplification, 10 speakers, diversity antenna system, 6-disc CD changer, BMW cellular phone with voice-activated and remote operation, audio muting, dual illuminated vanity mirrors, locking illuminated velour-lined glovebox with rechargeable flashlight, velour-lined trunk with soft-close lid, luggage straps and drop-down toolkit, ski bag, full-use spare wheel and tire.

Accessories

—	**Electronic Damping Control**	1200	1500

850Ci COUPE

	Dealer	List
850Ci 2-Dr Coupe (auto)	69905	85500
Destination Charge:	NC	NC
Gas Guzzler Tax: Models w/auto trans	3000	3000

Standard Equipment

850Ci COUPE: 5.0L SOHC V12 engine, electronic fuel injection, electronic breakerless ignition system, dual Digital Motor Electronics engine-management systems with self-diagnosis capability, electronic throttle, electronically controlled 4-speed automatic transmission with economy, sport and manual shift modes, shift interlock, electronic cruise control, dual exhaust system with stainless steel components, 4-wheel independent suspension, twin-tube gas-pressure shock absorbers, anti-roll bars front and rear, engine-speed-sensitive variable-assist power steering, all season traction, 4-wheel disc brakes (ventilated front discs with aluminum calipers, hydraulic power assist), anti-lock braking system (ABS), 16x7.5J cast alloy wheels, 235/50ZR16 SBR tires, undercoating and cavity seal, hydraulic impact bumpers with front and rear compressible elements (damage control to 9 mph), retractable halogen lighting units with main high beams, super-ellipsoid low beams and foglights, additional flashers/high beams in bumper, 2-speed plus intermittent windshield wipers, heated windshield washer jets, dual power/heated outside mirrors, automatic positioning of right outside mirror for visibility of curb when backing up, heated driver's door lock, illuminating master key, central locking system with double-lock anti-theft feature, remote entry and security system with controls in head of master key, driveaway protection (disables engine when double-lock feature is engaged), metallic paint at no additional charge, power tilt/telescopic leather-covered steering wheel with automatic tilt-away for entry and exit, power front seats (driver - 12-way including power head restraint, power lumbar support; passenger - 8-way including power head restraint manual adjustment of head restraint angle), front seat integrated belt system, dual airbag supplementary restraint system, memory system for driver's seat, steering wheel and outside mirrors (three memory settings), automatic dimming inside rearview mirror, 2-stage heated front seats with timers, ergonomic rear seatbelt system, Nappa gathered leather upholstery (seats, lower instrument panel and center console, door inserts), bird's-eye maple interior trim, velour carpeting, rear center armrest, first-aid kit, time-delay courtesy light with fade-out feature, impact sensor (unlocks doors, switches on interior lights and 4-way hazard flashers in case of accident), map reading lights, rear reading lights, tinted glass with dark upper windshield and rear window bands, power windows (with power-off operation, one-touch of driver's and passenger's windows, automatic positioning of front windows for positive sealing), electronic speedometer and tachometer, LCD main and dual trip odometers, multi information display combining Service Interval Indicator, check control vehicle monitor system, onboard computer, 2-stage rear window defroster, automatic climate control with separate controls for left and right sides (CFC-free refrigerant), microfiltered ventilation, automatic ventilation system (can be programmed to switch on interior ventilation automatically when car is standing), power 2-way sunroof with one-touch operation, anti-theft AM/FM stereo radio/cassette audio system with 10x25-watt (250-watt peak power) amplification, 12 speakers, diversity antenna system, 6-disc CD changer, BMW cellular phone with voice activated and remote operation, audio muting, dual illuminated vanity mirrors, split fold-down rear seats, ski bag, color-keyed velour-lined trunk, drop-down toolkit in trunklid, full-use spare wheel and tire.

Accessories

—	**Electronic Damping Control**	1200	1500
—	**Forged Alloy Wheels**	880	1100

COLT

PE21	Base 2-Dr Sedan	8714	9120
PL21	ES 2-Dr Sedan	9571	10060
PL41	Base 4-Dr Sedan	10644	11428
PH41	ES 4-Dr Sedan	11472	12181
Destination Charge: Alaska		550	550
	Other States	430	430

Standard Equipment

COLT 2 DOOR - BASE: Black outside door handles, gray fascias, black side window opening moldings, 5-mph bumper system, passenger compartment carpeting, instrument panel coin holder, center floor console with armrest and storage, side window demisters, vinyl door/quarter trim, stainless steel exhaust system, driver side foot rest, flush aero-style halogen headlights, single note horn, flood instrumentation cluster illumination, dome lamps, outside left manual mirror, vinyl seat trim with cloth insert, reclining high-back front bucket seats, lowback rear bench seat, 4-spoke steering wheel, carpeted floor trunk trim, four argent styled steel wheels with bright center cap, 2-speed windshield wipers, 1.5 liter SMPI 4-cylinder engine, 5-speed manual transmission, power front disc/rear drum brakes, manual rack and pinion steering.

2 DOOR ES (in addition to or instead of 2-DR BASE equipment): Body color outside door handles, body color fascias, body color bodyside moldings, rear spoiler, assist grips, cigarette lighter, instrument panel dual sliding cupholder, cloth and vinyl door/quarter trim with map pockets, back lighting instrument cluster illumination, outside dual manual remote mirrors, passenger side covered visor mirror, cloth and vinyl seat trim, reclining front bucket seats with adjustable head restraint, passenger side rear-seat easy entry, four full-wheel covers.

COLT 4 DOOR - BASE: Black outside door handles, body color fascias, black side window opening moldings, rear armrest, three assist grips, 5-mph bumper system, passenger compartment carpeting, instrument panel coin holder, center floor console with armrest and storage, instrument panel dual sliding cupholder, side window demisters, child protection door locks, cloth and vinyl door/quarter trim with map pockets, stainless steel exhaust system, driver side foot rest, rear seat heater ducts, flush aero-style halogen headlights, single note horn, back lighting instrument cluster illumination, dome lamps, outside dual manual non-remote mirrors, cloth and vinyl seat trim, reclining front bucket seats with adjustable head restraints, lowback rear bench seat, 4-spoke steering wheel, carpeted floor trunk trim, four full-wheel covers, 2-speed windshield wipers, 1.8 liter SMPI 4-cylinder engine, 5-speed manual transmission, power front disc/rear drum brakes, power rack and pinion steering.

4 DOOR ES (in addition to or instead of 4-DR BASE equipment): Outside body color door handles, body color bodyside moldings, rear spoiler, cigarette lighter, remote fuel filler door release, dual note horn, outside dual manual remote mirrors, driver/passenger side covered visor mirrors, full cloth seat trim, split folding rear bench seat with center armrest, tilt/height control driver's seat, remote trunk release with override feature, side trunk trim, intermittent windshield wipers.

Accessories

CODE	DESCRIPTION	DEALER	LIST
C	**Pkg C** — Base 2-Dr..	360	419
	incls rear window defroster, tinted glass, dual ext mirrors, radio (AM/FM w/clock & 4 spkrs		
C	**Pkg C** — Base 4-Dr..	499	580
	incls rear window defroster, convenience group #2 (fixed time intermittent wipers, black dual remote mirrors, cigar lighter, pass side vanity mirror, remote fuel filler door release, remote trunk release, trunk trim dress-up, trunk light), floor mats, tinted glass, black bodyside moldings, radio (AM/FM w/clock & 4 spkrs)		
D	**Pkg D** — Base 2-Dr..	1057	1229
	incls rear window defroster, tinted glass, dual exterior mirrors, radio (AM/FM w/clock & 4 spkrs, air conditioning)		
D	**Pkg D** — Base 4-Dr..	1195	1390
	incls rear window defroster, convenience group #2 (fixed time interval wipers, black dual remote mirrors, cigar lighter, pass side vanity mirror, remote fuel filler door release, remote trunk release, trunk trim dress-up, trunk light), floor mats, tinted glass, black bodyside molding, radio (AM/FM w/clock & 4 spkrs), air conditioning		
G	**Pkg G** — ES 2-Dr..	86	100
	incls rear window defroster, tinted glass, radio (AM/FM w/clock & 4 spkrs)		
H	**Pkg H** — ES 2-Dr..	1192	1386
	incls pkg G contents plus air cond, convenience group #1 (split folding rear seat, fixed time intermittent wipers, remote fuel filler door release, remote trunk release, trunk trim dress-up, trunk light), pwr steering, radio (AM/FM w/cassette, clock & 4 spkrs)		
K	**Pkg K** — ES 2-Dr..	1577	1834
	incls pkg H contents plus sport group (frt vented disc brakes, dual tip exhaust, touring tuned susp'n, tach [man trans only], P185/65R14 tires, 14" aluminum wheels), 1.8 liter engine		
K	**Pkg K** — ES 4-Dr..	1043	1213
	incls air conditioning, rear window defroster, convenience group #3 (tilt steering column, color-keyed dual pwr remote mirrors, variable intermittent wipers, cruise control), floor mats, tinted glass, radio		
L	**Pkg L** — ES 4-Dr..	1717	1996
	incls air cond, rear window defroster, convenience group #3 (tilt steering column, color-keyed dual pwr remote mirrors, variable intermittent wipers, cruise control), floor mats, tinted glass, radio (AM/FM w/cassette, clock & 4 spkrs), pwr door locks, cast aluminum wheels, pwr windows		
HAA	**Air Conditioning** — ES 2-Dr..	697	810
BGF	**Brakes** — anti-lock - ES 4-Dr..	601	699

CODE	DESCRIPTION	DEALER	LIST
GFA	**Rear Window Defroster**	57	66
NAE	**California Emissions**	NC	NC
NBY	**New York Emissions**	NC	NC
MJC	**Bodyside Molding** — gray - Base 2-Dr...............................	46	54
RAW	**Radio** — Base 2-Dr w/pkg C or D	156	181
	Base 4-Dr w/pkg C or D	156	181
	ES 2-Dr w/pkg G..	156	181
	incls AM/FM stereo w/cass, clock & 4 spkrs		
RAT	**Radio** — Base 4-Dr	233	271
—	**Paint**	NC	NC
EJB	**Engine** — 1.5L MPI 4 cyl - Base 2-Dr	STD	STD
	GL 2-Dr	STD	STD
EJA	**Engine** — 1.8L MPI 4 cyl - Base 4-Dr	STD	STD
	ES 4-Dr..	STD	STD
	ES 2-Dr - included in Pkg K		
DDR	**Transmission** — 5-spd manual	STD	STD
DGA	**Transmission** — 3-spd automatic - ES 2-Dr w/pkg G or H	445	518
DGB	**Transmission** — 4-spd automatic - Base 4-Dr w/pkg C or D...................	603	701
	ES 2-Dr w/pkg K...	551	641
	ES 4-Dr w/pkg K or L..	551	641

COLT VISTA

CODE	DESCRIPTION	DEALER	LIST
PM52	Base Wagon (5-spd)	12036	12979
PH52	SE Wagon (5-spd)	13130	14194
MM52	AWD Wagon (5-spd)	13751	14884
	Destination Charge:...	430	430

Standard Equipment

COLT VISTA - BASE: Body color fascias, black side window opening moldings, gray bodyside moldings, upper black tailgate applique, 5-mph bumpers, cigarette lighter, cupholders, side sliding door, child protection sliding door locks, stainless steel exhaust system, remote release fuel filler door, halogen aero headlights, rear heat ducts, remote hood release, single horn, three assist grips, floor console, full vinyl front door trim, molded cloth covered headliner, driver's sun visor with ticket holder, inner tailgate assist handle, dome and cargo area lamps, passenger-side covered visor mirror, outside dual manual mirrors, lowback reclining front bucket seats with adjustable head rests, removable fold and tumble rear bench seat, full-face fabric seat trim, tilt steering column, door map pockets, flat cargo floor storage, four argent styled steel wheels with bright center caps, side and rear quarter vented windows, 2-speed variable intermittent wipers/washers, 1.8 liter SMPI 16-valve 4-cylinder engine, 5-speed manual transmission, power assisted rack and pinion steering, power front disc/rear drum brakes.

SE (in addition to or instead of BASE equipment): Upper red and black tailgate applique, two-tone paint with accent color fascias, bodyside moldings and lower tailgate applique; power door locks, tinted glass, dual horn, front door trim with cloth insert, driver foot rest, driver side covered visor mirror, outside dual power mirrors, front center armrest, reclining split back bench seat, Premium full-fabric seat trim (vinyl on back of front seats), passenger seat back pocket storage, left rear side shelf storage, power lock/unlock tailgate, four 7-spoke full-wheel covers, fixed rear intermittent wipers/washers, 2.4 liter SMPI 16-valve 4-cylinder engine.

AWD (in addition to or instead of SE equipment): Body color fascias, lower gray tailgate applique, single horn, front full vinyl door trim, front and rear mudguards, rear bench seat, full-face fabric seat trim, two-tone paint with accent color fascias deleted, power door locks deleted, tinted glass deleted, driver foot rest deleted, front seat center armrest deleted, passenger seat back pocket storage deleted, left rear side shelf deleted, power lock/unlock tailgate deleted.

Accessories

Code	Description	Dealer	List
C	**Pkg C** — Base Wagon .... *incls rear window defroster, air conditioning, tinted glass, pwr remote dual o/s mirrors, radio (AM/FM w/clock & 4 speakers), pwr remote tailgate lock, rear stabilizer bar, 9-spoke full wheel covers, rear window wiper/washer*	994	1156
D	**Pkg D** — Base Wagon .... *incls Pkg C contents plus pwr door locks, floor mats, radio (AM/FM w/cassette, clock & 4 speakers), speed control*	1545	1796
K	**Pkg K** — SE Wagon .... *incls air conditioning, cargo security cover, rear window defroster, floor mats, radio (AM/FM w/cassette, clock & 6 speakers)*	1384	1609
S	**Pkg S** — AWD Wagon .... *incls cargo security cover, custom group, rear window defroster, floor mats, tinted glass, keyless entry, radio (AM/FM w/clock & 4 speakers)*	579	673
W	**Pkg W** — AWD Wagon .... *incls Pkg S contents plus air conditioning, radio (AM/FM w/cassette, clock & 6 speakers), speed control, tach, pwr windows*	1839	2138
HAA	**Air Conditioning** — AWD Wagon...	679	790
BGF	**Brakes** — rear disc w/anti-lock - Base Wagon......................................	601	699
	SE Wagon...	601	699
BGF	**Brakes** — 4-wheel disc anti-lock - AWD Wagon	601	699
	SE Wagon...	57	66
	AWD Wagon..	57	66
NAE	**California Emissions**...	NC	NC
NBY	**New York Emissions**...	NC	NC
MWA	**Roof Rack**...	130	151

COLT VISTA

GEO

CODE	DESCRIPTION	DEALER	LIST
CLA	**Floor Mats** — Base Wagon w/Pkg C	47	55
RAT	**Radio** — Base Wagon...	248	288
	incls AM/FM w/clock & 4 speakers		
RAW	**Radio** — Base Wagon w/Pkg C...	156	181
	AWD Wagon..	156	181
—	**Paint** — two-tone	166	193
EJA	**Engine** — 1.8L MPI 16-valve 4-cyl - Base Wagon	STD	STD
EY7	**Engine** — 2.4L MPI 16-valve 4-cyl - SE Wagon......................................	STD	STD
	AWD Wagon..	STD	STD
	Base Wagon	156	181
DDR	**Transmission** — 5-spd manual	STD	STD
DGB	**Transmission** — 4-spd auto	622	723

METRO

1MS08	XFi 3-Dr Hatchback Coupe..	6706	7195
1MR08	3-Dr Hatchback Coupe	6706	7195
1MR68	5-Dr Hatchback Sedan...	7172	7695
Destination Charge:..		295	295

Standard Equipment

METRO: Radio antenna, power front disc/rear drum brakes, black front and rear bumpers (XFi), 1.0 liter single overhead camshaft 3-cylinder electronic fuel injection engine, stainless steel muffler and tailpipe exhaust, outside LH remote black mirror (XFi), rack and pinion steering, independent 4-wheel MacPherson strut front suspension, P145/80R12 all-season SBR BW tires, 5-speed manual transmission with 4th and 5th gear overdrive, styled steel wheels with center caps (XFi), cargo area trim, full carpeting (including cargo area), center console with cupholders and storage tray, front automatic door locks, rear child security door locks (1MR68), temperature gauge, 3-position dome light, lighter/power socket, inside day/night rearview mirror, front automatic lap/shoulder belts, Scotchgard fabric protector on seats, full-folding rear seat, high-back reclining front bucket seats with integral head restraints, cloth covered seating surface with vinyl backs and sides, self-aligning steering wheel, driver's door storage bin, headlights on reminder

CODE	DESCRIPTION	DEALER	LIST

tone, rear-quarter swing-out window, body-color upper front/rear bumpers (NA - XFi), dual outside LH remote/RH manual black mirrors (NA - XFi), black bodyside moldings (NA - XFi), full wheel covers (NA - XFi), fixed intermittent wipers (NA - XFi).

Accessories

CODE	DESCRIPTION	DEALER	LIST
—	**Metro XFi Base Equipment Group 1** — 1MS08	NC	NC
	incld w/model		
—	**Metro XFi Preferred Equipment Group 2** — 1MS08	268	301
UL0	w/UL0 radio, add	174	195
	incls standard equipment, electronically tuned AM/FM stereo radio with seek, digital clock and four speakers		
—	**Metro Base Equipment Group 1** — 1MR08 & 1MR68	NC	NC
UL1	w/UL1 radio, add	268	301
UL0	w/UL0 radio, add	441	496
	incld w/model		
—	**Metro Preferred Equipment Group 2** — 1MR08 & 1MR68	909	1021
UL0	w/UL0 radio, add	174	195
	incls standard equipment, air conditioning, electronically tuned AM/FM stereo radio with seek, digital clock and four speakers		
—	**Radio Equipment** — see pkgs		
UL1	radio - see pkgs		
	incls electronically tuned AM/FM stereo radio with seek, digital clock and four speakers		
UL0	radio - see pkgs		
	incls electronically tuned AM/FM stereo radio with seek/scan, tone select, stereo cassette tape, digital clock, theft deterrent and four speakers		
H2	**Cloth & Vinyl Bucket Seats**	NC	NC
—	**Exterior Color** — paint, solid	NC	NC
LP2	**Engine** — 1.0 liter SOHC L3 EFI...........................	NC	NC
C60	**Air Conditioning** — CFC free	641	720
D42	**Cover, Cargo Security**....................................	45	50
C49	**Defogger** — rear window....................................	134	150
R9W	**Defogger** — rear window, delete............................	NC	NC
YF5	**California Emission Requirements**.........................	62	70
FE9	**Federal Emission Requirements**	NC	NC
NG1	**New York State Emission Requirements**.....................	62	70
B37	**Floor Mats** — front & rear................................	22	25
D35	**Mirrors, Dual Outside** — LH remote & RH manual, black	18	20
B84	**Moldings** — bodyside, black	45	50
U16	**Tachometer**	45	50
—	**Transmissions**		
MM5	5-speed manual w/4th & 5th gear overdrive....................	NC	NC
MX1	3-speed automatic...	441	495
C25	**Wiper/Washer** — rear window...............................	111	125

GEO

PRIZM

1SK19	4-Dr Sedan (except Calif.)	10215	10730
1SK19	4-Dr Sedan (Calif.)	9958	10460
1SK19/B4M	LSi 4-Dr Sedan (except Calif.)	10603	11500
1SK19/B4M	LSi 4-Dr Sedan (Calif.)	10354	11230
Destination Charge:		365	365

Standard Equipment

PRIZM: Radio antenna, power front disc/rear drum brakes, front and rear body-color bumpers, 1.6 liter dual overhead camshaft 16-valve 4-cylinder multi-port fuel injection engine, stainless steel exhaust, tinted glass, composite halogen headlights, dual outside LH remote/RH manual black mirrors, black bodyside moldings, rack and pinion steering, independent 4-wheel MacPherson strut front suspension, P175/65R14 all-season SBR BW tires, styled steel wheels with center cap, cargo area trim, full carpeting, center console includes cupholder and storage tray, rear child security door locks, cloth door trim, remote fuel door, molded cloth headliners, rear console heating ducts, 3-position dome light, lighter/power socket, inside day/night rearview mirror, headlights on reminder tone, restraint system (driver and passenger air bags, front lap/shoulder belts, rear center lap belt, rear outboard lap/shoulder belts), Scotchgard fabric protection on seats and door trim, reclining front bucket seats with adjustable head restraints, vinyl headrests/seatback with cloth bolsters, driver's door storage bin, door ajar warning light.

LSi (in addition to or instead of PRIZM equipment): Black center pillar, full wheel covers, front and rear passenger assist grips, trunk lid/cargo area trim, console with armrest, cargo area light, covered dual visor mirrors, split folding 60/40 rear seat, full-cloth facing seat trim/side bolsters with cloth/vinyl seatbacks, tilt steering wheel, driver and passenger door storage bins.

Accessories

—	**Prizm Base Equipment Group 1 — 1SK19**	NC	NC
UL1	w/UL1 radio, add	284	330
UL0	w/UL0 radio, add	452	525
—	**Prizm Preferred Group 2 — 1SK19**	507	590
UL0	w/UL0 radio, add	168	195
	incls standard equipment, electronically tuned AM/FM stereo radio with seek, digital clock and four speakers, power steering		
—	**Prizm LSi Preferred Equipment Group 1 — 1SK19/B4M**	NC	NC
UL1	w/UL1 radio, add	284	330

CODE	DESCRIPTION	DEALER	LIST
ULO	w/ULO radio, add	452	525
	incls LSi equipment		
—	**Prizm LSi Preferred Equipment Group 2** — 1SK19/B4M........................	1329	1545
ULO	w/ULO radio, add	168	195
UPO	w/UPO radio, add	488	568
	incls LSi equipment, air cond, electronically tuned AM/FM stereo radio w/seek, digital clock and four speakers, black dual outside electric remote mirrors, power steering, trunk release remote, variable intermittent wipers		
—	**Prizm LSi Preferred Equipment Group 3** — 1SK19/B4M........................	1926	2240
ULO	w/ULO radio, add	168	195
UPO	w/UPO radio, add	488	568
	incls LSi equipment, air conditioning, electronically tuned AM/FM stereo radio with seek, digital clock and four speakers, black dual outside electric remote mirrors, power steering, trunk release remote, variable intermittent wipers, cruise control w/resume speed, power door locks, power windows		
—	**Radio Equipment** — see pkgs		
UL1	radio - see pkgs		
	incls elec tuned AM/FM stereo radio w/seek, digital clock , four speakers		
ULO	radio - see pkgs		
	incls electronically tuned AM/FM stereo radio w/seek and scan, tone select, stereo cass tape, digital clock, theft deterrent and four speakers		
UPO	radio - see pkgs		
	incls elec tuned AM/FM stereo radio w/seek/scan, tone select, stereo cass tape, compact disc plyr, digital clock, theft deterrent, six ext range spkrs		
—	**Interior Trim**		
A2	cloth & vinyl bucket seats..	NC	NC
B2	custom cloth bucket seats (std on Prizm LSi model)...............................	NC	NC
—	**Exterior Color** — paint, solid..	NC	NC
C60	**Air Conditioning** — CFC free	684	795
JM4	**Brakes** — 4-wheel anti-lock brake system.....................................	512	595
K34	**Cruise Control w/Resume Speed**	151	175
C49	**Defogger** — rear window...	146	170
R9W	**Defogger** — rear window, delete...	NC	NC
AU3	**Door Locks** — power..	189	220
YF5	**California Emission Requirements**..	60	70
FE9	**Federal Emission Requirements**	NC	NC
NG1	**New York State Emission Requirements**....................................	60	70
B37	**Floor Mats** — front & rear, carpeted, color-keyed.........................	34	40
CA1	**Sun Roof** — electric w/map light & tilt-up feature........................	568	660
U16	**Tachometer**...	52	60
—	**Transmissions**		
MM5	5-speed manual w/4th & 5th gear overdrive.....................................	NC	NC
MX1	3-speed automatic...	426	495
MS7	4-speed electronically controlled automatic w/overdrive.......................	667	775
—	**Engines**		
LO1	1.6 liter DOHC 16-valve L4 MFI	NC	NC
LV6	1.8 liter DOHC 16-valve L4 MFI	303	352
	incls P185/65R14 all-season steel belted radial BW tires/rear stabilizer bar		
PG4	**Wheels** — 14" alloy...	288	335
CD4	**Wipers** — intermittent variable..	34	40

TRACKER

TRACKER 2WD
		DEALER	LIST
CE10367	2-Dr Convertible	10343	10865

TRACKER 4WD
CJ10316	2-Dr	11705	12295
CJ10367	2-Dr Convertible	11553	12135
CJ10316/B2Z	LSi 2-Dr	13104	13765
CJ10367/B2Z	LSi 2-Dr Convertible	12852	13500
Destination Charge:		300	300

Standard Equipment

TRACKER: Radio antenna, power front disc/rear drum brakes, rear-wheel anti-lock brakes, front and rear bumpers with integral black rub strip, 1.6 liter single overhead camshaft 4-cylinder electronic fuel injection engine (available with FE9 Federal Emission only), 1.6 liter single overhead camshaft 16-valve 4-cylinder multi-port fuel injection engine (available with YF5 California or NG1 New York Emission only), stainless steel muffler and tailpipe exhaust, composite halogen headlights, front manual locking hubs, dual outside black mirrors, spare tire cover, full-size outside rear-mounted lockable spare tire and wheel, front MacPherson strut suspension, rear solid axle coil spring suspension, swing-open right-hand hinged door tailgate with lock, P195/75R15 all-season SBR BW tires (2WD), P205/75R15 all-season SBR BW tires (4x4), front and rear tow hooks, transfer case, 5-speed manual transmission with 5th gear overdrive, styled steel wheels with center caps, fixed intermittent wipers, front and rear passenger assist grips, cargo area trim, full carpeting including cargo area, center console with cupholders and storage tray, rear window defogger (NA - Convertible), tachometer (4x4), trip odometer, 3-position dome light, lighter/power socket, inside day/night rearview mirror, restraint system (front lap/shoulder belts, rear outboard lap/shoulder belts), Scotchgard fabric protection on seats, fold-and-stow rear bench seat (4x4), driver and passenger easy-entry seats, high-back reclining front bucket seats with integral head restraints, cloth bolsters and vinyl seatbacks, self-aligning steering wheel, driver and passenger door storage bins.

Accessories

		DEALER	LIST
—	**Tracker 2WD Convertible Base Equipment Group 1** — CE10367	NC	NC
UL1	w/UL1 radio, add	272	306

CODE	DESCRIPTION	DEALER	LIST
UL0	w/UL0 radio, add	446	501
UP0	w/UP0 radio, add	798	897
	incls standard equipment		
—	**Tracker 2WD Convertible Preferred Equipment Group 2** — CE10367	517	581
UL0	w/UL0 radio, add	174	195
UP0	w/UP0 radio, add	526	591
	incls standard equipment, electronically tuned AM/FM stereo radio with seek, digital clock and four speakers, power steering		
—	**Tracker 4WD/Tracker 4WD Convertible Base Equip Group 1** — CJ10316 & CJ10367	NC	NC
UL1	w/UL1 radio, add	272	306
UL0	w/UL0 radio, add	446	501
UP0	w/UP0 radio, add	798	897
	incld w/model		
—	**Tracker 4WD/Tracker 4WD Convertible Preferred Equip Group 2** — CJ10316 & CJ10367	517	581
UL0	w/UL0 radio, add	174	195
UP0	w/UP0 radio, add	526	591
	incls standard equipment, electronically tuned AM/FM stereo radio with seek, digital clock and four speakers		
—	**Tracker 4WD LSi/Tracker 4WD LSi Convertible Base Equip Group 1** — CJ10316/B2Z & CJ10367/B2Z	NC	NC
UL0	w/UL0 radio, add	174	195
UP0	w/UP0 radio, add	526	591
	incld w/model		
—	**Radio Equipment** — see pkgs		
UL1	radio - see pkgs		
	incls elec tuned AM/FM stereo radio w/seek, digital clock/our speakers		
UL0	radio - see pkgs		
	incls electronically tuned AM/FM stereo radio with seek/can, tone select, stereo cassette tape, digital clock, theft deterrent and four speakers		
UP0	radio - see pkgs		
	incls electronically tuned AM/FM stereo radio with seek and scan, tone select, stereo cassette tape, compact disc player, digital clock, theft deterrent and four speakers		
—	**Interior Trim**		
L2	linear cloth bucket seats	NC	NC
E2	expressive cloth bucket seats	NC	NC
C2	custom cloth bucket seats - LSi & Tracker 4x4 LSi Convertible	NC	NC
—	**Exterior Color** — paint, solid	NC	NC
—	**Engines**		
LS5	1.6 liter SOHC L4 EFI (w/FE9 Emissions only)	NC	NC
L01	1.6 liter SOHC 16-valve L4 MFI (w/YF5 or NG1 Emissions only)	NC	NC
C60	**Air Conditioning** — CFC free	663	745
YF5	**California Emission Requirements**	62	70
FE9	**Federal Emission Requirements**	NC	NC
NG1	**New York State Emission Requirements**	62	70
B37	**Floor Mats** — front & rear - std on LSi models	25	28
B84	**Moldings** — bodyside - CJ10316 model (std on Tracker LSi)	53	59
	Convertible models (std on LSi Convertible)	76	85

CODE	DESCRIPTION	DEALER	LIST
—	**Seating**		
AP6	rear not desired - CE10367 model only	NC	NC
AM7	rear folding bench - CE10367 model only (std on 4x4 models)	396	445
NY7	**Skid Plates** — front differential & transfer case	67	75
N33	**Steering Wheel** — tilt	102	115
—	**Transmissions**		
MM5	5-speed manual w/5th gear overdrive	NC	NC
MX1	3-speed automatic	530	595
QA4	**Wheels** — 15" alloy w/steel spare	298	335

ACCORD COUPE

		DEALER	LIST
CD712R	DX 2-Dr (5-spd)	12011	14130
CD722R	DX 2-Dr (auto)	12648	14880
CD711R	DX 2-Dr w/ABS (5-spd)	12818	15080
CD721R	DX 2-Dr w/ABS (auto)	13456	15830
CD713R	LX 2-Dr (5-spd)	14476	17030
CD723R	LX 2-Dr (auto)	15113	17780
CD714R	LX 2-Dr w/ABS (5-spd)	15283	17980
CD724R	LX 2-Dr w/ABS (auto)	15921	18730
CD715R	EX 2-Dr (5-spd)	16618	19550
CD725R	EX 2-Dr (auto)	17255	20300
CD716R	EX 2-Dr w/Leather (5-spd)	17510	20600
CD726R	EX 2-Dr w/Leather (auto)	18148	21350
Destination Charge:		350	350

Standard Equipment

ACCORD COUPE - DX: 2.2L 130HP 16 valve engine with second-order balance system, aluminum-alloy cylinder head and block w/cast iron liners, electronic ignition, multi-point programmed fuel injection, driver and front passenger airbag SRS, torque-sensitive power rack-and-pinion steering, 5-speed manual transmission, power-assisted front disc/rear drum brakes, dual manual remote-operated mirrors, body side molding, multi-reflector halogen headlights, body-colored impact-absorbing bumpers, center console armrest w/storage compartment, front 3-point seat belts, rear 3-point seat belts w/center lap belt, adjustable steering column, fold-down rear seatback w/lock, quartz digital clock, passenger vanity mirror, trunk-open warning light, remote fuel filler door release, remote trunk release with lock, rear window defroster with timer, 2-speed intermittent windshield wipers, rear seat heater ducts, low fuel warning light, maintenance interval indicator.

LX (in addition to or instead of DX equipment): Integrated rear window antenna, body-colored dual power mirrors, air conditioning, power windows, power door locks, AM/FM high-power 4x12.5 watt stereo cassette, cruise control, beverage holder, driver and passenger vanity mirrors.

EX (in addition to or instead of LX equipment): 2.2L 145HP VTEC engine, anti lock brakes (ABS), power-assisted 4-wheel disc brakes, 15-inch alloy wheels, power moonroof, body-colored body side molding, driver's seat w/power height adjustment, driver's seat adjustable lumbar support, AM/FM high-power 4x20 watt stereo cassette w/6 speakers.

NOTE: *Honda accessories are dealer installed. Contact a Honda dealer for accessory availability.*

ACCORD SEDAN

CODE	DESCRIPTION	DEALER	LIST
CD552R	DX 4-Dr Sedan (5-spd)	12181	14330
CD551R	DX 4-Dr Sedan w/Anti-Lock Brakes (5-spd)	12988	15280
CD562R	DX 4-Dr Sedan (auto)	12818	15080
CD561R	DX 4-Dr Sedan w/Anti-Lock Brakes (auto)	13626	16030
CD553R	LX 4-Dr Sedan (5-spd)	14646	17230
CD554R	LX 4-Dr Sedan w/Anti-Lock Brakes (5-spd)	15453	18180
CD563R	LX 4-Dr Sedan (auto)	15283	17980
CD564R	LX 4-Dr Sedan w/Anti-Lock Brakes (auto)	16091	18930
CD555R	EX 4-Dr Sedan (5-spd)	16788	19750
CD556R	EX 4-Dr Sedan w/Anti-Lock Brakes (5-spd)	17680	20800
CD565R	EX 4-Dr Sedan (auto)	17425	20500
CD566R	EX 4-Dr Sedan w/Leather Pkg (auto)	18318	21550
Destination Charge:		350	350

CODE	DESCRIPTION	DEALER	LIST

Standard Equipment

ACCORD SEDAN - DX: 2.2L 130HP 16-valve engine w/second-order balance system, aluminum-alloy cylinder head and block w/cast iron liners, electronic ignition, multi-point programmed fuel injection, driver and front passenger airbag SRS, torque-sensitive power rack-and-pinion steering, 5 speed manual transmission, power assisted front disc/rear drum brakes, dual-manual remote-operated mirrors, body side molding, multi-reflector halogen headlights, body-colored impact-absorbing bumpers, center console armrest w/storage compartment, front 3-point seat belts w/adjustable shoulder anchors, rear 3-point seat belts w/center lap belt, adjustable steering column, fold-down rear seatback w/lock, quartz digital clock, passenger vanity mirror, trunk/tailgate-open warning light, remote fuel filler door release, remote trunk release w/lock, rear window defroster w/timer, 2-speed intermittent windshield wipers, rear seat heater ducts, low fuel warning light, maintenance interval indicator.

LX (also has in addition to or instead of DX equipment): Rear fender-mounted power antenna, body-colored dual power mirrors, air conditioning, power windows, power door locks, AM/FM high-power 4x12.5 watt stereo cassette, cruise control, fold-down rear seat center armrest, beverage holder, driver and passenger vanity mirrors.

EX (also has in addition to or instead of LX equipment): 2.2L 145HP VTEC engine, anti-lock brakes ABS, power assisted 4-wheel disc brakes, 15-inch alloy wheels, power moonroof, body-colored body side molding, driver's seat w/power height adjustment, driver's seat adjustable lumbar support, AM/FM high-power 4x20 watt stereo cassette w/6 speakers.

NOTE: Honda accessories are dealer installed. Contact a Honda dealer for accessory availability.

CIVIC COUPE

CODE	DESCRIPTION	DEALER	LIST
EJ212R	DX 2-Dr Coupe (5-spd)	9649	11220
EJ222R	DX 2-Dr Coupe (auto)	10492	12200
EJ112R	EX 2-Dr Coupe (5-spd)	11696	13600
EJ113R	EX 2-Dr Coupe w/Anti-Lock Brakes (5-spd)	12427	14450
EJ122R	EX 2-Dr Coupe (auto)	12341	14350
EJ123R	EX 2-Dr Coupe w/Anti-Lock Brakes (auto)	13072	15200
Destination Charge:		350	350

Standard Equipment

CIVIC COUPE - DX: 1.5L 102HP 16-valve SOHC engine, aluminum-alloy cylinder head and block w/cast iron cylinder liners, multi-point programmed fuel injection (PGM-FI), electronic ignition, 5-speed manual transmission, power-assisted front disc/rear drum brakes, driver and front passenger airbag supplemental restraint system (SRS), chin spoiler, impact-absorbing body-colored bumpers, body side molding, dual manual remote-operated mirrors, tinted glass, adjustable steering column, beverage holder, 2-speed intermittent windshield wipers, front 3-point seat belts, rear 3-point seat belts w/center lap belt, reclining front seatbacks, fold-down rear seatbacks w/lock, remote fuel filler door release, remote trunk release w/lock, trunk-open warning light, rear window defroster w/timer, child safety-seat anchors, coin box, power-assisted rack-and-pinion steering (with auto transmission only).

EX (also has in addition to or instead of DX equipment): 1.6L 125HP 16 valve SOHC VTEC engine, power-assisted rack-and-pinion steering, power moonroof w/tilt feature, body-colored dual power mirrors, full wheelcovers, AM/FM high-power 4x20 watt stereo cassette w/6 speakers, power windows and door locks, cruise control, quartz digital clock, tachometer, cargo area light, passenger vanity mirror.

NOTE: Honda accessories are dealer installed. Contact a Honda dealer for accessory availability.

CIVIC HATCHBACK

CODE	DESCRIPTION	DEALER	LIST
EH235R	CX 3-Dr Hatchback (5-spd)	8460	9400
EH236R	DX 3-Dr Hatchback (5-spd)	9288	10800
EH246R	DX 3-Dr Hatchback (auto)	10131	11780
EH237R	VX 3-Dr Hatchback (5-spd)	9890	11500
EH338R	Si 3-Dr Hatchback (5-spd)	11326	13170
EH339R	Si 3-Dr Hatchback w/Anti-Lock Brakes (5-spd)	12057	14020
Destination Charge:		350	350

Standard Equipment

CIVIC HATCHBACK - CX: 1.5L 70HP 8-valve SOHC engine, aluminum-alloy cylinder head and block w/cast iron cylinder liners, multi-point programmed fuel injection (PGM-FI), electronic ignition, 5-speed

CODE	DESCRIPTION	DEALER	LIST

manual transmission, power assisted front disc/rear drum brakes, driver and front passenger airbag supplemental restraint system (SRS), impact-absorbing body-colored bumpers, two-piece hatch, dual manual remote-operated mirrors, near-flush windshield and side windows, tinted glass, beverage holder, 3-point seat belts at all outboard seating positions, reclining front seatbacks, 50/50 split fold-down rear seatback, remote hatch and fuel filler door releases, hatch-open warning light, rear window defroster w/timer, child safety-seat anchors, coin box, variable-diameter tubular door reinforcing beams.

DX (also has in addition to or instead of CX equipment): 1.5L 102HP 16-valve SOHC engine, power assisted rack-and-pinion steering (auto transmission only), rear window wiper/washer, body side molding, adjustable steering column, cargo cover, 2-speed intermittent windshield wipers, rear magazine pocket.

VX (also has in addition to or instead of DX equipment): 1.5L 92HP 16-valve SOHC VTEC-E engine, power-assisted rack-and-pinion steering deleted, rear window wiper/washer deleted, chin spoiler, body side molding deleted, lightweight alloy wheels, cruise control deleted, quartz digital clock deleted, tachometer, adjustable steering column deleted, cargo cover deleted, 2-speed intermittent windshield wipers deleted, rear magazine pocket deleted.

Si (also has in addition to or instead of VX equipment): 1.6L 125HP 16-valve SOHC VTEC engine, power assisted rack-and-pinion steering, power-assisted 4-wheel disc brakes, power moonroof with tilt feature, rear window wiper/washer, chin spoiler deleted, body side molding, body-colored dual power mirrors, full wheel covers, lightweight alloy wheels deleted, cruise control, quartz digital clock, adjustable steering column, cargo cover, 2-speed intermittent windshield wipers, cargo area light, passenger vanity mirror, driver's footrest, rear magazine pocket.

NOTE: *Honda accessories are dealer installed. Contact a Honda dealer for accessory availability.*

HONDA

CIVIC SEDAN

		DEALER	LIST
EG854R	DX 4-Dr Sedan (5-spd)	10105	11750
EG864R	DX 4-Dr Sedan (auto)	10750	12500
EG855R	LX 4-Dr Sedan (5-spd)	11137	12950
EG856R	LX 4-Dr Sedan w/Anti-Lock Brakes (5-spd)	11868	13800

CODE	DESCRIPTION	DEALER	LIST
EG865R	LX 4-Dr Sedan (auto)	11782	13700
EG866R	LX 4-Dr Sedan w/Anti-Lock Brakes (auto).................................	12513	14550
EH959R	EX 4-Dr Sedan (5-spd)...	13536	15740
EH969R	EX 4-Dr Sedan (auto)...	14181	16490
Destination Charge:	....	350	350

Standard Equipment

CIVIC SEDAN - DX: 1.5L 102HP 16-valve SOHC engine, aluminum-alloy cylinder head and block w/cast iron cylinder liners, multi-point programmed fuel injection (PGM-FI), electronic ignition, 5-speed manual transmission, power assisted rack-and-pinion steering, power-assisted rack-and-pinion steering, power-assisted front disc/rear drum brakes, driver and front passenger airbag supplemental restraint system (SRS), impact absorbing body-colored bumpers, body side molding, dual manual remote-operated mirrors, tinted glass, adjustable steering column, beverage holder, 2-speed intermittent windshield wipers, 3-point front and rear seat belts, reclining front seatback, adjustable front seat belt anchors, fold-down rear seatback w/lock, remote trunk and fuel filler door releases, trunk-open warning light, rear window defroster w/timer, child safety-seat anchors, coin box, child-proof rear door locks, lined trunk w/under-floor storage compartment.

LX (also has in addition to or instead of DX equipment): Dual power mirrors, full wheel covers, AM/FM high-power 4x12.5 watt stereo cassette, power windows and door locks, cruise control, quartz digital clock, tachometer, front center armrest w/storage compartment, cargo area light, passenger vanity mirror, rear magazine pocket.

EX (also has in addition to or instead of LX equipment): 1.6L 125HP 16-valve SOHC VTEC engine, power-assisted 4-wheel disc brakes, anti-lock braking system (ABS), power moonroof w/tilt feature, body-colored dual power mirrors, air conditioning, AM/FM high-power 4x20 watt stereo cassette, driver's footrest.

NOTE: Honda accessories are dealer installed. Contact a Honda dealer for accessory availability.

CODE	DESCRIPTION	DEALER	LIST

CIVIC DEL SOL

CIVIC DEL SOL

Code	Description	Dealer	List
EG114R	S 2-Dr Coupe (5-spd)	12126	14100
EG124R	S 2-Dr Coupe (auto)	12926	15080
EH616R	Si 2-Dr Coupe (5-spd)	13846	16100
EH626R	Si 2-Dr Coupe (auto)	14491	16850
EG217R	VTEC 2-Dr Coupe (5-spd)	15050	17500
	Destination Charge:	350	350

Standard Equipment

CIVIC DEL SOL S: 1.5L 102HP 16-valve SOHC engine aluminum-alloy cylinder head and block w/cast iron cylinder liners, multi-point programmed fuel injection (PGM-FI), electronic ignition, 5-speed manual transmission, power-assisted ventilated front disc/rear drum brakes, driver and front passenger airbag supplemental restraint system (SRS), body-colored 5 mph impact-absorbing bumpers, body-colored dual manual mirrors, full wheel covers, removable roof panel, quartz halogen headlights, center armrest w/storage compartment/beverage holder/coin box, centrally locking rear storage compartments, driver's footrest, floor/trunk full carpeting, passenger-side sun visor w/vanity mirror, lockable remote fuel filler door release, power side windows, rear power window, 3-point seat belts, reclining seatbacks, trunk-open warning light, cigarette lighter and ashtray, pre-wired front speaker grilles, rear window defroster w/timer, 2-speed intermittent windshield wipers w/washer, adjustable steering column, tachometer, automatic transmission mode indicator, quartz digital clock, interior light, cargo area light, power rack-and-pinion steering (with auto transmission only).

Si (also has in addition to or instead of S equipment): 1.6L 125HP 16-valve SOHC VTEC engine, power-assisted rack-and-pinion steering, power-assisted 4-wheel disc brakes, alloy wheels, body-colored dual power mirrors, AM/FM high-power 4x20 watt stereo cassette, cruise control.

VTEC (also has in addition to or instead of Si equipment): 1.6L 160HP 16-valve DOHC VTEC engine.

NOTE: Honda accessories are dealer installed. Contact a Honda dealer for accessory availability.

CODE	DESCRIPTION	DEALER	LIST

PRELUDE

		DEALER	LIST
BA814R	S 2-Dr Coupe (5-spd)	15385	18100
BA824R	S 2-Dr Coupe (auto)	16023	18850
BB215R	Si 2-Dr Coupe (5-spd)	18190	21400
BB225R	Si 2-Dr Coupe (auto)	18828	22150
BB216R	Si 4WS 2-Dr Coupe (5-spd)	20536	24160
BB226R	Si 4WS 2-Dr Coupe (auto)	21174	24910
BB117R	VTEC 2-Dr Coupe (5-spd)	20825	24500
	Destination Charge:	350	350

Standard Equipment

PRELUDE S: 2.2L 135HP 16-valve SOHC engine w/second-order balance system, aluminum-alloy cylinder head and block w/cast iron liners, multi-point programmed fuel injection, driver and front passenger airbag (SRS), variable-assist power rack-and-pinion steering, 5-speed manual transmission, power-assisted 4-wheel disc brakes, power sunroof w/tilt feature, rear fender-mounted power antenna, body-colored dual power mirrors, multi-reflector halogen headlights, body-colored impact-absorbing bumpers, dual-outlet exhaust, AM/FM high-power 4x12.5 watt stereo cassette, center console armrest w/storage compartment, power windows, cruise control, digital clock, tachometer, adjustable steering column, 2-speed intermittent windshield wipers, 3-point front and rear seat belts, reclining front seatbacks, right-side fold-down rear seatback w/lock, remote trunk and fuel filler door releases, rear window defroster w/timer, cargo area light, child safety-seat anchors, driver/passenger vanity mirrors, beverage holder.

Si (also has in addition to or instead of S equipment): 2.3L 160HP 16-valve DOHC engine w/second-order balance system, aluminum-alloy cylinder head and block w/fiber-reinforced metal (FRM) cylinder walls, electronic ignition w/knock sensor, dual-stage induction system, alloy wheels, anti-lock braking system (ABS), chin spoiler, driver's seat adjustable lumbar support, air conditioning, ignition switch light, power door locks, AM/FM high-power 4x20 watt stereo cassette w/6 speakers.

4WS (also has in addition to or instead of Si equipment): Electronic 4-wheel steering, rear spoiler w/integral LED stoplight, leather-trimmed seats and door panel inserts, map lights.

VTEC (also has in addition to or instead of 4WS equipment): 2.2L 190HP 16-valve DOHC VTEC engine w/second-order balance system, electronic 4-wheel steering deleted, AM/FM high-power 5x20 watt stereo cassette w/7 speakers.

NOTE: *Honda accessories are dealer installed. Contact a Honda dealer for accessory availability.*

ELANTRA

40423	Base 4-Dr Sedan (5-spd)	8800	9749
40422	Base 4-Dr Sedan (auto)	9948	11024
40443	GLS 4-Dr Sedan (5-spd)	9669	10959
40442	GLS 4-Dr Sedan (auto)	10320	11684
Destination Charge:		405	405

Standard Equipment

ELANTRA - BASE: Front illuminated and dual rear ashtrays, front and rear assist grips, cargo area floor carpeting, cut pile carpeting, illuminated cigarette lighter, rotary-type climate controls, digital quartz clock, coin box, full center console w/storage box, dual cupholder, front side window defoggers, electric rear window defroster, rear child safety door locks, full door trim w/cloth inserts, temperature and trip odometer gauges, lockable glove box, rear seat heater ducts, cargo area illumination, overhead courtesy illumination, passenger visor vanity mirror, remote fuel door and hood releases, remote trunk release, color-keyed seatbelts, full face cloth seat trim, front reclining bucket seats w/adjustable headrests, color-keyed 4-spoke steering wheel w/airbag, collapsible steering column, door ajar/trunk open/low fuel warning lights, maintenance-free battery, unitized body construction, front ventilated power-assisted disc brakes, rear self-adjusting drum brakes, 1.6L DOHC 16 valve 4 cylinder dual bal shaft engine, front wheel drive, electronic multi-port fuel injection (MPI), front and rear stabilizer bars, power rack-and-pinion steering, front independent MacPherson Strut suspension, rear multi-link axle, 5-speed manual overdrive transmission, fixed mast antenna, bodycolor bumpers w/charcoal accent, bodycolor door handles, tinted glass, windshield sunshade band, bodycolor grille, aerodynamic halogen headlamps, dual remote-control black mirrors, bodycolor bodyside moldings w/black accent, P175/65R14 SBR w/full wheel covers, front variable intermittent wipers.

GLS (also has in addition to or instead of BASE equipment): AM/FM ETR 40 watt stereo cassette w/4 speakers, cargo area side trim, deluxe cut pile carpeting, full-center console w/covered storage box, power door locks, carpeted kick panel door trim, front courtesy lamp door trim,, front door map pocket trim, tachometer gauge, front map lights, deluxe full cloth seat trim, driver's 6-way adjustable seat, 60/40 split fold-down rear seats, tilt steering wheel, power windows, 1.8L DOHC 16 valve 4 cylinder dual bal

CODE	DESCRIPTION	DEALER	LIST

shaft engine, gas pressure shock absorbers, bodycolor bumpers w/bright accent, dual power remote-control bodycolor mirrors, bodycolor bodyside moldings w/bright accent, bright side window accents, bodycolor rocker panel molding, bright trim tailpipe, P185/60HR-14 SBR tires w/deluxe full wheelcovers.

Accessories

Code	Description	Dealer	List
CA	**California Emissions System**	NC	NC
CD	**Compact Disc Player**	290	395
CF	**Floor Mats**	38	58
AR	**Console**	70	108
DG	**Door Edge Guards**	23	36
MG	**Mud Guards**	47	78
WD	**Deflector**	30	52
02AB	**Base Package 2 — Base**	268	350
	incls AM/FM stereo radio w/cassette		
03AC	**Base Package 3 — Base**	998	1245
	incls AM/FM stereo radio w/cassette and air conditioning		
04AD	**Base Package 4 — Base**	1178	1465
	incls AM/FM stereo radio w/cassette, air conditioning and cruise control		
10AJ	**GLS Package 10 — GLS**	1053	1303
	incls AM/FM stereo radio w/cassette, air conditioning and cruise control		
11AK	**GLS Package 11 — GLS**	1330	1643
	incls AM/FM stereo radio w/cassette, air conditioning, cruise control and alloy wheels		
12AL	**GLS Package 12 — GLS**	1469	1813
	incls AM/FM stereo radio w/cassette, air conditioning, cruise control and sunroof		
13AM	**GLS Package 13 — GLS**	1764	2078
	incls AM/FM stereo radio w/cassette, air conditioning, cruise control, sunroof and anti-lock brakes		
14AN	**GLS Package 14 — GLS**	2605	3120
	incls AM/FM stereo radio w/cassette, air conditioning, cruise control, sunroof, anti-lock brakes and alloy wheels		
15AO	**GLS Package 15 — GLS**	1894	2345
	incls AM/FM stereo radio w/cassette, air conditioning, cruise control, sunroof and alloy wheels		

CODE	DESCRIPTION	DEALER	LIST

EXCEL

11303	Base 3-Dr Hatchback (4-spd)	6710	7190
11302	Base 3-Dr Hatchback (auto)	7271	7815
11353	GS 3-Dr Hatchback (5-spd)	7311	8099
11352	GS 3-Dr Hatchback (auto)	7872	8724
11423	GL 4-Dr Sedan (4-spd)	7476	8099
11422	GL 4-Dr Sedan (auto)	8037	8724
Destination Charge:		405	405

Standard Equipment

EXCEL - BASE HATCHBACK: Front illuminated/dual rear ashtrays, front assist grip, detachable cargo area cover, cargo area floor carpeting, cut pile carpeting, cigarette lighter, lever-type climate controls, center console w/coin holder, front side window defoggers, electric rear window defroster, full door trim w/armrests, temperature/trip odometer gauges, cargo area/overhead courtesy illumination, day/night mirror, remote hood release, color-keyed seatbelts, full face woven cloth seat trim, front reclining bucket seats w/adjustable headrests, passenger-side walk-in device, 60/40 split fold-down rear seats, color-keyed 2-spoke steering wheel, rear covered armrest storage bins, door ajar and hatch/trunk ajar warning lights, low fuel warning light, rear swiveling windows, maintenance-free battery, unitized body construction, ventilated power assisted front disc brakes, self-adjusting rear drum brakes, 1.5L SOHC 4-cylinder engine, transverse mounted front wheel drive, electronic multi-port fuel injection (MPI), front and rear stabilizer bars, rack-and-pinion steering, front independent MacPherson strut suspension, rear independent trailing arm suspension, 5-speed manual overdrive transmission, fixed mast antenna, bodycolor bumpers w/black rubstrips, black door handles, black grille, aerodynamic halogen headlamps, locking fuel filler door, dual remote-control black mirrors, black bodyside moldings, front mud flaps, rear stone guards, P155/80R13 SBR tires w/full wheelcovers, front variable intermittent wipers.

GS HATCHBACK (also has in addition to or instead of BASE HATCHBACK equipment): AM/FM ETR stereo cassette w/2 speakers, rotary-type climate controls, digital quartz clock, deluxe front console w/cassette storage, deluxe door trim w/cloth inserts and integrated armrests, front door map pocket trim, tachometer gauge, lockable glove box, rear seat heater ducts, front passenger visor vanity mirror, remote cargo area and fuel door releases, full sport cloth seat trim w/cloth bolster, driver's 5-way adjustable seat, soft-grip type steering wheel, bodycolor bumpers, bodycolor door handles, tinted glass, bodycolor grille, locking fuel filler door deleted, dual remote-control bodycolor mirrors, black back panel moldings, black rocker panel moldings, bodycolor bodyside moldings, rear spoiler, P175/70R13 SBR tires w/deluxe full wheelcovers, rear wiper w/washer.

GL SEDAN Front illuminated and dual rear ashtrays, front assist grip, AM/FM ETR stereo cassette w/2-speakers, cargo area floor carpeting, cut pile carpeting, cigarette lighter, lever-type climate controls, center console w/coin holder, front side window defoggers, electric rear window defroster, rear child safety door locks, deluxe door trim w/cloth inserts and integrated armrests, front door map pocket trim, temperature and trip odometer gauges, lockable glove box, cargo area/overhead courtesy illumination, day/night mirror, remote cargo area and fuel door releases, remote hood release, color-keyed seatbelts, full face woven cloth seat trim, front reclining bucket seats w/adjustable headrests, color-keyed 2-spoke steering wheel, door ajar/hatch/trunk ajar/low fuel warning lights, full roll-down rear window, maintenance-free battery, unitized body construction, ventilated power-assisted front disc brakes, self-adjusting rear drum brakes, 1.5L SOHC 4-cylinder engine, transverse-mounted front wheel drive, electronic multiport fuel injection (MPI), front and rear stabilizer bars, rack-and-pinion steering, independent MacPherson front strut suspension, rear independent trailing arm, 5-speed manual overdrive transmission, fixed mast antenna, bodycolor bumpers w/black rubstrips, black door handles, bodycolor grille, aerodynamic halogen headlamps, dual remote control black mirrors, black bodyside moldings, front mud flaps, rear stone guards, P175/70R13 SBR tires w/deluxe full wheelcovers, front variable intermittent wipers.

Accessories

CODE	DESCRIPTION	DEALER	LIST
CA	**California Emissions System**	NC	NC
CF	**Floor Mats**	38	58
AR	Console	64	105
MG	Rear Mud Guards	26	40
WD	Deflector — all except Base	30	52
02AB	Base Package 2 — Base	260	340
	incls AM/FM stereo radio w/cassette		
03AC	**Base Package 3** — Base	541	660
	incls AM/FM stereo radio w/cassette, tinted glass and power steering		
04AD	**Base Package 4** — Base	1263	1545
	incls AM/FM stereo radio w/cassette, tinted glass, power steering and air conditioning		
05AE	**GL Package 5** — GL	232	260
	incls power steering		
06AF	**GL Package 6** — GL	994	1155
	incls power steering and air conditioning		
10AJ	**GS Package 10** — GS	232	260
	incls power steering		
11AK	**GS Package 11** — GS	994	1155
	incls power steering and air conditioning		
12AL	**GS Package 12** — GS	1394	1645
	incls power steering, air conditioning and sunroof		

SCOUPE

30223	Base 2-Dr Coupe (5-spd)	8575	9499
30222	Base 2-Dr Coupe (auto)	9188	10174
30243	LS 2-Dr Coupe (5-spd)	9351	10599
30242	LS 2-Dr Coupe (auto)	9964	11274
30253	Turbo 2-Dr Coupe (5-spd)	10057	11399
Destination Charge:		405	405

Standard Equipment

SCOUPE - BASE: Front illuminated ashtray, front assist grip, cargo area floor carpeting, cut pile carpeting, illuminated cigarette lighter, rotary type climate controls, digital quartz clock, full console w/coin holder, front side window defoggers, electric rear window defroster, front door map pocket trim, full door trim w/cloth inserts, tachometer/temperature/trip odometer gauges, illuminated locking glove box, rear seat heater ducts, cargo area/overhead courtesy illumination, front map lights, day/night mirror, front passenger visor vanity mirror, remote fuel door/hood/trunk releases, color-keyed front passive seatbelts w/manual lap, full face deluxe cloth seat trim, front reclining bucket seats w/adjustable headrests, passenger-side walk-in device, 60/40 split fold-down rear seat, color-keyed 3-spoke steering wheel, collapsible steering column, door ajar/trunk ajar/low fuel warning lights, maintenance-free battery, unitized body construction, ventilated power assisted front disc brakes, self-adjusting rear drum brakes, 1.5L SOHC 4-cylinder engine, transverse mounted layout front wheel drive, electronic multi-port fuel injection (MPI), front and rear stabilizer bars, rack-and-pinion steering, independent MacPherson front strut suspension, rear independent trailing arm, 5-speed manual overdrive transmission, manual telescopic antenna, bodycolor bumpers, black door handles, green tinted glass, windshield sunshade band, bodycolor air inlet grille, aerodynamic halogen headlamps, dual remote control black mirrors, black rocker panel moldings, bodycolor bodyside moldings, rear spoiler, dual tailpipes w/chrome finishers, P175/65R14 SBR tires w/full wheelcovers, front variable intermittent wipers.

LS (also has in addition to or instead of BASE equipment): Deluxe AM/FM stereo cassette w/4 speakers, cargo area side trim carpeting, deluxe cut pile carpeting, dual cupholders, full sporty cloth seat trim, driver's 6-way adjustable seat, passenger's 4-way adjustable seat, front reclining bucket seats w/adjustable headrests deleted, soft-grip type steering wheel, tilt steering column, power windows, power rack-and-

CODE	DESCRIPTION	DEALER	LIST

pinion steering, bodycolor door handles, dual power remote-control bodycolor mirrors, bodycolor body-side cladding, Michelin P185/60HR14 performance radial tires w/deluxe full wheelcovers.

TURBO (also has in addition to or instead of LS equipment): LED turbo boost meter gauge, turbo badged full sporty cloth seat trim, leather wrapped steering wheel w/leather wrapped gear shift knob, turbocharged 1.5L SOHC 4-cylinder engine, sport tuned package, fog lamps, Michelin P185/60HR14 performance radials w/aluminum alloy wheels.

Accessories

CODE	DESCRIPTION	DEALER	LIST
CA	**California Emissions System**	NC	NC
CD	**Compact Disc Player**	290	395
CF	**Floor Mats**	38	58
AR	**Console**	64	105
DG	**Door Edge Guards**	15	23
SH	**Sunshade**	38	58
02AB	**Base Package 2** — Base	496	610
	incls AM/FM stereo radio w/cassette and power steering		
03AC	**Base Package 3** — Base	1235	1505
	incls AM/FM stereo radio w/cassette, power steering and air conditioning		
10AJ	**LS Package 10** — LS	739	895
	incls air conditioning		
11AK	**LS Package 11** — LS	983	1190
	incls air conditioning and sunroof		
12AL	**LS Package 12** — LS	1405	1715
	incls AM/FM stereo radio w/cassette, air cond, sunroof and alloy wheels		
15AO	**Turbo Package 15** — Turbo	1132	1385
	incls AM/FM stereo radio w/cassette, air conditioning and sunroof		

SONATA

21423	Base 4-Dr Sedan (5-spd)	11418	12799
21422	Base 4-Dr Sedan (auto)	12182	13579
21432	Base V6 4-Dr Sedan (auto)	12867	14369
21443	GLS 4-Dr Sedan (5-spd)	12383	14199
21442	GLS 4-Dr Sedan (auto)	13147	14979
21452	GLS V6 4-Dr Sedan (auto)	13832	15769
Destination Charge:		405	405

Standard Equipment

SONATA - BASE: Air conditioning, front illuminated and dual rear ashtrays, front and rear assist grips, AM/FM ETR stereo cassette w/6 speakers, cargo area floor carpeting, cut pile carpeting, illuminated cigarette lighter, rotary type climate controls, digital quartz clock, full center console w/coin holder and storage box, dual cupholders, front side window defoggers, electric rear window defroster w/timer, rear child safety door locks, front door map pocket trim, full door trim w/cloth inserts. tachometer/temperature/trip odometer gauges, illuminated locking glove box, rear seat heater ducts, delay-out w/illuminated ignition, cargo area/overhead courtesy illumination, dual visor vanity mirrors, remote fuel door and hood release, remote trunk release w/lock-out feature, color-keyed seatbelts, passive motorized front seatbelts, full cloth seat trim, driver's 4-way adjustable seat, front reclining bucket seats, rear integral headrests, tilt/color-keyed 3-spoke steering wheel, warning lights for door ajar/trunk ajar/low fuel, full roll-down rear window, maintenance-free battery, unitized body construction, ventilated power assisted front disc brakes, self-adjusting rear drum brakes, 2.0L DOHC 16 valve 4-cylinder dual bal shaft engine, front wheel drive, electronic multi-port fuel injection (MPI), front and rear stabilizer bars, power rack-and-pinion steering, independent MacPherson front strut suspension, rear multi-link axle suspension, 5-speed manual overdrive transmission, fixed mast antenna, bodycolor bumpers w/dark charcoal accents, bodycolor door handles, tinted glass, bodycolor grille, aerodynamic halogen headlamps, dual remote-control black mirrors, bodycolor bodyside moldings w/dark charcoal accents, P195/70R14 SBR tires w/full wheelcovers, front variable intermittent wipers.

GLS (also has in addition to or instead of BASE equipment): Deluxe AM/FM ETR stereo cassette w/6 speakers, cargo area side trim, deluxe cut pile carpeting, armrest box cover and cassette tape holder, carpeted

CODE	DESCRIPTION	DEALER	LIST

kick panel door trim, front courtesy lamps, oil pressure and voltmeter gauges, front map lights, front passenger visor vanity mirror, cruise control, power door locks, power dual remote-control bodycolor mirrors, power telescopic antenna, power windows, deluxe full cloth seat trim, driver's 6-way adjustable seat, 60/40 split fold-down rear seat w/center armrest, soft-grip steering wheel, front seatback storage pockets, 4-speed elec controlled auto overdrive transmission w/lock-up torque converter and dual mode selector, power telescopic antenna, bodycolor bumpers w/bright accents, windshield sunshade band, bodycolor grille w/dark charcoal insert, dual power remote-control bodycolor mirrors, bodycolor bodyside moldings w/bright accents, bright window accents, P195/70R14 SBR tires w/deluxe full wheelcovers.

Accessories

Code	Description	Dealer	List
CA	**California Emissions System**	NC	NC
CF	**Floor Mats**	43	67
AR	**Console**	89	130
DG	**Door Edge Guards**	27	43
MG	**Mud Guards**	58	93
WD	**Deflector**	26	52
03AC	**Base Package 3** — Base	694	850
	incls cruise control and power package		
04AD	**Base Package 4** — Base	490	600
	incls sunroof		
06AF	**Base Package 6** — Base	1184	1450
	incls cruise control, power package and sunroof		
10AJ	**GLS Package 10** — GLS	388	475
	incls alloy wheel package		
11AK	**GLS Package 11** — GLS	1372	1680
	incls alloy wheel package, sunroof and high AM/FM stereo radio w/cass		
12AL	**GLS Package 12** — GLS V6	2135	2560
	incls alloy wheel package, sunroof, high AM/FM stereo radio w/cassette and anti-lock brakes		
13AM	**GLS Package 13** — GLS V6	2254	2715
	incls alloy wheel package, sunroof, premium AM/FM stereo radio w/compact disc player and leather package		
14AN	**GLS Package 14** — GLS V6	3017	3595
	incls alloy wheel package, sunroof, premium AM/FM stereo radio w/compact disc player, leather package and anti-lock brakes		
15AO	**GLS Package 15** — GLS	2022	2430
	incls alloy wheel package, sunroof, high AM/FM stereo radio w/cassette and leather package		
16AP	**GLS Package 16** — GLS V6	2785	3310
	incls alloy wheel package, sunroof, high AM/FM stereo radio w/cassette, leather package and anti-lock brakes		

CODE	DESCRIPTION	DEALER	LIST

G20 (1993.5)

92353	4-Dr Sedan (5-spd)	17835	21750
92313	4-Dr Sedan (auto)	18655	22750
Destination Charge:		450	450

Standard Equipment

G20: In-line 4-cylinder 16-valve DOHC engine, sequential multi-point fuel injection, front wheel drive, 5-speed manual transmission, all-steel unit body construction, front suspension (independent, multi-link with coil springs and stabilizer bar), rear suspension (independent, strut-type with reinforced parallel links, coil springs and stabilizer bar), rack and pinion steering with power assist, 4-wheel disc brakes with anti-lock braking system, power heated outside mirrors, tinted glass, halogen headlights, body-colored bumpers and moldings, power-assisted contoured front bucket seats, driver's seat lumbar support and seat height adjustment, leather-wrapped steering wheel and shift knob, carpeted floor mats, non-CFC R134a air conditioning, cruise control, tilt steering column, driver's and passenger's windows with "one-touch down" feature, power door locks, power trunk release, power fuel filler door release, rear window defroster with timer, driver's and passenger's front seat back pockets, illuminated driver's and passenger's vanity mirrors, fade out interior lamp, cargo net in trunk, driver's and passenger's side air bags, child safety rear door locks, energy-absorbing front and rear bumpers, anti-theft system, six-speaker premium audio system with two A-pillar mounted tweeters, 160-watt amplifier, auto-reverse cassette deck, automatic power antenna and diversity antenna system, electronic speedometer, analog tachometer, coolant temperature and fuel gauges, trip odometer, digital quartz clock, 6.0 JJ-14 polished cast aluminum wheels, P195/65HR14 performance radial tires.

Accessories

V01	**Leather Upholstery**	1804	2200
	incls leather interior, power sunroof, 4-way power seats, keyless remote entry system w/2 transmitters		
J01	**Power Sunroof**	820	1000

J30

97014	4-Dr Sedan (auto)	29930	36950
	Destination Charge:	450	450

Standard Equipment

J30: V6 4-cam 24-valve engine, sequential multi-point fuel injection, electronically controlled four-speed automatic transmission with lockup torque converter and interactive engine control system, front suspension (extended-travel MacPherson strut type with stabilizer bar), rear suspension (double-isolated multi-link type with stabilizer bar), speed sensitive power rack and pinion steering, 4-wheel disc brakes with anti-lock braking system, 6.5JJ-15 cast aluminum alloy wheels, 215/60R15 all-season radial tires, power sunroof, tinted glass, fully contoured projector beam headlights, leather appointed interior, leather-wrapped steering wheel and shift knob, walnut accents on center console and driver's door, rear center armrest, carpeted and illuminated trunk, carpeted floor mats, power windows, power door locks with keyless remote entry system, power trunk release, power fuel filler door release, 8-way power driver's and front passenger's seats, limited slip differential, heated front seats, manual tilt steering column, cruise control, automatic temperature control with non-CFC R134a refrigerant, center console cupholder, cargo net in trunk, driver side and passenger side air bags, 5-mph energy-absorbing body-colored front and rear bumpers, theft deterrent system with keyless remote entry, child safety rear door locks, six-speaker Bose audio system with four amplifiers including two A-pillar tweeters, AM/FM stereo tuner with auto reverse/full logic cassette deck, in-dash CD player, pre-wiring for dealer-installed cellular phone with antenna laminated in rear window glass, analog speedometer and tachometer, trip odometer, analog quartz clock, warning lights.

Accessories

R01	**Touring Pkg**	1863	2300
	incls 215/60HR15 SBR high performance tires, performance alloy wheels, super HICAS 4-wheel steering, rear decklid spoiler, recalibrated springs and stabilizer bar		

INFINITI

Q45

94214	Q45 4-Dr Sedan (auto)	40055	49450
94614	Q45A 4-Dr Sedan w/Full-Active Suspension (auto)	44510	54950
	Destination Charge:	450	450
	Gas Guzzler Tax: Q45	1000	1000
	Q45A	2100	2100

Standard Equipment

Q45: V8 4-cam 32-valve engine, sequential multi-point fuel injection, dual exhaust, electronically-controlled four-speed automatic transmission, limited slip differential, unit-body construction, front suspension (independent multi-link with coil springs and stabilizer bar), rear suspension (independent multi-link with coil springs), rack and pinion steering with speed-sensitive power assist, 4-wheel disc brakes with anti-lock braking system, 6.5JJ-15 cast aluminum wheels, P215/65VR15 tires, power sunroof, power heated outside mirrors, tinted glass, halogen headlights, 10-way driver/8-way passenger power seats, driver entry/exit system with two-position memory, leather seating surfaces and head restraints, leather-wrapped steering wheel and shift knob, front center console with storage compartment, rear center armrest, illuminated trunk, carpeted floor mats, wood appointments, air conditioning with automatic temperature control with non-CFC R134a refrigerant, cruise control, tilt and telescoping steering column, power windows with "one-touch down" driver's window, power door locks, power trunk release, power fuel filler door release, rear window defroster with timer, illuminated entry/exit system with time delay fade-out, anti-glare rear view mirror, cargo net in trunk, driver's side and passenger's side air bags, front/rear head restraints, child safety rear door locks, energy-absorbing body colored front/rear bumpers, anti-theft system, pick-resistant door lock cylinders, keyless remote entry system (or electronic key), 5-mph type energy-absorbing front and rear bumpers, six-speaker Bose audio system with four amplifiers and two A-pillar tweeters, AM/FM stereo tuner with auto reverse/full logic cassette deck, automatic power antenna, diversity antenna system, pre-wiring for Infiniti cellular phone and CD autochanger, electro-luminescent analog speedometer and tachometer, dual trip odometers, gauges (fuel level, coolant, temperature), analog quartz clock, 10-point diagnostic information display system.

Accessories

| U01 | **All-Season Tires** | NC | NC |

CODE	DESCRIPTION	DEALER	LIST
R02	**Touring Pkg** — Q45	2511	3100
	incls rear decklid spoiler, performance alloy wheels, performance tires, heated headrests, performance steering ratio and 4-wheel steering, revised front stabilizer bar, rear stabilizer bar		
B01	**Traction Control** — Q45	1296	1600
	incls traction control, heated front seats and all-season tires		
B02	**Traction Control** — Q45 (NA w/touring pkg)	1215	1500
	incls traction control, all-season tires		

AMIGO

B15	2WD S (5-spd)	13067	14849
B25	2WD XS (5-spd)	13639	15499
C15	4WD S (5-spd)	14783	16799
C25	4WD XS (5-spd)	15135	17199
	Destination Charge:	350	350

Standard Equipment

AMIGO S: Cargo area mat, center console, cigarette lighter, floor mats, dome lamp, day/night rearview mirror, remote hood opener, reclining front bucket seats with see-thru headrests, rear bench seat with headrests, gauges (water temp, oil pressure, battery, brake system, low fuel, trip odometer), 3-spoke steering wheel, dual sunvisors, 2-speed wiper/washer with mist, power brakes with ventilated discs, rear wheel ABS, front manual locking hubs (4WD), power black OS mirrors, recirculating ball steering with power assist, fuel tank skid plate, transfer case skid plates (4WD), radiator skid plate (4WD), oil pan skid plate (4WD), maintenance-free battery, single note horn, 3/4 molded resin door/side trim, warning/indicator lamps, assist grips.

XS (in addition to or instead of S equipment): Full molded vinyl covered door/side trim, sporty shift knob, oil pressure gauge, voltmeter, tachometer, tilt steering wheel, 2-speed intermittent wiper/washer.

ISUZU

CODE	DESCRIPTION	DEALER	LIST

Accessories

		DEALER	LIST
AA	**Air Conditioning**	706	830
H1	**Sunroof**	256	300
B1	**California Emissions**	135	150
C1	**New York Emissions**	135	150
FBA	**AM/FM Stereo Radio w/Cassette**	284	405
	incls 2 speakers		
FCA	**AM/FM Stereo Radio w/Cassette**	376	520
	incls 4 speakers		

ISUZU PICKUPS

Code	Description	DEALER	LIST
Q16	2WD 2.3L S Regular Cab Std Bed (5-spd)	8506	9399
Q46	2WD 2.3L S Regular Cab Long Bed (5-spd)	9620	10809
S14	2WD 2.6L S Regular Cab Std Bed (auto)	10679	11999
S75	2WD 2.6L S Spacecab (5-spd)	11311	12709
T15	4WD 2.6L S Regular Cab Std Bed (5-spd)	11897	13519
U15	4WD 3.1L S Regular Cab Std Bed (5-spd)	12654	14379
	Destination Charge:	350	350

Standard Equipment

S PICKUP: Cigarette lighter, cut-pile carpeting, molded headliner, dome lamp, day/night rearview mirror, remote hood opener, special instrumentation gauges [water temp, oil pressure (4WD), voltmeter (4WD), tachometer (4WD), trip odometer], warning/indicator lamps [oil pressure, battery, brake system, 4WD engagement (4WD), low fuel], 3-passenger bench seat (Regular Cab), reclining buckets seats (Spacecab), forward facing jump seats (Spacecab), see-thru headrests, 3-spoke steering wheel, dual sunvisors, semi-concealed 2-speed windshield wiper/washer with mist wipe, retractable cargo cover (Spacecab), assist grip, glove box with lock, automatic transmission interlock, power front disc brakes, rear disc brakes (4WD), rear wheel ABS, manual locking front hubs (4WD), power assisted recirculating ball steering (except 2.3L models), fuel tank skid plate (4WD), transfer case skid plate (4WD), radiator skid plate (4WD), oil pan skid plate (4WD), maintenance-free battery, single note horn.

ISUZU

CODE	DESCRIPTION	DEALER	LIST

Accessories

Code	Description	Dealer	List
C2	**California/New York Emissions** — w/2.3L engine	225	250
C3	**California/New York Emissions** — w/2.6L engine	135	150
A2/AF	**Air Conditioning** — NA on 2WD 2.6L models	706	830
M1	**Tire/Wheel Pkg** — 4WD	974	1145
	incls 31-10.5R15 off-road tires, alum wheels, mud flaps and fender flares		
GRP	**Brush/Grille Guard** — 4WD	216	305
G2	**Power Steering** — 2WD Reg Cab w/2.3L engine	276	325
ID	**Black Rear Step Bumper**	116	165
FBP	**AM/FM ETR Radio w/Cassette**	284	405
P1	**Bright Pkg** — 2WD	447	525
	incls bright grille/trim rings/mirrors/bumpers/door handles		
P2	**Bright Pkg** — 4WD	1421	1670
	incls tire/wheel pkg plus bright bumpers/grille/wheel opening moldings/dual mirrors		

RODEO

Code	Description	Dealer	List
E45	2WD S (5-spd)	13472	14969
G45	2WD S V6 (5-spd)	15311	17499
G44	2WD S V6 (auto)	16099	18399
G64	2WD LS V6 (auto)	19887	22729
H45	4WD S V6 (5-spd)	16746	19249
H44	4WD S V6 (auto)	17703	20349
H65	4WD LS V6 (5-spd)	20705	23799
H64	4WD LS V6 (auto)	21662	24899
	Destination Charge:	375	375

Standard Equipment

RODEO S: Child-safe rear door locks, cigarette lighter, console (V6), cut-pile carpeting, carpeted floor

68   EDMUND'S IMPORT CAR PRICES

mats (V6), lockable glove box, dome lamps, cargo lamps, day/night rearview mirror, remote hood opener, front bench seat with headrest and center armrest (4 cyl), front bucket seats with recliner and headrest (V6), tachometer (V6), trip odometer, gauges [fuel, water, oil (V6), volt (V6)], warning/indicator lamps, 3-spoke steering wheel, dual sunvisors, passenger assist grips, automatic transmission interlock, power assisted front ventilated disc brakes, rear drum brakes (4 cyl), rear ventilated disc brakes (V6), rear wheel anti-lock, 2-speed transfer case (4WD), automatic locking front hubs (4WD), manual black OS mirrors, rear defogger, rear intermittent wiper/washer (V6), gas pressurized shock absorbers, radiator skid plate (V6), exhaust cross-over pipe and transmission oil pan skid plates (V6), fuel tank skid plate, transfer case skid plate (4WD), inside mounted spare tire (4 cyl), outside spare tire carrier (V6), power recirculating ball steering, 2-speed windshield wiper with mist control, maintenance-free battery, single note horn.

LS (in addition to or instead of S equipment): Illuminated cigarette lighter, digital clock (in radio), cargo area convenience net, carpeted floor mats, map light, rear hatch opener, bucket seats with recliner and headrest, rear bench seat with split back and headrest, sport type shift knob, leather-wrapped steering wheel, tilt steering column, passenger side vanity mirror, illuminated instrument panel ashtray, air conditioning, AM/FM ETR stereo radio with cassette and four speakers, rear ventilated disc brakes, cruise control, bright power OS mirrors with defogger, intermittent rear wiper/washer, radiator skid plate, exhaust cross-over pipe and transmission oil pan skid plate, outside spare tire carrier, 2-speed windshield wiper/washer with intermittent feature, power windows, power door locks, dual note horn, center console.

Accessories

Code	Description	Dealer	List
B4	California Emissions	135	150
C4	New York Emissions	135	150
A3/AN	Air Conditioning — S	722	850
H2	Sunroof — LS	255	300
L1	Limited Slip Differential — 4WD LS	210	260
E1	Rear Window Wiper/Washer — 2WD S 4-Cyl	158	185
HR	Aero Luggage Rack — S	137	195
R1	Outside Spare Tire Carrier — 2WD S 4-Cyl	234	275
M2	Wheel Pkg — 4WD S	847	990
	incls limited slip differential and 16" aluminum wheels		
GRR	Brush/Grille Guard	216	305
JRG	Floor Mats — 2WD S 4-Cyl	39	55
FDY	CD Player — LS	385	550
FBY	AM/FM Stereo Radio w/Cassette — S	410	585
P3	Preferred Equipment Pkg — S V6	1690	1990
	incls air conditioning, power windows, roof luggage rack, cruise control, power door locks, AM/FM stereo radio w/cassette and 4 speakers, cargo net, intermittent rear window wiper/washer		

ISUZU

ISUZU

TROOPER

		DEALER	LIST
L45	4WD S 4-Dr (5-spd)	18381	21250
L44	4WD S 4-Dr (auto)	19376	22400
M65	4WD LS 4-Dr (5-spd)	22822	26850
M64	4WD LS 4-Dr (auto)	23800	28000
M05	4WD RS 2-Dr (5-spd)	21120	24000
M04	4WD RS 2-Dr (auto)	22132	25150
Destination Charge:		400	400

Standard Equipment

TROOPER S: Roof-mounted air deflector, mast type antenna, rear step bumper with pad, blue tinted glass, dual passenger side convex mirrors, clearcoat paint, chip-resistant coating, full-size spare tire, spare tire vinyl cover, styled steel wheels, tie-down hooks, center console, rear seat heater ducts, cut-pile carpeting, carpeted floor mats, storage compartment under rear seat, lockable glove box with lamp, full instrumentation (tachometer, water temp, oil pressure and volt gauges, trip odometer, low fuel warning lamp, 4WD engagement lamp), room lamp, cargo lamp, cigarette lighter and ashtray, day/night rearview mirror, driver and passenger visor vanity mirrors with lid, remote hood opener, remote fuel door opener, passenger assist grips headlamps-on reminder, reclining bucket seats with adjustable headrests and passenger seatback storage pocket, rear folding bench seat, height adjustable headrests, soft grip steering wheel, tilt steering column, full door trim with cloth insert, front door storage pockets, molded felt headliner, four speakers, maintenance-free battery, power assisted 4-wheel ventilated disc brakes with rear wheel anti-lock, rear defogger, part-time 4WD, automatic locking front hubs, dual note horn, skid plates (radiator, exhaust cross-over pipe and transmission, oil pan, fuel tank, transfer case, catalytic converter), recirculating ball power steering.

LS (in addition to or instead of S equipment): Power antenna, fog lamps, bronze tinted glass, privacy tint glass (rear, side, back and quarter windows), electric remote mirrors with defogger, bright window surround moldings, rocker moldings with integral mud flaps, aluminum wheels, retractable cargo cover, convenience net, floor rails, rear seat foot rest, dual map lights, inboard folding armrests, 60/40 split folding/reclining rear seat with center armrest, leather-wrapped steering wheel, carpeted lower doors, air conditioning, 75 amp alternator, anti-theft device, premium high power AM/FM stereo cassette system with six speakers, 4-wheel ABS, cruise control, rear defogger with auto cancel timer, headlamp wiper/washer, limited slip differential, power windows and power door locks.

RS (in addition to or instead of LS equipment): Flip-out quarter windows, bright window surround molding deleted, two-tone paint, storage compartment under rear seat deleted, rear seat foot rest deleted, passenger side walk-in device, rear folding/reclining seat with center armrest, 4-wheel ABS deleted, gas pressurized shock absorbers.

Accessories

Code	Description	Dealer	List
B5	**California Emissions**...	135	150
C5	**New York Emissions**...	135	150
A3	**Air Conditioning** — S	720	900
Z1	**Two-Tone Paint** — LS	225	280
P5	**Appearance Pkg** — S	600	750
	incls color-keyed bumpers and 16" aluminum wheels w/locks and bright grille (req's Preferred Equipment Pkg)		
H3	**Power Sunroof** — LS...	880	1100
L2	**Limited Slip Differential** — S................................	210	260
	req's Preferred Equipment Pkg		
L3	**Anti-Lock Brakes** — S & RS.................................	880	1100
RC	**Retractable Cargo Cover** — S...............................	84	120
J2	**Seats** — split fold-down rear - S...........................	200	250
J3	**Seats** — heated leather power - LS........................	1915	2250
P4	**Preferred Equipment Pkg** — S..............................	1600	1880
	incls AM/FM ETR stereo radio w/cassette and 6 speakers, air conditioning, power windows, cruise control, split fold-down rear bench seat, power door locks, cargo cover, power mirrors, convenience net		

ISUZU

XJ12

		DEALER	LIST
—	4-Dr Sedan w/Single Airbag (auto)	58548	71750
—	4-Dr Sedan w/Dual Airbag (auto)	59731	73200
Destination Charge:		580	580

Standard Equipment

XJ12: Power steering, digital clock, trip computer, alarm system, tinted glass, Pirelli P4000E 225/60ZR16 SBR BW tires, remote decklid release, power windows with driver's side express-down, anti-lock power 4-wheel disc brakes, limited slip differential, leather-wrapped steering wheel, lattice alloy wheels, 6.0 liter V12 EFI engine, power sunroof, variable intermittent wipers, cruise control, door/front seatback map pockets, burl walnut interior trim, door trim panels with walnut inserts, heated windshield washer nozzles, automatic air conditioning, power antenna, tilt steering column, front stabilizer bar, dual power heated mirrors, dual illuminated visor vanity mirrors, glove box mirror, carpeting (includes trunk), electric rear window defroster, remote entry system, retractable sunscreens on rear windows, walnut center console with storage and cassette holder, premium leather-faced seats, power door locks with central locking system, 4-speed ECT automatic transmission, door courtesy lights with time delay, dual front and rear reading/courtesy lights, AM/FM ETR stereo radio with cassette/CD autochanger/Dolby/8 speakers; map light, trunk light, power front bucket seats with memory and 12-way adjustment including lumbar support.

Accessories

		DEALER	LIST
—	California Emission	25	30
—	Non-Standard Color/Trim Option	1200	1500
—	All-Weather Pkg	400	500
—	Compact Disc Player	580	725

JAGUAR

XJS

		DEALER	LIST
—	4.0L 2-Dr Coupe (auto)	42391	51950
—	4.0L 2-Dr Convertible (auto)	48919	59950
—	6.0L 2-Dr Coupe (auto)	57079	69950
—	6.0L 2-Dr Convertible (auto)	65239	79950
Destination Charge:		580	580

Standard Equipment

4.0L COUPE & CONVERTIBLE: Power steering, color-keyed bumpers, walnut trim, tinted glass, variable intermittent wipers, driver and front passenger air bags, 4.0 liter DOHC 6-cylinder 24-valve EFI engine, security system, leather upholstery, electric rear window defroster with timer, convertible top (Convertible), leather-wrapped steering wheel, fog lights, metallic paint, Goodyear P235/60ZR15 SBR BW tires, automatic air conditioning, Alpine AM/FM ETR stereo radio with cassette and four speakers, power windows, front stabilizer bar, cruise control, lattice alloy wheels, heated power reclining sport front buck-et seats with power lumbar support and driver's side memory, limited slip differential, remote entry system, trip computer, map lights, 4-speed ECT automatic transmission, trunk light, tilt steering column, door lights, anti-lock power 4-wheel disc brakes, courtesy lights with delay feature, stowage bag (Convertible), door locks with power central locking system feature (includes trunk), dual power heated mirrors with driver's 2-position memory, dual illuminated visor vanity mirrors.

6.0L COUPE & CONVERTIBLE (in addition to or instead of 4.0L COUPE & CONVERTIBLE equipment): Color-keyed grille, burl walnut trim, rear decklid spoiler, prem leather upholstery, 6.0 liter SOHC V12 EFI engine, Pirelli P4000 225/60ZR16 tires, dual color-keyed heated pwr mirrors w/driver's side 2-position memory.

Accessories

		DEALER	LIST
—	All-Weather Pkg	160	200
—	Compact Disc Player	580	725
—	California Emissions	25	30
—	Manual 5-Speed Transmission — 4.0L	NC	NC
—	Non-Standard Color/Trim Option	1200	1500
—	Sport Handling Pkg — 4.0L	800	1000
	incls spt suspension, Pirelli P6000 225/55ZR16 tires, 5-spoke alloy wheels		
—	Rear Seat Delete — 4.0L	(1200)	(1500)

JAGUAR

LAND ROVER

RANGE ROVER

CODE	DESCRIPTION	DEALER	LIST
SXVC	County 4-Dr (auto)	41000	46900
SXLB	County LWB (auto)	43700	50200
	Destination Charge:	625	625

Standard Equipment

RANGE ROVER COUNTY: 3.9 liter 182 horsepower V8 OHV engine, Lucas/Bosch multi-point electronic fuel injection, 4-speed automatic transmission with overdrive, 4WD, front suspension (variable rate air springs, automatic self leveling, radius arms, Panhard rod, 25mm anti-sway bar), rear suspension (variable rate air springs, automatic self leveling, trailing links, 18.5 mm anti-sway bar), Michelin XM + S 244 all-purpose 205R16 tubeless tires, 7.0 x 16" alloy wheels, power assisted worm and roller steering, power four-wheel disc brakes with anti-lock braking system, 23.4 gallon fuel tank, air conditioning, power tilt/slide glass sunroof with sunshade, 3-spoke alloy wheels, leather seating, Pioneer ETR AM/FM stereo radio with cassette and CD changer, diversity antenna, cruise control, 8-way power heated front bucket seats, split fold-down rear seat, electronic traction control, alarm system with keyless entry, power windows with one-touch feature on front windows, rear loadspace cover, integral trailer tow hitch receiver, tinted glass, automatic dimming rearview mirror, dual power/heated OS mirrors, central locking system, remote fuel filler door release, burl walnut trim on fascia/door cappings/center console; rear window washer/wiper, rear window defroster, side window defoggers, full instrumentation including tachometer, removable carpeting, halogen headlights.

RANGE ROVER COUNTY LWB (in addition to or instead of RANGE ROVER COUNTY equipment): 4.2 liter 200 horsepower V8 OHV engine, dual preset memory driver's seat, mediterranean poplar wood trim on fascia/door cappings/center console; "cyclone"-style alloy wheels with "Quicksilver" finish.

Accessories

CODE	DESCRIPTION	DEALER	LIST
—	**California Emissions System**	100	100
—	**Paint** — Beluga Black - County	250	250
BSE	**Black Sable Edition** — County LWB	875	1050
	incls Beluga Black paint and Dark Sable Connolly leather seats		

CODE	DESCRIPTION	DEALER	LIST
LSE	**Light Stone Edition** — County LWB .... incls Brooklands Green or Cornish Cream paint and Light Stone Connolly leather seats	625	750
MSE	**Montpellier Sable Edition** — County LWB .... incls Montpellier Red paint and Dark Sable Connolly leather seats	625	750

LEXUS ES 300

9000	Base 4-Dr Sedan (auto)	25092	30600
	Destination Charge:	470	470

Standard Equipment

ES 300: 3.0L 188HP 4-cam 24 valve V6 engine, 4-speed electronically controlled automatic transmission with intelligence (ECT-i), vehicle-speed-sensing progressive power rack and pinion steering, front-wheel drive, 4-wheel independent MacPherson strut-type suspension, MacPherson struts, front and rear stabilizer bars, 4-wheel power-assisted ventilated disc brakes, 4-wheel anti-lock braking system (ABS), 15" aluminum alloy wheels, 205/65R15 V-rated tires (choice of Goodyear Eagle GA radials, Dunlop SP Sport DSO V4 all season, or Firestone Firehawk FTX all season), halogen double projector low-beam headlamps, halogen double projector high-beam headlamps, dual power remote-controlled and color coordinated outside mirrors with defoggers, variable intermittent full-area windshield wipers with mist control, color keyed lower bodyside cladding, remote entry system, electronic analog instrumentation, driver and front passenger airbag supplemental restraint system (SRS), 3-point safety belts (front and outboard rear), rear center lap belt, automatic locking retractor (ALR)/emergency locking retractor (ELR) safety belts for all outboard positions except driver, manual tilt steering wheel with driver side airbag, driver and front passenger power seat adjustments (seat fore/aft movement, recline, front and rear vertical height, manual headrest fore/aft, driver's seat manual lumbar support), power window with driver's side "auto-down" feature, retained accessory power for windows and optional moonroof, power door locks with driver's door two-turn unlock feature, R-134a CFC-free air conditioning system, walnut wood trim, automatic climate control, automatic on/off headlamps, rear window defogger with timer, vehicle theft-deterrent system, dual illuminated visor vanity mirrors, center sun visor, remote electronic trunk lid and fuel-filler door releases, outside temperature indicator, Lexus/Pioneer AM/FM ETR with auto-reverse cassette and 8 speakers, automatic AM/FM power mast antenna with FM diversity antenna on rear window glass, pre-wired for optional Lexus cellular telephone, toolkit, first aid kit.

Accessories

CODE	DESCRIPTION	DEALER	LIST
DC	**Remote 6-CD Auto Changer**	750	1000
FT	**All-Season Tires**	NC	NC
HH	**Heated Front Seats**	320	400
LA	**Leather Trim Pkg**	1040	1300
SR	**Power Tilt & Slide Moonroof w/Sunshade**	720	900

GS 300

CODE	DESCRIPTION	DEALER	LIST
9300	Base 4-Dr Sedan (auto)	32718	39900
	Destination Charge:	470	470

Standard Equipment

GS 300: 3.0L 220HP twin-cam 24-valve in-line 6 cylinder engine, 4-speed electronically controlled automatic transmission with intelligence (ECT-i), vehicle-speed-sensing progressive power rack and pinion steering, rear-wheel drive, 4-wheel independent double-wishbone suspension, gas pressurized shock absorbers, front and rear stabilizer bars, 4-wheel power-assisted ventilated disc brakes, 4-wheel anti-lock braking system (ABS), 16" aluminum alloy wheels, 215/60R16 V-rated tires (Goodyear or Bridgestone), halogen projector low beam headlamps, halogen high beam headlamps, dual power remote controlled and color coordinated outside mirrors with defoggers, variable intermittent full-area windshield wipers with mist control, monotone lower body side cladding (except white), remote entry system, electronic analog instrumentation, driver and front passenger airbag supplemental restraint system (SRS), 3-point safety belts (front and outboard rear), rear center lap belt, "easy access" front seat belts, automatic locking retractor (ALR)/emergency locking retractor (ELR), safety belts for front and rear outboard passengers, power tilt and telescoping steering column with automatic tilt-away, driver and front passenger power seat adjustments (fore/aft movement, seatback for/aft movement, cushion height, lumbar support), power windows with driver's side "auto-down" feature, retained accessory power for windows and optional moonroof, power door locks with driver's door two-turn unlock feature, R-134a CFC-free air conditioning system, walnut wood trim, automatic climate control, automatic on/off headlamps, rear window defogger with auto-off timer, vehicle and audio theft-deterrent systems, illuminated entry system, dual illuminated visor vanity mirrors, center sun visor, remote electric trunk lid and fuel-filler door releases, outside temperature indicator, Lexus Premium Audio System with AM/FM cassette (7 speakers including 10" bi-amplified subwoofer and 225-watts maximum power), automatic 3-position AM/FM power mast antenna and FM diversity antenna system, pre-wired for Lexus cellular telephone, tookit, first-aid kit.

Accessories

CODE	DESCRIPTION	DEALER	LIST
DC	**Remote 12-CD Auto Changer**	750	1000
FT	**All-Season Tires**	NC	NC
LA	**Leather Trim Pkg**	1040	1300
NK	**Lexus/Nakamichi Premium Audio System**	825	1100
SR	**Power Tilt & Slide Moonroof w/Sunshade**	720	900
TN	**Traction Control System (TRAC) w/Heated Seats**	1440	1800

LS 400

CODE	DESCRIPTION	DEALER	LIST
9100	Base 4-Dr Sedan (auto)	39920	49900
	Destination Charge:	470	470

Standard Equipment

LS 400: 4.0L 250 HP 4 cam 32 valve V8 engine, 4-speed electronically controlled automatic transmission with intelligence (ECT-i), vehicle-speed-sensing progressive-power rack and pinion steering, rear-wheel drive, 4-wheel independent double-wishbone suspension, gas filled shock absorbers, front and rear stabilizer bars, 4-wheel power-assisted ventilated disc brakes, 4-wheel anti-lock braking system (ABS), 16" aluminum alloy wheels, 225/60R16 V-rated tires (choice of Goodyear Eagle GA radials, Bridgestone Turanza GR 30, Dunlop SP Sport 400 all season, Goodyear Invicta GAL all season), halogen projector low-beam headlamps, halogen high-beam headlamps, dual power remote controlled and color coordinated outside mirrors with defoggers, monotone lower body side cladding, remote entry system, electronic analog instrumentation, driver and front passenger airbag supplemental restraint system (SRS), 3-point safety belts (front and outboard rear), rear center lap belt, automatic locking retractor (ALR)/emergency locking retractor (ELR) safety belts for front and rear outboard passengers, power tilt and manual telescopic steering column with automatic tilt-away driver and front passenger power seat adjustments (fore/aft movement, seatback fore/aft movement, cushion height, lumbar support), power windows with driver's side "auto-down" feature, retained accessory power for windows and optional moonroof, power door locks with driver's two-turn unlock feature, R-134a CFC-free air conditioning system, walnut wood trim, automatic climate control system, automatic on/off headlamps, rear window defogger with auto-off timer, vehicle and audio theft-deterrent systems, dual illuminated visor vanity mirrors, center sun visor, remote electric trunk lid and fuel-filler door releases, outside temperature indicator, Lexus premium audio system with AM/FM cassette (7 speakers including 8" bi-amplified subwoofer and 225-watts maximum power), automatic three-position AM/FM power mast antenna and FM diversity antenna system, pre-wired for Lexus cellular telephone, toolkit, first-aid kit.

Accessories

CODE	DESCRIPTION	DEALER	LIST
DC	**Remote 6-CD Auto Changer**	750	1000
FT	**All-Season Tires**	NC	NC
MO	**Lexus Memory System**	640	800
NK	**Lexus/Nakamichi Premium Audio System**	825	1100
SA	**Electronic Air Suspension w/Lexus Ride Control**	1360	1700
SR	**Power Tilt & Slide Moonroof w/Sunshade**	800	1000
TN	**Traction Control System (TRAC) w/Heated Front Seats**	1520	1900

SC 300

CODE	DESCRIPTION	DEALER	LIST
9201	Base 2-Dr Coupe (5-spd)	31160	38000
9200	Base 2-Dr Coupe (auto)	31898	38900
	Destination Charge:	470	470

CODE	DESCRIPTION	DEALER	LIST

Standard Equipment

SC 300: 3.0L 225HP twin-cam 24 valve in-line 6 cylinder engine, 5-speed manual transmission, vehicle speed-sensing-progressive power rack and pinion steering, rear-wheel drive, 4-wheel independent double-wishbone suspension, gas pressurized shock absorbers, front and rear stabilizer bars, 4-wheel power-assisted ventilated disc brakes, 4-wheel anti-lock braking system (ABS), 15" aluminum alloy wheels, 215/60R15 V-rated tires (choice of Goodyear Eagle GA or Bridgestone Potenza RE88), halogen projector low-beam headlamps, independent halogen high-beam headlamps, dual power remote controlled and color coordinated outside mirrors with defoggers, variable intermittent full-area windshield wipers with mist control, remote entry system, electronic analog instrumentation, driver and front passenger airbag supplemental restraint system (SRS), 3-point front safety belts for all seating positions, front passenger-slide power walk-in seat feature for easier entry/exit of rear seat passengers, automatic locking retractor (ALR)/emergency locking retractor (ELR) safety belts for front and rear passengers, front seat belt assisting arm, standard manual tilt and telescopic steering column, driver and front passenger power seat adjustments (fore/aft movement, seatback fore/aft movement, cushion height, lumbar support), power windows with driver's side "auto-down" feature, power door locks with driver's door two-turn unlock feature, R-134a CFC-free air conditioning system, maple wood trim, automatic climate control, automatic on/off headlamps, rear window defogger with auto-off timer, vehicle theft-deterrent system, illuminated entry system, dual illuminated visor vanity mirrors, center sun visor, remote electric trunk lid and fuel-filler door releases, Lexus Premium Audio System with AM/FM cassette (7 speakers including 8" bi-amplified subwoofer and 170-watts maximum power), automatic 3-position MA/FM power mast antenna and FM diversity antenna system, pre-wired for Lexus cellular telephone, toolkit, first-aid kit.

Accessories

CODE	DESCRIPTION	DEALER	LIST
DC	**Remote 12-CD Auto Changer**	750	1000
HH	**Heated Front Seats**	320	400
	req's manual transmission		
LA	**Leather Trim Pkg w/Lexus Memory System**	1440	1800
NK	**Lexus/Nakamichi Premium Audio System**	825	1100
SR	**Power Tilt & Slide Moonroof w/Sunshade**	720	900
TN	**Traction Control System (TRAC) w/Heated Front Seats**	1440	1800
	req's automatic transmission		

LEXUS

LEXUS

CODE	DESCRIPTION	DEALER	LIST

SC 400

9220	Base 2-Dr Coupe (auto)	36080	45100
	Destination Charge:	470	470

Standard Equipment

SC 400: 4.0L 250HP 4 cam 32 valve V8 engine, 4-speed electronically controlled auto transmission w/intelligence (ECT-i), vehicle-speed-sensing progressive power rack/pinion steering, rear-wheel drive, 4-wheel independent sport-tuned double-wishbone suspension, gas-filled shock absorbers, front and rear stabilizer bars, 4-wheel power assisted ventilated disc brakes, 4-wheel anti-lock braking system (ABS), 16" alum alloy wheels, 225/55R16 V-rated tires (choice of Goodyear Eagle GSD or Bridgestone Potenza RE93), halogen projector low-beam headlamps, independent halogen high-beam headlamps, dual power remote-controlled/color coordinated outside mirrors w/defoggers, variable intermittent full-area windshield wipers w/mist control, remote entry system, elec analog instrumentation, driver and front passenger airbag supplemental restraint system (SRS), 3-point safety belts for all seating positions, front passenger-side power walk-in seat feature for easier entry/exit of rear seat passengers, auto locking retractor (ALR)/emergency locking retractor (ELR) safety belts for front and rear passengers, front seatbelt assisting arms, power tilt and telescopic steering column with power automatic tilt-away, driver and front passenger power seat adjustments (fore/aft movement, seatback fore/aft movement, cushion height, lumbar support), power windows w/driver's side "auto-down" feature, power door locks with driver's door two-turn unlock feature, R-134a CFC-free air conditioning system, maple wood trim, automatic climate control, automatic on/off headlamps, rear window defogger with auto-off timer, vehicle theft-deterrent systems, illuminated entry system, dual-illuminated visor-vanity mirrors, center sunvisor, remote electric trunk lid and fuel-filler door releases, Lexus premium audio system w/AM/FM cassette (7-speakers including 8" bi-amplified subwoofer and 170-watts maximum power), automatic 3-position AM/FM power mast antenna /FM diversity antenna system, pre-wired for Lexus cellular telephone, toolkit, first-aid kit.

Accessories

DC	**Remote 12-CD Auto Changer**	750	1000
NK	**Lexus/Nakamichi Premium Audio System**	825	1100
RF	**Color-Keyed Rear Spoiler**	320	400
SR	**Power Tilt & Slide Moonroof w/Sunshade**	720	900
TN	**Traction Control System (TRAC) w/Heated Front Seats**	1440	1800

MAZDA

323

—	Base 3-Dr Hatchback (5-spd)	7609	7995
	Destination Charge: Alaska..	575	575
	Other States..	375	375

Standard Equipment

323: 1.6L SOHC 8-valve 4-cylinder engine (16-valve in California), 5-speed manual transmission w/overdrive, rack and pinion steering, power-assisted front disc/rear drum brakes, 13-inch styled wheels w/bright center caps, driver's side remote mirror, reclining front bucket seats w/adjustable head restraints, fold-down rear seatback, breathable vinyl upholstery, center console w/forward storage tray, rigid removable cargo cover, locking glove compartment, engine coolant temperature gauge, resettable trip odometer, heater/defroster with 4-speed blower, rear window defogger.

Accessories

Code	Description	DEALER	LIST
AT1	**Automatic Transmission — 4-speed**	653	725
ACA	**Air Conditioning**	672	840
PS1	**Power Steering**	213	250
FLM	**Floor Mats**	45	65
CE1	**California or New York Emissions**	NC	NC
1PL	**Plus Pkg**	556	650
	incls cloth upholstery, 60/40 split fold-down rear bench seat, full wheel covers and AM/FM ETR radio w/cassette		
1FL	**Fleet Pkg**	764	940
	incls air conditioning and cloth upholstery		

MAZDA

626

		DEALER	LIST
—	DX 4-Dr Sedan (5-spd)	13134	14255
—	ES 4-Dr Sedan (5-spd)	18761	21545
—	LX 4-Dr Sedan (5-spd)	14737	16540
—	LX V6 4-Dr Sedan (5-spd)	16472	18700
Destination Charge: Alaska		575	575
	Other States	375	375

Standard Equipment

626 DX: 2.0L DOHC 16-valve 4-cylinder engine, 5-speed manual transmission w/overdrive, rack and pinion steering w/variable power assist, power-assisted front disc/rear drum brakes, 14-inch wheels with full wheel covers, 195/65R14 88S all season radial tires, front mud guards, variable intermittent windshield wipers, driver and passenger side airbag, adjustable seatbelt anchors, reclining front bucket seats w/adjustable thigh support, 60/40 split fold-down rear seatback with center armrest, driver and passenger door map pockets, center console w/covered storage and cupholders, child safety rear-door locks, remote trunk and fuel-door releases, courtesy lights, illuminated ignition-lock keyhole, 8,000-rpm tachometer gauge, engine coolant temperature gauge, rear window defogger with automatic shut-off.

LX (in addition to or instead of DX equipment): Driver and passenger visor vanity mirrors, power windows w/driver's side one-touch-down feature, dual map/reading lights for front-seat passengers, cruise control w/steering-wheel-mounted controls, air conditioning, AM/FM cassette stereo w/anti-theft coding, automatic power antenna.

LX - V6 (in addition to or instead of LX equipment): 2.5L DOHC 24-valve V6 engine, power-assisted four-wheel disc brakes, 15-inch aluminum alloy wheels, 205/55R15 87V all season radial tires, dual-outlet exhaust, anti-theft alarm system.

ES (in addition to or instead of LX - V6 equipment): Anti-lock braking system (ABS), heated outside door mirrors, leather seating surfaces.

Accessories

		DEALER	LIST
AT1	**Automatic Transmission — 4-speed**	696	800
AB1	**Anti-Lock Brakes — LX V6**	680	800

MAZDA

CODE	DESCRIPTION	DEALER	LIST
AB1	**Anti-Lock Brakes w/Rear Disc** — DX & LX	808	950
FLM	**Floor Mats**	49	70
CE1	**California or New York Emissions**	NC	NC
1LX	**Luxury Pkg** — LX..	1140	1425
	incls power moonroof, alloy wheels, anti-theft system and heated mirrors		
1P0	**Fleet Pkg** — DX	1671	2070
	incls power windows, cruise control, air conditioning, power door locks and AM/FM ETR radio w/cassette		
2LX	**Premium Pkg** — LX V6..	1440	1800
	incls power moonroof, anti-theft system, heated mirrors, power driver's seat and anti-lock brakes		

929

—	4-Dr Sedan (auto)	25940	30500
	Destination Charge: Alaska...	575	575
	Other States..	375	375

Standard Equipment

929 3.0L DOHC 24-valve V6 engine, 4-speed electronically controlled automatic transmission, rack-and-pinion steering with variable power assist, power assisted four-wheel ventilated disc brakes, four-wheel anti-lock braking system (ABS), four-wheel independent multi-link suspension, 15-inch aluminum alloy wheels, P205/65R15 radial tires, 5 mph front and rear bumpers, auto-off headlights, dual body color power mirrors with heated mirror glass, concealed windshield wipers w/variable intermittent feature, fully integrated halogen fog lights, driver and front passenger airbag supplemental restraint system (SRS), adjustable upper front seat belt anchors, automatic climate control system, fold-down rear seat center armrest, power glass moonroof with tilt-up ventilation features, illuminated driver and passenger sun visor vanity mirrors, power windows with driver's one-touch down feature, power door locks with central locking feature on front doors, leather-wrapped steering wheel and shift lever grip, rear window defogger with automatic shut-off, AM/FM cassette stereo with 6 speakers and anti-theft coding, remote fuel door and trunk releases, center console with dual cupholders.

MAZDA

MAZDA

CODE	DESCRIPTION	DEALER	LIST

Accessories

Code	Description	Dealer	List
FLM	**Floor Mats**	70	100
MR2	**Solar Ventilation System**	533	650
	req's Premium Pkg		
1PR	**Premium Pkg**	3198	3900
	incls leather pkg, solar glass, keyless entry system, unique alloy wheels, pre-wiring for cellular telephone, premium audio system w/multi-disc compact disc changer		
1LE	**Leather Pkg**	1353	1650
	incls leather upholstery, power passenger seat, rear center armrest		
1CO	**Cold Pkg**	498	600
	incls heated front seats, all-season tires, limited slip differential, upgraded battery, heavy duty windshield wipers and larger washer tank		

MPV

4 CYLINDER

Code	Description	Dealer	List
LV521	MPV 2-Row Wagon/Van (auto)	15957	17795
LV521	MPV 3-Row Wagon (auto)	17204	19195

6 CYLINDER

Code	Description	Dealer	List
LV522	MPV 3-Row Wagon (incls Pkg A & B) (auto)	17917	19995
LV522	MPV 3-Row Wagon (incls Pkg D) (auto)	17917	19995
LV523	MPV 4WD 3-Row Wagon (incls Pkg C) (auto)	20590	22995
LV523	MPV 4WD 3-Row Wagon (incls Pkg D) (auto)	20590	22995
	Destination Charge:	425	425

Standard Equipment

MPV 5-PASSENGER WAGON/VAN 4 CYLINDER: 2.6L SOHC 12-valve 4 cylinder engine, 4-speed auto trans w/overdrive, rack-and-pinion steering w/variable assist, power assisted front and rear disc brakes, rear wheel anti-lock braking system (ABS), 15-inch wheels w/full wheel covers, P195/75R15 tires, protective bodyside moldings, dual manual mirrors, variable intermittent wipers w/rear wiper washer, tinted glass w/dark-tinted windshield sunshade band, high-mount stop light, 5-passenger seating w/3-passenger 2nd row seat, reclining front bucket seats w/adjustable head restraints, driver side airbag supplemental restraint system, child safety lock on rear side door, remote hood and fuel door releases, tachometer, tilt steering column, rear window defogger w/auto shut-off, AM/FM cassette stereo w/4 speakers.

MPV 7-PASSENGER WAGON 4 CYLINDER (in addition to or instead of MPV 5-PASSENGER WAGON/VAN 4 CYLINDER equipment): Dual power mirrors, 7-passenger seating w/2-passenger 2nd row seat & 3-passenger 3rd row, removable 2nd row seat w/recline, easy-fold and flip-forward 3rd row seats, fold-flat function for 2nd and 3rd row seats, AM/FM cassette stereo w/6 speakers.

MPV 7-PASSENGER WAGON V6 (in addition to or instead of MPV 7-PASSENGER WAGON 4 CYLINDER equipment): 3.0L SOHC 18-valve V6 engine, 4-speed electronically controlled auto trans w/overdrive.

MPV 7-PASSENGER 4WD WAGON V6 (in addition to or instead of MPV 7-PASSENGER WAGON V6 equipment): Multi-mode four-wheel-drive system w/lockable center diff, 15-inch aluminum alloy wheels, P215/65R15 tires.

Accessories

CODE	DESCRIPTION	DEALER	LIST
ACB	**Dual Air Conditioning** — LV522, LV523	1230	1500
ACA	**Single Air Conditioning** — NA on models w/Pkg D	705	860
MR1	**Power Moon Roof** — LV522, LV523	820	1000
	models w/Pkg A & B require dual air cond, towing pkg and alloy wheel pkg		
1TP	**Towing Pkg** — LV522	430	500
	LV523	344	400
	models w/Pkg A & B require alloy wheels		
1CO	**Cold Pkg**	258	300
	incls 65 amp battery, 5.1 liter washer tank, rear heater		
CD1	**CD Player** — models w/Pkg D	560	700
1TR	**Touring Pkg** — LV522	490	570
	incls 8-pass seating, 2nd row w/3 seats, fold-down armrests, beverage holders, outboard armrests [models w/Pkg A & B require FLE floor mats]		
JCP	**Two-Tone Paint**	205	250
	std on LV522 w/Pkg D; NA on LV523 w/Pkg D		
FLM	**Floor Mats** — 2-Row	47	65
	3-Row	65	90
FLE	**Floor Mats** — 3-Row	69	95
1PA	**Pkg A** — LV521 3-Row	872	1050
	incls power windows, power door locks, cruise control, rear privacy glass, bronze tinted windows		
1PB	**Pkg B** — std on LV522 w/Pkg A & B model		
	incls Pkg A items plus body-color grille and license plate illumination bar, keyless entry system		
1PC	**Pkg C** — std on LV523 w/Pkg C model		
	incls Pkg A items plus body-color grille and license plate illumination bar and keyless entry		
2LX	**Pkg D** — std on models w/Pkg D		
	incls Pkg B & C items plus lace alloys wheels, leather seating surfaces, wheel special two-tone paint, color-keyed bodyside moldings [dual air conditioning mandatory, towing pkg mandatory, moonroof mandatory]		

MAZDA

CODE	DESCRIPTION	DEALER	LIST

MX-5 MIATA

		DEALER	LIST
—	2-Dr Convertible (5-spd)	14753	16450
Destination Charge: Alaska		575	575
	Other States	375	375

Standard Equipment

MX-5: 1.8L 16-valve DOHC 4 cylinder engine, multi-port fuel injection, 5-speed manual transmission w/overdrive, power plant frame (PPF), rack-and-pinion steering, power assisted 4-wheel disc brakes, dual bodycolor mirrors, 14-inch styled steel wheels w/bright mini-caps, 185/60R14 82H SBR tires, 2-speed wipers w/intermittent feature and 1-wipe feature, tinted glass, driver and passenger side airbags, reclining bucket seats, AM/FM auto reverse cassette stereo system w/anti-theft coding, full center console w/lockable storage compartment/removable cupholder, remote fuel door and trunk release, double-fold sun visors w/passenger vanity mirror, 8,000 rpm tachometer with 7,000 rpm redline, engine coolant temperature/oil pressure/fuel gauges, air conditioning (CFC free).

Accessories

Code	Description	DEALER	LIST
AT1	**Automatic Transmission** — 4-speed	739	850
	req's Pkg A, B or C		
1PA	**Pkg A** — models w/5-spd	1436	1710
	models w/auto	1109	1320
	incls limited slip differential (models w/5-spd), power steering, leather-wrapped steering wheel, alloy wheels w/locks, speakers in headrests and power OS mirrors		
1PB	**Pkg B** — models w/5-spd	2024	2410
	models w/auto	1697	2020
	incls Pkg A contents plus cruise control, power windows/power antenna		
1PC	**Pkg C** — models w/5-spd	2612	3110

CODE	DESCRIPTION	DEALER	LIST
	models w/auto..	2285	2720
	incls Pkg B contents plus tan top and tan leather upholstery		
ACA	**Air Conditioning**..	640	830
HT1	**Detachable Hard Top**..	1215	1500
	req's Pkg A, B or C		
RA4	**Sensory Sound System**..	560	700
	req's Pkg B or C		
AB1	**Anti-Lock Brakes**...	765	900
	req's Pkg A, B or C		
FLM	**Floor Mats**...	47	65

MX-6

—	Base 2-Dr Coupe (5-spd)...	15147	17195
—	LS 2-Dr Coupe (5-spd)..	18456	21195
Destination Charge: Alaska..		575	575
	Other States...	375	375

Standard Equipment

MX-6: 2.0L 16-valve DOHC 4 cylinder engine, 5-speed manual transmission w/overdrive, fully indepen-dent suspension, rack and pinion steering w/variable power assist, power assisted front disc/rear drum brakes, 14" wheels w/full wheel covers, P195/65R14 all season radial tires, front mud guards, dual body-color power mirrors, illuminated driver's door lock keyhole, intermittent windshield wipers w/variable con-trol, tinted glass w/upper windshield sunshade band, reclining bucket seats w/driver's adjustable thigh support, 60/40 split fold-down rear seatback, driver and passenger side airbags, AM/FM full logic auto-reverse cassette stereo, dual visor vanity mirrors, center console w/covered storage and cupholder, power windows w/driver's side one-touch-down feature, power door locks, dual overhead map lights, illuminat-ed ignition-lock keyhole, 8,000 RPM tachometer, tilt steering wheel, cruise control.

LS (in addition to or instead of MX-6 equipment): 2.5L 24-valve DOHC V6 engine, power assisted 4-wheel

MAZDA

disc brakes, 15-inch aluminum alloy wheels, P205/55R15 all season radial tires, halogen fog lights, dual-outlet exhaust, anti-theft alarm system, power sunroof w/tilt up ventilation feature, air conditioning (CFC-free), leather-wrapped steering wheel.

Accessories

CODE	DESCRIPTION	DEALER	LIST
AT1	**Automatic Transmission** — 4-speed - Base	696	800
AC1	**Air Conditioning** — Base	680	850
RS1	**Rear Spoiler**	300	375
1LE	**Leather Pkg** — LS	800	1000
	incls leather upholstery, dual heated OS mirrors and power driver's seat		
10P	**Popular Equipment Group** — Base	960	1200
	incls power sunroof, anti-theft alarm system and alloy wheels w/locks		
AB1	**Anti-Lock Brakes** — LS	680	800
AB1	**Anti-Lock Brakes w/Rear Discs** — Base	808	950
CE1	**California or New York Emissions**	NC	NC
FLM	**Floor Mats**	49	70

MAZDA PICKUPS

		DEALER	LIST
B2300	2WD Base Short Bed (5-spd)	8090	8780
B2300	2WD SE Short Bed (5-spd)	9294	10550
B2300	2WD Base Cab Plus (5-spd)	10566	11995
B3000	2WD SE Long Bed (5-spd)	10059	11420
B3000	2WD SE Long Bed (auto)	11447	12995
B3000	2WD SE Cab Plus (5-spd)	11535	13095
B4000	2WD SE Long Bed (5-spd)	10258	11645
B4000	2WD LE Cab Plus (auto)	13341	15145
B4000	4WD SE Short Bed (5-spd)	13341	15145
B4000	4WD SE Cab Plus (5-spd)	14618	16595
B4000	4WD LE Cab Plus (auto)	16380	18595
Destination Charge: Alaska & Hawaii		600	600
Other States		460	460

CODE	DESCRIPTION	DEALER	LIST

Standard Equipment

2WD TRUCK - BASE: 2.3L SOHC 8-valve 4 cylinder engine, electronic fuel injection, 5-speed manual transmission w/overdrive, power assisted front disc/rear drum brakes, rear wheel anti-lock braking system (ABS), steel wheels, P195/70R14 radial tires, double-wall cargo bed w/one-touch tailgate release, tinted glass, rear step bumper, high-mount rear stop light, dual side mirrors, full-size spare tire, rear mud guards, 3-passenger bench seat, 60/40 split reclining bench seat w/fold-down armrest (Cab Plus), vinyl upholstery, full instrumentation includes coolant temperature/voltmeter/oil pressure, trip odometer, AM/FM electronically tuned stereo (Cab Plus), floor console w/dual cupholders (Cab Plus).

SE 2WD TRUCK (in addition to or instead of BASE 2WD TRUCK equipment): Variable power assisted steering, full-faced styled steel wheels, P225/70R14 radial tires, flip-open rear quarter window (Cab Plus), dual aero-style mirrors, 3-passenger bench seat deleted, reclining bucket seats, 60/40 split reclining bench seat w/fold-down armrest deleted, cloth upholstery, fold-down rear jump seats (Cab Plus), full carpeting, AM/FM cassette stereo w/digital clock, tachometer, leather-wrapped steering wheel.

LE 2WD TRUCK (in addition to or instead of SE 2WD TRUCK equipment): 4.0L 12-valve V6 engine, 4-speed automatic transmission w/overdrive, sliding rear window, dual aero-style power mirrors, reclining bucket seats deleted, 60/40 split reclining bench seat w/fold-down armrest, Premium AM/FM cassette stereo w/digital clock, rear cargo cover (Cab Plus), tilt steering, cruise control, power windows and locks.

4WD TRUCK - SE: 4.0L 12-valve V6 engine, elec fuel injection, 5-speed manual transmission, shift-on-the fly 2-speed transfer case w/auto locking front hubs, variable power assisted steering, power assisted front disc/rear drum brakes, rear wheel anti-lock braking system (ABS), protective underbody skid plates, styled steel wheels, P235/75R15 all terrain radial tires, double-wall cargo bed with one-touch tailgate release, tinted glass, flip-open rear quarter window (Cab Plus), rear step bumper, high-mount rear stop light, dual aero-style mirrors, front/rear mud guards, reclining sport bucket seats w/thigh and lumbar support, cloth upholstery, fold-down rear jump seats (Cab Plus), full carpeting, full instrumentation includes coolant temperature/voltmeter/oil pressure gauges, trip odometer, AM/FM cassette stereo w/digital clock, floor console w/dual cupholders, tachometer, leather-wrapped steering wheel, sliding rear window.

LE 4WD TRUCK (in addition to or instead of SE 4WD TRUCK equipment): 4-speed auto transmission w/overdrive, dual aero-style power mirrors, reclining sport bucket seats w/thigh and lumbar support deleted, Premium AM/FM cass stereo w/digital clock, tilt steering, cruise control, power windows and locks.

Accessories

CODE	DESCRIPTION	DEALER	LIST
AC1	**Air Conditioning**	640	780
AW1	**Alloy Wheels** — NA on Base models	205	250
BLN	**Bed Liner**	150	250
PS1	**Power Steering** — Base Short Bed	226	275
FLM	**Floor Mats**	42	60
CE1	**California Emissions**	NC	NC
HA1	**High Altitude Emissions**	NC	NC
JCP	**Two-Tone Paint** — LE	230	280
RA1	**AM/FM Radio w/Clock** — Base Short Bed	144	175
CD1	**Compact Disc Player** — LE	242	295
1VP	**Value Pkg** — 2WD Base Cab Plus	NC	NC
	incls P215/70R14 all-season tires, styled steel wheels, fold-down center armrest, map pockets, 60/40 split bench seat, upgraded door trim, LE cloth upholstery, carpeting		
1PP	**Performance Pkg** — Long Bed	205	250
	2WD SE Cab Plus	254	310

MAZDA

CODE	DESCRIPTION	DEALER	LIST
1WP	**Alloy Wheel Pkg** — 4WD Cab Plus..	500	610
	incls alloy wheels, P265/75R15 all-terrain tires, performance axle		
1LU	**LE Upgrade Pkg** — 4WD LE Cab Plus w/o alloy wheel pkg......................	492	600
	incls sport bucket seats and performance axle		
2LU	**LE Upgrade Pkg** — 4WD LE Cab Plus w/alloy wheel pkg........................	287	350
	incls sport bucket seats		
1SU	**SE Upgrade Pkg**		
	2WD SE Long Bed..	549	670
	incls sport bucket seats, dual power mirrors, power windows, power door locks and sliding rear window		
	2WD SE Cab Plus..	590	720
	incls sport bucket seats, dual power mirrors, power windows, power door locks, sliding rear window and cargo cover		
	4WD SE Short Bed...	623	760
	incls performance axle, dual power mirrors, power windows and power door locks		
	4WD SE Cab Plus w/o alloy wheels..	664	810
	incls performance axle, dual power mirrors, power windows, power door locks and cargo cover		
2SU	**SE Upgrade Pkg** — 4WD SE Cab Plus w/alloy wheels...........................	459	560
	incls dual pwr mirrors, pwr windows, pwr door locks and cargo cover		

PROTEGE

—	DX 4-Dr Sedan (5-spd)	10293	11295
—	LX 4-Dr Sedan (5-spd)	11711	12995
Destination Charge: Alaska..		575	575
	Other States	375	375

Standard Equipment

PROTEGE BASE: 1.8L SOHC 16-valve 4 cylinder engine, 5-speed manual transmission w/overdrive, rack-and-pinion steering with variable power assist, power assisted ventilated front disc/rear drum brakes, front and rear stabilizer bars, 13-inch wheels w/center cap, P175/70R13 all season radial tires, stone guards, body-color front grille, protective bodyside moldings, left side remote mirror, 2-speed windshield wipers w/one-wipe feature, reclining front bucket seats, 60/40 split fold-down rear seatback, cloth seating surfaces, center console w/covered storage compartment.

DX (in addition to or instead of BASE equipment): 13-inch wheels w/full wheel covers, body-color bumpers, dual remote mirrors, intermittent windshield wipers, cloth door trim inserts, cut-pile carpeting, remote trunk and fuel door releases.

LX (in addition to or instead of DX equipment): 1.8L DOHC 16-valve 4 cylinder engine, power assisted 4-wheel disc brakes, 14-inch wheels w/full wheel coves, P185/60R14 all season radial tires, dual-outlet muffler w/bright tail pipes, dual body-color power mirrors, adjustable driver's thigh support, fold-down rear center armrest, power windows and door locks, tachometer, trunk light, AM/FM cassette stereo w/four speakers, tilt steering column.

Accessories

CODE	DESCRIPTION	DEALER	LIST
AT1	**Automatic Transmission** — 4-speed	653	725
ACA	**Air Conditioning**	672	840
FLM	**Floor Mats**	45	65
1WP	**Alloy Wheels w/Locks** — LX	340	425
CE1	**California or New York Emissions**	NC	NC
SR1	**Power Sunroof** — LX	448	560
RA1	**AM/FM ETR Radio** — fleet only	251	330
1DX	**DX Convenience Group** — DX	520	650
	incls AM/FM ETR radio w/cassette, tilt steering wheel, tachometer, trunk light and warning lights		
1FL	**DX Fleet Pkg** — DX (fleet only)	977	1190
	incls power windows, power door locks, air conditioning, molded door trim and courtesy lights		

RX-7

		DEALER	LIST
—	2-Dr Coupe (5-spd)	29059	34000
Destination Charge:		375	375

Standard Equipment

RX-7: Two-rotor inline rotary engine w/sequential twin turbochargers/air-to-air intercooler/elec fuel injection, 5-speed manual trans w/overdrive, engine oil cooler, power plant frame (PPF), Torsen torque-sensing limited slip differential, 4-wheel independent double-wishbone suspension, rack-and-pinion steering with engine-speed variable power assist, power assisted 4-wheel ventilated disc brakes, anti-lock braking system (ABS), 16-inch aluminum alloy wheels, 225/50VR16 radial tires, dual aerodynamic bodycolor power mirrors, tinted glass, retractable halogen headlights, light weight aluminum hood, illuminated driver's lock keyhole, intermittent windshield wipers w/variable control, driver and passenger side airbags, power windows w/driver's side one-touch down feature, power door locks, remote liftgate and fuel-door releases, seat back storage pockets, dual storage compartment behind seats, 9,000 RPM tachometer w/8,000 RPM redline, oil pressure/engine coolant temperature gauges, leather-wrapped steering wheel and shift knob, cruise control w/steering wheel mounted controls, drilled aluminum clutch and brake pedals, anti-theft alarm system, AM/FM cass stereo w/5 speakers and automatic power antenna, air cond.

Accessories

		DEALER	LIST
AT1	**Automatic Transmission**	740	850
	NA w/Popular Equipment Group or R-2 Pkg		
1RP	**R-2 Pkg** — NA w/Touring Pkg	1640	2000
	incls Pirelli P zero Z-rated tires, twin engine oil coolers, dedicated front brake air ducts, special RZ1 suspension, rear spoiler, front airdam, front shock tower support brace, unique cloth seat upholstery, cruise control deleted		
1TR	**Touring Pkg**	3198	3900
	incls leather seating surfaces, power glass moonroof, halogen fog lights, rear window wiper/washer, Bose acoustic wave stereo music system w/compact disc player, upgraded sound insulation, rear cargo cover		
1PE	**Popular Equipment Pkg** — NA w/R-2 Pkg	1230	1500
	incls leather seating surfaces, power steel sunroof and rear cargo cover		
FLM	**Floor Mats**	51	70

CODE	DESCRIPTION	DEALER	LIST

C-CLASS

		DEALER	LIST
—	C220 4-Dr Sedan (auto)	25440	29900
—	C280 4-Dr Sedan (auto)	29690	34900
	Destination Charge:	475	475

Standard Equipment

C220: Front and rear stabilizer bars, alloy wheels, power steering, power windows driver and front passenger air bags, cruise control, first aid kit, tinted glass, power steel sunroof with pop-up feature, 195/65R15 tires, leather-wrapped steering wheel, power automatic antenna, door locks with power central locking system, velour carpeting (trunk included), outside temperature indicator, M-B tex upholstery, automatic air conditioning, front seatback map pockets, AM/FM ETR stereo radio with cassette, 8 speakers and pre-wiring for CD; 4-speed ECT automatic transmission, dual heated remote mirrors (right power), dual illuminated visor vanity mirrors, halogen fog lights, anti-lock power 4-wheel disc brakes, cellular telephone pre-wiring, electric rear window defroster, 2.2 liter 4 cylinder EFI 16 valve engine, front bucket seats with power driver seat.

C280 (in addition to or instead of C220 equipment): Dual power front bucket seats, AM/FM ETR stereo radio with cassette, 8 speakers, Bose sound system and pre-wiring for CD; 2.8 liter EFI 24 valve engine.

Accessories

CODE	DESCRIPTION	DEALER	LIST
551	**Anti-Theft Alarm System**	477	575
—	**Leather Upholstery** — C280	1311	1580
—	**Metallic Paint**	469	565
116	**C1 Pkg** — C220	1295	1560
	incls heated front seats, auto locking differential, headlight wipers/washers		
117	**C1 Pkg** — C280	2283	2750
	incls heated frt seats, auto traction control sys, headlight wipers/washers		
118	**C2 Pkg**	266	320
	incls trunk pass-through with ski sack, split fold-down rear seat		
119	**C3 Pkg** — C280	1419	1710
	incls power glass sunroof w/pop-up feature, retractable rear head restraints, leather seats		
873	**Heated Front Seats**	457	550
221	**Power Passenger Seat** — C220	465	560

CODE	DESCRIPTION	DEALER	LIST
—	**Power Orthopedic Back Rest**		
404	left front..	295	355
405	right front..	295	355
287	**Split Fold-Down Rear Seat**............................	224	270
282	**Rear Seat** — w/trunk pass-through & ski sack............	108	130
211	**Automatic Locking Differential** — C220	921	1110
430	**Head Restraints** — rear seats.........................	274	330
414	**Roof** — power glass sunroof w/pop-up feature	183	220
471	**Automatic Traction Control System** — C280	2170	2615
600	**Headlight Wipers/Washers**............................	257	310
810	**Radio** — high-performance sound system - C220..........	403	485
	incls 8-speaker Bose sound system		

E-CLASS

		DEALER	LIST
—	E300D 4-Dr Diesel Sedan (auto)	34030	40000
—	E320 4-Dr Sedan (auto).................................	36160	42500
—	E320 2-Dr Coupe (auto)................................	51130	61600
—	E320 2-Dr Cabriolet (auto)	64160	77300
—	E320 5-Dr Wagon (auto)...............................	39310	46200
—	E420 4-Dr Sedan (auto)................................	43390	51000
—	E500 4-Dr Sedan (auto)................................	67060	80800
	Destination Charge:......................................	475	475
	Gas Guzzler Tax: E500 Sedan	1700	1700

Standard Equipment

E300D, E320 SEDAN & WAGON: 195/65R15 tires, power windows, driver and front passenger air bags, cruise control, anti-theft alarm system, first aid kit, tinted glass, power steering, alloy wheels, AM/FM ETR stereo radio with cassette and active bass speaker system (CD compatible), velour carpeting (trunk included), dual heated power mirrors, dual illuminated visor vanity mirrors, pre-wiring for cellular telephone, door locks with power central locking system, power steel sunroof with pop-up feature, automat-

MERCEDES-BENZ

ic air conditioning, luggage rack (Wagon), M-B Tex upholstery (E300D, E320 Wagon), leather upholstery (E320 Sedan), automatic power antenna, halogen fog lights, 4-speed automatic transmission, front seat-back map pockets, outside temperature indicator, anti-lock power 4-wheel disc brakes, leather-wrapped steering wheel, electric rear window defroster, dual power front bucket seats, rear-facing third seat (Wagon), 3.0 liter diesel engine (E300D), 3.2 liter 6 cylinder EFI 24 valve engine (E320).

E320 COUPE & CABRIOLET (in addition to or instead of E320 SEDAN equipment): Rear console storage box (Coupe), tilt steering column w/memory, AM/FM ETR stereo w/cass/high-performance sound system, air deflector (Cabriolet), dual power front bucket seats w/driver seat memory, headlight wipers/washers.

E420 SEDAN (in addition to or instead of E320 SEDAN equipment): Headlight wipers/washers, tilt steering column with memory, AM/FM ETR stereo radio with cassette and high-performance sound system, dual power front bucket seats with driver seat memory, 4.2 liter V8 EFI 32 valve engine.

E500 SEDAN (in addition to or instead of E420 SEDAN equipment): Metallic paint, heated front seats, automatic traction control system, 5.0 liter V8 EFI 32 valve engine, rear console storage box, level control rear axle suspension, rear reading lights, rear window power sunshade.

Accessories

CODE	DESCRIPTION	DEALER	LIST
810	**Radio** — AM/FM stereo w/cassette & high-performance sound system - E300D, E320 Sedan	403	485
441	**Power Tilt Steering Column** — E300D, E320 Sedan & Wagon	295	355
—	**Leather Upholstery** — E300D, E320 Wagon	1311	1580
111	**E1 Pkg** — E300D	1295	1560
	incls headlight wipers/washers, auto locking differential, heated front seats		
112	**E1 Pkg** — E320 Sedan & Wagon	2283	2750
	incls headlight wipers/washers, auto traction control sys, heated frt seats		
113	**E1 Pkg** — E320 Coupe & Cabriolet, E420	2075	2500
	incls heated front seats, automatic traction control system		
114	**E2 Pkg** — E300D, E320 Sedan	872	1050
	incls high-performance sound system, driver seat memory, power tilt steering column		
115	**E3 Pkg** E320 Wagon	830	1000
	incls driver seat memory, cargo area cover and partition net, power tilt steering column		
541	**Cargo Area Cover & Partition Net** — E320 Wagon	390	470
873	**Heated Front Seats** — E-Class (std E500)	457	550
241	**Driver Seat** — incls memory feature - E300D, E320 Sedan & Wagon	374	450
404	**Left Front Seat** — back rest, power orthopedic - E-Class except E500	295	355
405	**Right Front Seat** — back rest, power orthopedic - E-Class except E500	295	355
952	**Sportline Pkg** — E320 Sedan	1536	1850
	E320 Coupe	880	1060
	incls sport suspension, sport steering, 4-place sport seats		
877	**Rear Reading Lights** — E-Class Sedans (std E500)	71	85
211	**Automatic Locking Differential** — E300D	921	1110
480	**Rear Axle Level Control Suspension** — E320, E420	560	675
—	**Metallic Paint** — E300D, E320 Sedan & Wagon	535	645
	E320 Coupe & Cabriolet, E420	NC	NC
471	**Automatic Traction Control System** — E320, E420	2170	2615
600	**Headlight Wipers/Washers** — E300D, E320 Sedan & Wagon	257	310
540	**Power Sunshade** — rear window - E320 Coupe	332	400
	E-Class Sedans (std on 500)	332	400

S-CLASS

		DEALER	LIST
—	S320 4-Dr Sedan (auto)	58600	70600
—	S350D 4-Dr Turbo Diesel Sedan (auto)	58600	70600
—	S420 4-Dr Sedan (auto)	65990	79500
—	S500 4-Dr Sedan (auto)	79100	95300
—	S500 2-Dr Coupe (auto)	82830	99800
—	S600 4-Dr Sedan (auto)	108150	130300
—	S600 2-Dr Coupe (auto)	110640	133300
	Destination Charge:	475	475
	Gas Guzzler Tax: S420	1700	1700
	S500	2100	2100
	S600 Coupe	3000	3000
	S600 Sedan	3700	3700

Standard Equipment

S350D, S320 & S420 SEDANS: Anti-theft alarm system, tachometer, power decklid pull-down, vehicle-speed-sensitive wipers, tinted glass, power steering, leather upholstery, clock, front door/front seatback map pockets, first aid kit, front seat center fold-down armrest, 12-way power front bucket seats with memory, driver and front passenger air bags, power windows, power anti-lock 4-wheel disc brakes, outside temperature indicator, AM/FM ETR stereo radio with cassette and Bose sound system, automatic air conditioning, leather-wrapped steering wheel, 3.5 liter 6 cylinder turbo diesel engine (S350D), 3.2 liter 6 cylinder EFI engine (S320), 4.2 liter V8 EFI 32-valve engine (S420), front and rear stabilizer bars, infrared remote locking system, 4-speed automatic transmission (S350D & S420), 5-speed automatic transmission (S320), electric rear window defroster, cruise control, alloy wheels, automatic power antenna, door locks with power central locking system and power closing assist, pre-wiring for cellular telephone, 225/60VR16 SBR tires (S350D & S320), 235/60ZR16 SBR tires (S420), halogen fog lights, front courtesy lights with time delay, front and rear reading and door courtesy lights, velour carpeting (trunk included), dual heated power mirrors with memory, automatic dimming day/night rearview mirror, dual visor vanity mirrors, power tilt steering column with memory, headlight wipers with heated washers.

S500 SEDAN & S500 COUPE (in addition to or instead of S320 SEDAN equipment): 4-speed automatic transmission, 235/60ZR16 SBR tires, active charcoal filter, 12-way power heated front bucket seats with memory, heated power rear seat (Sedan), rear reading lights deleted (Coupe), 5.0 liter V8 EFI 32-valve engine, rear axle level control suspension, rear console storage box (Coupe), auto traction control system.

S600 SEDAN & S600 COUPE (in addition to or instead of S320 SEDAN equipment): 235/60ZR16 SBR tires, 4-speed automatic transmission, rear window power sunshade, active charcoal filter, trunk-mounted compact disc changer, 6.0 liter V12 EFI 48-valve engine, rear console storage box (Coupe), cellular telephone, rear reading lights deleted (Coupe), automatic air conditioning (Coupe), automatic front and rear air conditioning (Sedan), automatic traction control system, rear adaptive damping system suspension with rear axle level control, 12-way power heated front bucket seats with memory and power orthopedic backrests, heated rear seat (Sedan).

Accessories

Code	Description	Dealer	List
873	**Heated Front Seats** — S320, S350D, S420	481	575
224	**Four-Place Seating** — S320, S350D, S420	4333	5220
	S500 Sedan	3303	3908
	incls four power seats		
872	**Heated Rear Seats** — S320, S350D, S420	481	580
306	**Active Charcoal Filter** — S320, S350D, S420	415	500
480	**Rear Axle Level Control Suspension** — S320, S350D, S420	714	860
217	**Adaptive Damping Suspension System** — incls rear axle level control -		
	S320, S350D, S420	2283	2750
	S500	1693	2040
—	**Metallic Paint**	NC	NC
582	**Rear Air Conditioning** — S320, S350D, S420, S500 Sedan	1527	1840
404	**Left Front Seat** — back rest, power orthopedic (std S600)	295	355
405	**Right Front Seat** — back rest, power orthopedic (std S600)	295	355
223	**Rear Seatback** — power - S320, S350D, S420	863	1040
471	**Traction Control System** — automatic - S320, S420	2170	2615
412	**Power Sliding Steel Sunroof**	NC	NC
414	**Power Sliding Glass Sunroof**	324	390
211	**Automatic Locking Differential** — S350D	921	1110
540	**Rear Window Sunshade** — power (std S600)	332	400

SL-CLASS

CODE	DESCRIPTION	DEALER	LIST
—	SL320 2-Dr Coupe/Roadster (auto)	70720	85200
—	SL500 2-Dr Coupe/Roadster (auto)	82590	99500
—	SL600 2-Dr Coupe/Roadster (auto)	99680	120100
	Destination Charge: SL500	1300	1300
	SL600	3000	3000

Standard Equipment

SL320: Power windows, power steering, air deflector, clock, first aid kit, tachometer, leather-wrapped steering wheel, front courtesy lights w/time delay, front reading lights, door courtesy lights, tinted glass, auto pwr antenna, dual heated pwr mirrors w/memory, auto dimming day/night rearview mirror, dual illuminated visor vanity mirror, auto pop-up roll bar, outside temperature indicator, leather upholstery, vehicle speed-sensitive wipers, infrared remote locking system, halogen fog lights, cruise control, anti-lock power 4-wheel disc brakes, driver and front passenger air bags, door locks w/power central locking system, velour carpeting (trunk included), front and rear stabilizer bars, power convertible top or removable hardtop, alloy wheels, 5-speed automatic transmission, automatic air conditioning, front seat fold-down center armrest, electric rear window defroster (Hardtop), headlight wipers with heated washers, front door map pockets, 225/55ZR16 SBR tires, AM/FM ETR stereo radio with cassette and Bose Acoustimass sound system, anti-theft alarm system, 3.2 liter 6 cylinder EFI 24-valve engine, 10-way power front bucket seats with dual 3-position memory, tilt steering column with memory, pre-wiring for cellular telephone.

SL500 (in addition to or instead of SL320 equipment): 4-speed automatic transmission, automatic traction control system, 5.0 liter V8 EFI 32-valve engine, control area network data management system.

SL600 (in addition to or instead of SL500 equipment): Cellular telephone, 6.0 liter V12 48-valve engine, trunk-mounted compact disc changer, adaptive damping suspension system with 4-wheel level control, 10-way power heated front bucket seats with dual 3-position memory.

Accessories

CODE	DESCRIPTION	DEALER	LIST
216	**Adaptive Damping Suspension System** — SL320, SL500	3332	4015
—	**Metallic Paint**	NC	NC
471	**Automatic Traction Control** — SL320	2170	2615
873	**Heated Front Seats** — SL320, SL500	457	550
404	**Left Front Seat** — back rest, power orthopedic	295	355
405	**Right Front Seat** — back rest, power orthopedic	295	355

3000GT

Code	Description	Dealer	List
T24-N	GT Base 2-Dr Coupe (5-spd)	22286	27175
GT24-N	GT Base 2-Dr Coupe (auto)	22998	28050
GT24-P	SL 2-Dr Coupe (5-spd)	25955	31650
GT24-P	SL 2-Dr Coupe (auto)	26667	32525
GT24-T	VR-4 Turbo 2-Dr Coupe (5-spd)	33529	40900
Destination Charge:		470	470

Standard Equipment

3000 GT: 6-way adjustable front bucket seats w/memory recline, sport knit upholstery w/knit bolster, leather-wrap steering wheel/manual transmission shift knob/parking brake lever, passenger area cut-pile carpeting, cargo area carpeting, cloth insert door trim w/carpeted lower section, carpet floor mats, dual bi-level heater/defroster with rear seat heater ducts and variable speed fan, CFC-free refrigerant air conditioning w/manual controls, power windows w/one-touch driver's auto down, power door locks w/one-touch keyless locking, electric rear window defroster w/timer, tilt steering column, full-function cruise control, courtesy lamps: dome/trunk/map/glove compartment, rear cargo cover, center console w/storage areas/cupholders/coin holder/armrest; remote hood latch/fuel-door/trunk lid releases, dual sunvisors w/vanity mirror, driver and front passenger airbags, 4-wheel disc brakes, full instrumentation includes 160 mph speedometer, 7,000 RPM redline tachometer, fuel-level gauge, oil pressure gauge, coolant temperature gauge/tripmeter/voltmeter; warning lights for check engine/brake system/low oil pressure, low fuel, door/trunk ajar/charging system/low coolant/economy-power overdrive indicator; warning chime, 4-spoke sport steering wheel, rear window wiper/washer, digital quartz clock, ETR AM/FM stereo cassette w/6 speakers, graphic equalizer and anti-theft feature; power antenna, ETACS-IV, color keyed 5 mph bumpers, color keyed rear spoiler w/high mounted stop lamp, bright sport dual exhaust outlets, tinted glass, halogen headlamps w/auto-off and flash-to-pass, projection fog lamps, power remote dual aero-type sideview mirrors, convex right sideview mirror, upper windshield shade band, 16 x 8.0 aluminum alloy wheels w/locks, 225/55R16 V-rated SBR performance tires, 3.0L DOHC V6 engine w/MVIC, electronic multi-point fuel injection, automatic valve-lash adjusters, roller-type cam followers, stainless steel dual exhaust system, 5-speed manual transmission w/overdrive, strut-type independent front suspension, multi-link independent rear suspension, power assist rack and pinion steering, on-board diagnostic system, color-coded under hood service item identification.

CODE	DESCRIPTION	DEALER	LIST

3000 GT SL (in addition to or instead of 3000 GT equipment): 7-way adjustable driver seat w/5-way power adjustments, auxiliary 12-volt power outlet, steering wheel mounted audio controls, cargo tie-down straps, remote keyless entry system, dual sunvisors w/illuminated vanity mirror, anti lock braking system (ABS), Mitsubishi/Infinity audio system (AM/FM cassette w/graphic equalizer/8 speakers/separate amplifier and steering wheel remote audio controls), power and diversity antenna, electric sideview mirror defroster, ECS-electronically controlled suspension, security system.

3000 GT VR-4 (in addition to or instead of 3000 GT SL equipment): Leather front seating surfaces, cloth insert door trim w/carpeted lower section deleted, automatic climate control w/air conditioning (CFC-free refrigerant) and electric pictographic controls, 180 mph speedometer, turbocharger boost gauge replaces voltmeter, economy/power overdrive indicator deleted, active aero system front airdam extension and rear spoiler, 17 x 8.5 aluminum alloy wheels w/locks, 245/45R17 Z-rated SBR performance tires, 3.0L DOHC V6 engine w/twin turbochargers and intercoolers, engine oil cooler, active exhaust system, Getrag 6-speed manual transmission w/overdrive, four-wheel steering, limited slip rear differential, full-time AWD w/VCU and center differential.

Accessories

Code	Description	Dealer	List
Y99	**Yellow Pear Paint** — all except Base	250	313
EA	**Compact Disc Auto Changer**	530	799
CW	**Chrome Wheels** — VR-4	400	500
LS	**Leather Pkg** — SL	960	1120
	incls leather seating surfaces		
SR	**Manual Sunroof** — all except Base	300	375
MG	**Mud Guards**	92	142

DIAMANTE

		Dealer	List
DM42-P	ES 4-Dr Sedan (auto)	21431	25525
DM42-U	LS 4-Dr Sedan (auto)	26006	32500
—	4-Dr Wagon (auto)	NA	NA
Destination Charge:		470	470

CODE	DESCRIPTION	DEALER	LIST

Standard Equipment

DIAMANTE ES/WAGON: 7-way adjustable front seats (6-way on Wagon), velour upholstery, high-gloss woodgrain accents on instrument panel and front armrests, cutpile carpeting, fold-down rear center armrest, cargo-area carpeting, front and rear door armrests, adjustable front and rear headrests, air conditioning (CFC-free refrigerant) w/automatic climate control, power windows, power door locks, electric rear window defroster w/auto shut-off, center console w/integral armrest, dual cupholder, rear seat heater ducts, door key illumination, courtesy lamps, ignition key w/delay light, digital quartz clock, cruise control, remote fuel door and power deck lid release, height-adjustable steering column, driver and front passenger airbags, height-adjustable front shoulder belts, four-wheel disc brakes, full instrumentation: 150 mph speedometer/tachometer/fuel-level gauge/tripmeter/coolant temperature gauge, warning lights: engine check/brake system/low oil pressure/charging system/low fuel/automatic trans position indicator/economy-power overdrive/and door/trunk ajar; key-in-ignition warning chime, variable intermittent wipers, ETACS-IV, ETR AM/FM stereo cassette w/6 speakers/graphic equalizer/anti-theft feature/steering wheel remote controls (7 speakers on Wagon), diversity antenna system - power antenna and rear in-glass antenna, color-keyed 5 mph bumpers, bodyside molding, integral front air dam, bright dual exhaust tips (N/A on Wagon), tinted glass, prism-type headlamps, dual power remote aero type sideview mirrors, convex right sideview mirror, upper windshield shade band, 15 x 6 7-spoke alloy wheels w/locks (5-spoke on Wagon), 205/65R15 SBR performance tires (H rated tires on Wagon), conventional spare tire, 3.0L SOHC V6 engine, electronic multi-point fuel injection, automatic valve lash adjusters, roller-type rocker arms, variable induction control system (MVIC), stainless steel exhaust system, 4-speed automatic transmission w/power-economy modes, ELC-M engine and transmission management system (N/A on Wagon), 4-wheel independent suspension (N/A on Wagon), strut-type independent front suspension, multi-link independent rear suspension (N/A on Wagon), 5-link tube axle rear suspension (Wagon only), front and rear stabilizer bars, power assist rack and pinion steering, security system, on-board diagnostic system, color coded under hood service item identification.

LS (in addition to or instead of ES/WAGON equipment): Power driver's seat adjustments w/two position memory, power passenger seat, leather interior trim, classic style analog clock, remote keyless entry system, anti-lock braking system (ABS), Mitsubishi Infinity audio system includes AM/FM stereo cassette w/graphic equalizer/separate amplifier/8 speakers/steering wheel remote controls; side sill extension, dual power remote aero-type heated sideview mirrors, automatic day/night mirror, 15 x 6 5-spoke alloy wheels w/locks, 3.0L DOHC V6 engine w/twin spray fuel injectors, 5-link tube axles rear suspension deleted, EPS II speed and steering wheel velocity sensitive power steering.

Accessories

CODE	DESCRIPTION	DEALER	LIST
TM	**Trunk Mat** — ES	46	71
TN	**Traction Control** — LS..	556	678
WD	**Sunroof Air Deflector**..	37	57
	req's power tilt/slide sunroof		
PL	**Leather Seat Pkg** — ES...	1548	1888
	incls door trim panels w/leather trim, power driver's seat w/memory,		
	leather seating surfaces, leather-wrapped console lid		
EA	**Compact Disc Auto Changer**	488	699
PE	**Power Passenger Seat** — w/memory - LS...	295	369
EI	**Infinity Audio Sound System Radio** — ES	300	429
PI	**Power Tilt/Slide Sunroof**	690	863
	incls inner sunshade		
AB	**Four-Wheel Anti-Lock Brakes** — ES	880	1100
KE	**Keyless Entry System** — ES..	157	242

ECLIPSE

CODE	DESCRIPTION	DEALER	LIST
EC24-M	Base 3-Dr Coupe (5-spd)	10482	11979
EC24-M	Base 3-Dr Coupe (auto)	11075	12659
EC24-N	GS 1.8L 3-Dr Coupe (5-spd)	12256	14089
EC24-N	GS 1.8L 3-Dr Coupe (auto)	12849	14769
EC24-P	GS 2.0L DOHC 3-Dr Coupe (5-spd)	13764	15819
EC24-P	GS 2.0L DOHC 3-Dr Coupe (auto)	14357	16499
EC24-T	GS 2.0L Turbo 3-Dr Coupe (5-spd)	16117	18529
EC24-T	GS 2.0L Turbo 3-Dr Coupe (auto)	16827	19339
EC24-U	GSX 2.0L Turbo 4WD 3-Dr Coupe (5-spd)	18504	21269
EC24-U	GSX 2.0L Turbo 4WD 3-Dr Coupe (auto)	19214	22089
Destination Charge:		420	420

Standard Equipment

ECLIPSE - BASE: Cloth upholstery, split fold-down rear seat, heating/ventilating system w/4-speed fan, dial type controls and dual bi-level output; tilt steering column, courtesy lamps, dome lamps w/fade-out feature, remote hood-latch/fuel door/trunk lid releases; motorized front shoulder belts, 4-wheel disc brakes, integrated fog lamps, full instrumentation: 145 mph speedometer, tachometer, fuel-level gauge, tripmeter, coolant temperature gauge, oil pressure gauge; warning lights: engine check, brake system, low oil pressure, low fuel, door/trunk ajar/charging system/economy-power overdrive (w/automatic transmission)/low coolant, ETR AM/FM stereo w/4 speakers, digital quartz clock, color keyed 5 mph bumpers, color keyed door handles/tail lamp trim, full profile color keyed air dam, hood w/power bulge, wrap around color keyed bodyside molding, tinted glass, aero-type halogen headlamps, electric rear window defroster, dual remote aero-type sideview mirrors, 14 x 5.5 styled steel wheels, 185/70R14 all-season radial tires, 1.8L SOHC 4 cylinder engine, dual engine stabilizers, electronic multi-point fuel injection, automatic valve-lash adjusters, stainless steel exhaust system, 5-speed manual overdrive transmission, ventilated front disc/rear disc brakes, strut-type independent front suspension, twist-beam rear axle 3-link suspension, on-board diagnostic system.

GS (in addition to or instead of BASE equipment): Driver's seat lumbar support, cloth insert door trim w/carpeted lower section, rear cargo cover, center console with storage areas/cupholders/coin holder/armrest; cruise control "on" light (with cruise control), ETR AM/FM cassette w/6 speakers, sculpted side sill cladding, color keyed rear spoiler, dual remote aero-type sideview mirrors deleted, 14 x 5.5 aluminum alloy wheels, power assist rack and pinion steering.

GS DOHC (in addition to or instead of GS equipment): Air conditioning, power antenna, cruise control, rear window wiper/washer, ETR AM/FM cassette w/6 speakers, black roof and B pillar, bright dual exhaust outlets, full wheel covers, 14 x 5.5 aluminum alloy wheels deleted, 205/55R16 performance H rated tires, 2.0L DOHC 16-valve 4 cylinder engine.

GS TURBO (in addition to or instead of GS DOHC equipment): 6-way adjustable driver's seat, leather-wrapped steering wheel and manual transmission shift knob, power windows and door locks, turbo boost gauge, A/T oil temperature warning light (w/automatic transmission), ETR AM/FM cassette w/6 speakers/compact disc/diversity antenna; color keyed side sill extensions, 16 x 6 aluminum alloy wheels, full wheel covers deleted, 205/55R16 V-rated performance tires, 2.0L DOHC 16-valve 4 cylinder turbocharged intercooled engine, engine oil cooler, gas-charged shock absorbers.

GSX (in addition to or instead of GS TURBO equipment): Full-time AWD, limited-slip rear differential, double wishbone/semi-trailing.

Accessories

CODE	DESCRIPTION	DEALER	LIST
CW	**Alloy Wheels** — GS 2.0L	271	330
MG	**Mud Guards**	80	123
AC	**Air Conditioning** — Base, GS 1.8L	685	835
PP	**Power Pkg** — GS (std Turbo)	387	472
	incls power door locks, power windows		
LS	**Leather Pkg** — GS Turbo, GSX	368	448
	incls leather front seat surfaces		
PS	**Power Steering** — Base	225	274
EC	**AM/FM Stereo Radio w/Cassette** — Base	146	178
	incls four speakers		
ED	**Compact Disc Player** — all except Turbo models	417	642
	Base req's AM/FM ETR stereo radio w/cassette		
EW	**AM/FM ETR Stereo Radio w/Graphic Equalizer & Cassette** — GS 2.0L	205	250
	incls diversity antenna, six speakers		
EX	**AM/FM ETR Stereo w/Compact Disc Player & Cassette** — GS 2.0L	607	740
	incls diversity antenna, six speakers		
CC	**Cruise Control** — GS 1.8L	181	221
PA/GA	**Lower Body Paint** — GS 2.0L	105	125
	incls graphic accent		
TL	**Wheels Locks** — GS 2.0L	21	33
KE	**Keyless Entry System** — all except Base	157	242
	req's Power Pkg		
WC	**Wheel Covers** — Base	87	106
AB	**Four-Wheel Anti-Lock Power Disc Brakes** — GS Turbo	781	952
MW	**Rear Window Wiper/Washer** — GS 1.8L	111	135
FM	**Floor Mats**	38	58
SR	**Removable Sunroof** — all except Base	309	377

EXPO

		DEALER	LIST
EX35-L	LRV Base 3-Dr Liftback (5-spd)	11716	13019
EX35-L	LRV Base 3-Dr Liftback (auto)	12474	13859
EX35-N	LRV Sport 3-Dr Liftback (5-spd)	14619	16799
EX35-N	LRV Sport 3-Dr Liftback (auto)	15219	17489
EX45-N	4-Dr Liftback (5-spd)	13648	15689
EX45-N	4-Dr Liftback (auto)	14248	16379
EX45-W	4-Dr AWD Liftback (5-spd)	14900	17129
EX45-W	4-Dr AWD Liftback (auto)	15500	17819
Destination Charge:		445	445

Standard Equipment

EXPO LRV: Removable/tumbling rear bench with 50/50 split folding/reclining seatbacks, rear seat head-rests, full-face cloth upholstery, heating/ventilation system w/4-speed fan, dial-type controls and dual bi-level output; rear window defogger w/heavy-duty timer, tilt steering column, sliding rear passenger door w/inner rail sliding mechanism, dome and cargo area lights, remote fuel filler door w/tethered cap, low fuel warning light, analog instrumentation: 140 mph speedometer/fuel-level gauge/tripmeter/coolant temperature gauge; warning lights: engine check/brake system/low oil pressure/charging system/door-hatch ajar; driver side airbag, child protection rear door locks, variable intermittent wipers, 5 mph bumpers, protective bodyside molding, two-tone paint, dual manual remote sideview mirrors, 185/75R14 all-season tires, 14 x 5.5 full wheel covers, 1.8L SOHC 16V 4 cylinder engine, electronic multi-point fuel injection, stainless steel exhaust system, 5-speed manual overdrive transmission, power assist front disc/rear drum brakes, power assist rack and pinion steering, strut-type independent front suspension, semi-trailing arm independent rear suspension, front stabilizer bar, on-board diagnostic system.

EXPO LRV SPORT (in addition to or instead of EXPO LRV equipment): Rear-seat heater ducts (2nd seat), CFC-free refrigerant air conditioning, Power Package includes power windows w/driver side auto down/remote keyless entry system/dual power remote side view mirrors/cruise control; rear window wiper/washer with intermittent, power tailgate release, digital quartz clock, Convenience Package includes: center armrest/upgraded door trim w/cloth inserts and map pockets/rear cargo cover/power door and tailgate lock; tachometer, rear cargo cover, ETR AM/FM cassette w/4 speakers, tailgate deflector w/LED stop lamp, dual power remote sideview mirrors, 205/70R14 all season tires, 14 x 5.5 alloy wheels, 2.4L SOHC 16V 4 cylinder eng, dual eng stabilizers, auto valve lash adjusters, rear stabilizer bar.

EXPO/EXPO AWD (in addition to or instead of EXPO LRV SPORT equipment): 2nd and 3rd row seats w/50/50 folding/reclining; rear seat heater ducts (2nd and 3rd seat), air conditioning deleted, Power Package deleted, underseat front passenger tray, remote keyless entry system deleted, sliding rear passenger door w/inner rail sliding mechanism deleted, cruise control deleted, Convenience Package deleted, ETR AM/FM cassette w/4 speakers deleted, tailgate deflector w/LED stop lamp deleted, 14 x 5.5 full wheel covers, 14 x 5.5 alloy wheels deleted, rear stabilizer bar deleted.

Accessories

CODE	DESCRIPTION	DEALER	LIST
FM	**Floor Mats** — LRV	47	73
	4-Door	55	85
AW	**Alloy Wheels** — AWD models	233	291
AC	**Air Conditioning** — std LRV Sport	680	829
RR	**Luggage Rack**	178	274
KC	**Cargo Kit Pkg** — LRV	70	99
	incls cargo area net, cargo tray		
PP	**Power Pkg** — LRV Base	575	719
	incls dual power mirrors, cruise control, remote keyless entry system, power windows (req's 4-speed automatic transmission)		
PP	**Power Pkg** — 4-Door	715	894
	incls cruise control, remote keyless entry sys, pwr door locks, pwr windows		
CP	**Convenience Pkg** — LRV Base	477	596
	incls digital clock, power door locks, power tailgate locks, rear tonneau cover, rear window wiper/washer, front seat center armrest, door trim panels w/cloth inserts		
ER	**AM/FM ETR Stereo Radio** — LRV Base	217	334
	incls four speakers		
EQ	**AM/FM ETR Stereo Radio w/Cassette** — std LRV Sport	312	466
	incls four speakers		
ED	**Compact Disc Player**	407	626
PI	**Power Tilt/Slide Sunroof** — LRV Sport, 4-Door FWD	548	685
	incls inner sunshade		
AB	**Four-Wheel Anti-Lock Power Brakes** — all except LRV Base	800	976
TL	**Wheel Locks** — 4-Door FWD	24	37
MG	**Front & Rear Mud Guards**	54	84

MITSUBISHI

GALANT

CODE	DESCRIPTION	DEALER	LIST
GA41-N	S 4-Dr Sedan (5-spd)	12104	13600
GA41-N	S 4-Dr Sedan (auto)	12905	14500
GA41-P	ES 4-Dr Sedan (auto)	14259	16775
GA41-T	LS 4-Dr Sedan (auto)	15483	18215
GA41-R	GS 4-Dr Sedan (5-spd)	17420	20494
GA41-R	GS 4-Dr Sedan (auto)	18086	21277
	Destination Charge:	420	420

Standard Equipment

GALANT S: 5-way adjustable front driver's seat (recline, for/aft, front and rear tilt, headrest height), woven cloth seating surfaces (vinyl sides and backs), needle punch interior carpet, heating/ventilation system with 4-speed fan/dial type controls/dual bi-level output, electric rear window defroster, side window defroster, digital quartz clock, tilt steering column, courtesy lamps, trunk lamp, center console w/armrest and storage, door map pockets (driver's door only), trunk storage bin, valet trunk lockout, cupholders, remote hood/fuel door/trunk lid releases; one-touch keyless door locking, in-dash storage bin (NA w/CD player), dual sunvisors w/driver's ticket holder, driver's visor vanity mirror w/flip-up cover, driver's side footrest, driver and front passenger air bags, child protection rear door locks, 140 mph speedo-meter/tachometer/fuel level gauge/coolant temperature gauge: intermittent wipers, radio accommodation package w/4 speakers, color-keyed 5 mph bumpers, gray molding, day/night rearview mirror, dual black manual remote sideview mirrors, convex right sideview mirror, tinted glass, dual aero-type halogen head-lamps, 14 x 5.5 steel wheels w/full wheel cover, 185/70R14 H-rated SBR all season tires, 2.4L SOHC 16-valve 4 cylinder engine, multi point electronic fuel injection, dual engine stabilizers, roller rocker arms, auto lash valve adjusters, stainless steel exhaust system, 5-speed manual transmission w/overdrive, ventilated front disc brakes, rear drum brakes, power assist rack and pinion steering, front stabilizer bar.

ES (in addition to or instead of S equipment): Fold down lockable rear seat w/center armrest, deluxe full cloth upholstery, molded door panels w/cloth inserts and carpeted lower section, cut-pile interior carpet, CFC-free refrigerant air conditioning, rear-seat heater duct, power windows and door locks, glove compartment lamp, door lamps, under floor trunk storage compartment, in-dash storage bin w/cover (NA w/CD player), passenger visor vanity mirror w/flip-up cover, full function cruise control, ETR AM/FM stereo cassette w/6 speakers, automatic power and diversity antenna, color-keyed bodyside molding, color-

CODE	DESCRIPTION	DEALER	LIST

keyed dual power remote sideview mirrors, 4-speed electronic control automatic transmission w/overdrive and fuzzy logic shift control.

LS (in addition to or instead of ES equipment): 6-way adjustable front seat (recline, fore/aft, front/rear tilt, headrest height/tilt), luxury full cloth upholstery, electric rear window defroster w/auto timer, power glass sunroof w/shade, floor mats, dome lamp w/time delay, front seatback storage pockets, lighted passenger visor vanity mirror w/flip up cover, center sunvisor, ETACS-IV, fog lamps, variable intermittent wipers, upper windshield shade band, 15 x 6 alloy wheels w/wheel locks, 195/60R15 H-rated SBR all season tires.

GS (in addition to or instead of LS equipment): Sport full cloth upholstery, leather wrapped steering wheel and manual transmission shift knob, in-dash storage bin w/cover deleted, 150 mph speedometer, ETR AM/FM stereo cassette/CD w/6 speakers; rear spoiler w/LED stop lamp, 2.4L DOHC 16 valve 4 cylinder engine, dual coil distributorless ignition, knock sensor, 5-speed manual transmission w/overdrive, rear disc brakes, EPS-II electronic control power steering, rear stabilizer bar.

Accessories

MG	**Mud Guards**..	76	117
WD	**Sunroof Air Deflector** — LS, GS	34	52
KE	**Remote Keyless Entry System** — ES, LS, GS...........	145	223
AB	**Four-Wheel Anti-Lock Brakes** — ES, LS, GS...........	758	924
EC	**AM/FM ETR Stereo Radio w/Cassette** — S	297	457
ED	**Compact Disc** — S	449	641
	req's AM/FM ETR stereo radio w/cassette		
EX	**Compact Disc** — single play - ES, LS.................	449	641
AC	**Air Conditioning** — S	678	827
FM	**Floor Mats** — S, ES	47	73

MIGHTY MAX PICKUPS

MIGHTY MAX PICKUPS

TK27-G	2WD Regular Cab (5-spd)	8512	9429
TK27-G	2WD Regular Cab (auto)...	9109	10349
TK27-J	2WD Macrocab (5-spd)..	9595	10899

MITSUBISHI

CODE	DESCRIPTION	DEALER	LIST
TK27-J	2WD Macrocab (auto)	10192	11579
TF27-G	4WD Regular Cab (5-spd)	12510	14219
	Destination Charge:	420	420

Standard Equipment

MIGHTY MAX 2WD REGULAR CAB: Bench seat, full face cloth seat trim, adjustable head restraints, full carpeting, color-coordinated headliner, behind-seat storage area, bi-level heating/ventilation system, side window defoggers, remote hood release, tilt steering column, 2-speed windshield wipers, dual sunvisors, one-touch keyless locking doors, fuel level gauge, tripmeter, coolant temperature gauge, sport-type steering wheel, warning lights for: brakes/battery charge/low fluid/seatbelts/low oil pressure; front air dam extension, welded double-wall cargo box, steel tie-down hooks, one-hand tailgate release, chrome grille, black front bumper, rectangular headlamps, tinted glass, dual sideview mirrors, passenger-side convex mirror, P195/75R14 radial tires, 2.4L SOHC 4 cylinder engine, dual engine stabilizers, electronic ignition system, automatic valve lash adjusters, stainless steel exhaust system, 5-speed manual overdrive transmission, independent front suspension, front stabilizer bar, rigid rear axle with leaf springs, recirculating ball steering, power assisted vented front disc/rear drum brakes, self-adjusting rear brakes, load sensing brake proportion valve, sealed brake fluid reservoir, underhood service item I.D., on-board diagnostic system, 13.7 gallon fuel tank.

MIGHTY MAX 2WD MACROCAB (in addition to or instead of 2WD REGULAR CAB equipment): Split bench seat w/adjustable seat back, concealed storage compartment, cargo strap, lower section cab back trim, rear quarter windows, P205/75R14 radial tires, 18.2 gallon fuel tank.

MIGHTY MAX 4WD MACROCAB (in addition to or instead of 2WD MACROCAB equipment): Bench seat, concealed storage compartment deleted, cargo strap deleted, lower section cab back trim deleted, passenger assist grips, rear anti-lock braking system (ABS), 4WD engaged warning light, ABS warning light, large flared fenders, front and rear mudguards, skid plates: front end/transfer case/fuel tank; front towing hook, rear quarter windows deleted, P225/75R15 all terrain M & S radial tires, 3.0L SOHC V6 engine, dual engine stabilizers deleted, automatic locking front hubs, part-time 4WD system, 2-speed transfer case, power assist steering, anti-lock braking system ABS (2-wheel rear), 15.7 gallon fuel tank.

Accessories

CODE	DESCRIPTION	DEALER	LIST
DC	**Digital Clock**	60	92
AC	**Air Conditioning**	598	729
RA	**Radio Accommodation Pkg** — w/4 speakers - Macrocab	53	76
RT	**Radio Accommodation Pkg** — w/2 speakers - 2WD Regular Cab	33	47
EVPK	**Port Installed Value Pkg** — 2WD	759	759
	incls color-keyed rear step bumpers, digital clock, air conditioning, bodyside stripes, AM/FM ETR stereo radio w/cassette (req's Sport Pkg)		
SP	**Sport Pkg** — 2WD	356	445
	incls day/night rearview mirror, bright windshield molding, halogen headlights, door map pockets, cut-pile carpeting, color-keyed front bumpers, full door trim panel w/large armrests & lower carpeting, chrome grille, sliding rear window, full instrumentation, cloth bench seat, tachometer, Radio Accommodation Pkg (RT - Regular Cab, RA - Macrocab) (req's Port Installed Value Pkg)		
SW	**Sliding Rear Window** — 4WD	71	89
ER	**AM/FM ETR Radio** — 2WD	210	321
EQ	**AM/FM ETR Radio** — w/cassette	327	481
NB	**Black Rear Step Bumper**	113	162

CODE	DESCRIPTION	DEALER	LIST
BB	**Color-Keyed Front Bumper** — 4WD	30	38
CB	**Color-Keyed Rear Bumper** — 4WD	143	204
	req's color-keyed front bumper		
FM	**Floor Mats**	34	52
SM	**Bodyside Molding** — 2WD	72	111
TR	**Wheel Trim Rings** — 4WD	49	76
SC	**Chrome Rear Bumper**	141	201
	NA w/Sport Pkg on 2WD models		
CM	**Dual Chrome Sport Mirrors** — 4WD	77	118
LD	**Limited Slip Differential** — 4WD..	181	226
PS	**Power Steering** — 2WD...	232	290

MITSUBISHI

MIRAGE

MG21-E	S 2-Dr Coupe (5-spd)..	8268	8989
MG41-L	S 4-Dr Sedan (5-spd)	10237	11369
MG41-L	S 4-Dr Sedan (auto)	10667	11849
MG21-L	ES 2-Dr Coupe (5-spd)..	9324	10359
MG21-L	ES 2-Dr Coupe (auto)	9754	10839
MG41-M	ES 4-Dr Sedan (5-spd)	10740	11929
MG41-M	ES 4-Dr Sedan (auto)	11322	12579
MG21-M	LS 2-Dr Coupe (5-spd)..	10688	11879
MG21-M	LS 2-Dr Coupe (auto)	11215	12459
MG41-H	LS 4-Dr Sedan (auto)	12788	14529
	Destination Charge:..	420	420

Standard Equipment

MIRAGE S COUPE: Highback front bucket seats, textured vinyl upholstery w/cloth inserts, soft-touch wrap around dash, passenger area carpeting, front and rear armrests, heating/ventilating system with 4-speed fan/dial-type controls/dual bi level output; electric rear window defroster w/auto shut-off, 2-speed wipers, center console w/storage bin, remote hood-latch release, keyless locking, driver side airbag, motorized front passenger shoulder belt w/manual lap belt, height adjustable driver's shoulder belt, analog instrumentation: speedometer/fuel level gauge/coolant temperature gauge/backglow instrument illumination; warning lights: engine check/emergency brake on/low oil pressure/door ajar; 5 mph bumpers, black door handles, flush mount door handles, locking fuel-filler door with cap tether, semi concealed windshield wipers, aero-quad halogen headlamps, dual aero-type sideview mirrors, 145/80R13 all season SBR tires, styled steel wheels w/black center cap, 1.5L SOHC 12 valve 4 cylinder eng, elec multi point fuel injection, roller-type cam followers, stainless steel exhaust system, 4-wheel independent multi-link rear suspension, 5-speed man trans w/overdrive, power assist front disc/rear drum brakes, rack and pinion steering.

ES COUPE (in addition to or instead of S COUPE equipment): Lowback front bucket seats, height adjustable driver's seat, adjustable front headrests, full face cloth upholstery, cargo area carpeting, day/night rearview mirror, door map pockets, remote fuel-filler and hatch release, low fuel warning light, trip odometer, radio accommodation package includes: antenna/full harness/radio bracket/4 speakers; color keyed integrated front and rear bumpers, color keyed grille, color keyed bodyside molding, black door sash accent, color keyed door handles, locking fuel-filler door with cap tether and remote release, tinted glass, dual remote aero-type sideview mirrors, 155/80R13 all season SBR tires, steel wheels w/full wheel covers, power steering.

LS COUPE (in addition to or instead of ES COUPE equipment): Sport front bucket seats, split fold-down rear seat, full cloth upholstery, cloth insert door trim, 2-speed intermittent wipers, tilt steering column, digital clock, Convenience Package includes: Coupe digital clock/intermittent wiper/cloth door trim/split fold-down rear seat/full trunk trim/lamp: tachometer (w/5-speed only), ETR AM/FM cassette w/4 speakers, rear spoiler, dual power remote aero-type sideview mirrors, 185/65R14 all season SBR tires, alloy wheels, 1.8L SOHC 16 valve 4 cylinder engine.

MIRAGE S 4-DR: Highback front bucket seats, full face cloth upholstery, soft-touch wrap-around dash, passenger area carpeting, cargo area carpeting, front and rear armrests, heating/ventilating system w/4-speed fan/dial-type controls/dual bi-level output, electric rear window defroster w/auto shut-off, 2-speed wipers, day/night rearview mirror, digital clock, center console w/storage bin, remote hood/latch release, keyless locking, door map pockets, driver side airbag, motorized front passenger shoulder belt w/man lap belt, height adjustable driver's shoulder belt, child protection rear door locks, analog instrumentation: speedometer/fuel level gauge/coolant temperature gauge, backglow instrument illumination; warning lights for: eng check/emergency brake system/low oil pressure/low fuel/door ajar/trip odometer; radio accommodation pkg: antenna/full harness/radio bracket/4 speakers; 5 mph bumpers, black door handles, flush mount door handles, locking fuel-filler door w/cap tether, semi concealed windshield wipers, aero-quad halogen headlamps, dual aero-type sideview mirrors, 175/70R13 all season SBR tires, steel wheels w/full wheel covers, 1.5L SOHC 12 valve 4 cylinder eng, elec multi-point fuel injection, roller-type cam followers, stainless steel exhaust system, 4-wheel independent/multi-link rear suspension, 5-speed man trans w/overdrive, power assist front disc/rear drum brakes, rack and pinion steering, power steering.

ES 4-DR (in addition to or instead of S 4-DR equipment): Lowback front bucket seats, height adjustable driver's seat, adjustable front headrests, cloth insert door trim, 2-speed intermittent wipers, remote fuel filler and hatch release, color-keyed integrated front and rear bumpers, color-keyed grille, black door sash accent, locking fuel-filler door w/cap tether and remote release, tinted glass, dual remote aero-type mirrors, 185/65R14 all season SBR tires, 1.8L SOHC 16 valve 4 cylinder engine.

LS 4-DR (in addition to or instead of ES 4-DR equipment): Sport front bucket seats, split fold-down rear seat, full cloth upholstery, cruise control, variable intermittent wipers, tilt steering column, Convenience Package: 4-Dr sport front seats/tilt steering column/split fold-down rear seat with center armrest/full cloth upholstery; power windows and door locks, ETR AM/FM cassette w/4 speakers, color-keyed bodyside molding, color-keyed door handles, dual power remote aero-type sideview mirrors, alloy wheels, 4-speed automatic transmission with overdrive and lock-up torque conv.

CODE	DESCRIPTION	DEALER	LIST

Accessories

CODE	DESCRIPTION	DEALER	LIST
RS	**Rear Spoiler** — ES Coupe	170	213
AC	**Air Conditioning**	660	805
MG	**Mud Guards** — ES Coupe, LS Coupe	67	99
	Sedans	64	98
RA	**Radio Accommodation Pkg** — S Coupe	53	76
	incls four speakers		
CP	**Convenience Pkg** — ES Coupe	172	215
	incls intermittent wipers, full trunk trim, digital clock, split fold-down rear seat, trunk courtesy light, door trim panels w/cloth inserts		
CP	**Convenience Pkg** — ES Sedan	135	169
	incls upgraded seat upholstery, split fold-down rear seat, luxury front and rear seats, rear seat center armrest, tilt steering column		
PP	**Power Pkg** — ES Sedan	425	531
	incls power door locks, power windows		
ED	**Compact Disc Player**	407	626
	req's AM/FM ETR stereo radio w/cassette		
EQ	**AM/FM ETR Stereo Radio w/Cassette** — S, ES	312	466
ER	**AM/FM ETR Stereo** — S, ES	217	334
TR	**Wheel Trim Rings** — S Coupe	44	68
FM	**Floor Mats**	41	64
CC	**Cruise Control** — ES Sedan	180	225
	incls variable intermittent wipers		
TL	**Wheel Locks** — LS	21	33

MONTERO

MONTERO

	DEALER	LIST
MP45-N LS 4WD 4-Dr (5-spd)	20505	23975
MP45-N LS 4WD 4-Dr (auto)	21219	24825
MP45-W SR 4WD 4-Dr (auto)	26290	31475
Destination Charge:	445	445

MITSUBISHI

CODE	DESCRIPTION	DEALER	LIST

Standard Equipment

MONTERO LS: Sport type reclining front bucket seats, adjustable/see-thru headrests, reclining 2nd row seat w/headrests, fold down/tumble forward 2nd row bench seat, folding 3rd row seats w/headrests, full passenger compartment carpeting, cargo area carpeting, full interior trim, dual bi-level heating/vent system, rear-seat heater ducts, tilt steering column, sport-style steering wheel, Power Package includes: power window with auto down/power door locks/cruise control; center console w/storage and cupholders, cargo tie-down hooks, front and rear passenger assist grips, locking glove box, map/spot lights, inspection lamp w/front 12V auxiliary socket, dual sunvisors w/passenger visor vanity mirror, 2-speed intermittent windshield wiper/washer, rear window defroster w/timer, intermittent rear wiper/washer, side window defoggers, rear door mounted tool kit, driver side airbag, height adjustable front shoulder belts, four-wheel disc brakes, warning and indicator lights for: brakes/battery charge/door ajar/seatbelt reminder/cruise "on"/active trac 4WD mode indicator/low oil pressure/low fuel/low fluid/high beam indicator/parking brake on/hazard; resettable tripmeter, inclinometer, oil pressure gauge, voltmeter, digital quartz clock, ETR AM/FM stereo cassette w/6 speakers, fixed length whip antenna, skid plates: front end/transfer case/fuel tank; locking fuel filler door w/remote, side-opening rear door, front and rear tow hooks, front and rear mudguards, halogen headlamps, tinted glass, dual power sideview mirrors, convex passenger-side mirror, 15 x 6 styled-steel wheels w/center cap, 235/75R15 all season SBR tires, rear-mounted full-size spare tire w/lock, 3.0L SOHC V6 engine, automatic valve lash adjusters, ECI electronic multi-point fuel injection, stainless steel exhaust system, 5-speed manual overdrive transmission, Active Trac 4WD system, 2-speed transfer case, independent front suspension, front and rear stabilizer bars, coil spring rear suspension, clutch/starter override (for M/T only), power assisted recirculating ball steering.

SR (in addition to or instead of LS equipment): Driver's suspension seat, CFC-free refrigerant air conditioning, lighted driver's side visor vanity mirror, side window defoggers deleted, remote keyless entry, multi-mode anti-lock braking system (ABS), Multi-meter: LCD compass/interior and exterior thermometer/inclinometer/altimeter; ETR AM/FM stereo cassette w/EQ and 6 speakers, power and diversity antenna, wide body fender flares, headlamp washers, aluminum alloy wheels w/locks, 265/70R15 all-weather radial tires, spare tire cover, 3.5L DOHC V6 engine, 4-speed automatic overdrive transmission.

Accessories

Code	Description	Dealer	List
—	**Pkg A** — LS	754	754
	incls air conditioning, AM/FM stereo radio w/cassette and CD, luggage rack, remote control keyless entry, cargo mat, spare tire cover		
—	**Pkg B** — LS	1337	1337
	incls Pkg A plus power antenna and CD auto changer, graphic equalizer		
LP	**Leather & Wood Pkg** — SR	1398	1748
PI	**Power Sunroof**	550	688
AB	**Anti-Lock Brakes** — LS	950	1188
KC	**Cargo Cover** — LS	70	108
QW	**Sliding Rear Window**	100	125
RL	**Locking Rear Differential** — SR	320	400
AW	**Alloy Wheels** — LS	264	331
CW	**Chrome Wheels** — SR	500	625
RB	**Side Step**	219	335
FK	**Fog Lights**	148	228
EA	**CD Auto Changer** — SR	598	899
RO	**Luggage Rack** — SR	180	277

CODE	DESCRIPTION		DEALER	LIST

ALTIMA

15654	XE 4-Dr Sedan (5-spd)	12122	13739
15614	XE 4-Dr Sedan (auto)	12969	14699
15754	GXE 4-Dr Sedan (5-spd)	12958	14859
15714	GXE 4-Dr Sedan (auto)	13678	15684
15954	SE 4-Dr Sedan (5-spd)	15761	18179
15914	SE 4-Dr Sedan (auto)	16476	19004
15814	GLE 4-Dr Sedan (auto)	16628	19179
Destination Charge:		375	375

Standard Equipment

ALTIMA XE: 2.4L DOHC 16-valve 4 cylinder engine, sequential multi-point elec fuel injection, 5-speed man overdrive trans, power-assisted rack-and-pinion steering, 4-wheel independent suspension, super toe control rear suspension, front and rear stabilizer bars, power-assisted brakes (front vented disc/rear drum), full aerodynamic wheel covers, flush-mounted halogen lamps, semi-concealed windshield wipers /washers, tinted glass, dual power remote-controlled outside mirrors with passenger-side convex mirror, body-color wide protective bodyside moldings, contoured reclining front bucket seats with adjustable headrests, cloth seat trim, dual front door map pockets, full cut-pile carpeting, tilt steering column, 2-speed intermittent windshield wipers/twin-stream washers, electric rear window defroster with timer, side window defoggers, dual cupholders, remote trunk/fuel-filler door/hood releases, center console with covered storage area, lockable glove box, visor vanity mirror, interior courtesy lights (cigarette lighter, ashtray, glovebox, trunk), tachometer, trip odometer, speedometer, coolant temperature and low-fuel level gauges, digital quartz clock, driver and passenger side airbags (SRS), steel side-door guard beams, 3-point front manual seatbelts with height adjustment, 3-point outboard rear man seatbelts (center lap belt), child-safety rear door locks, energy-absorbing front and rear bumpers, energy-absorbing steering column.

GXE (in addition to or instead of XE equipment): Dark upper windshield band, rear seat center armrest w/ trunk pass-through, wood pattern trim, pwr windows w/driver-side auto-down feature, power door locks.

SE (in addition to or instead of GXE equipment): Aluminum alloy wheels, cornering lamps, fog lamps, body color wide protective bodyside moldings deleted, power sliding tinted glass sunroof with rear tilt feature and sunshade, rear spoiler and side sill extensions, front sport seats, leather-wrapped steering wheel and gear shift knob, air conditioning (with non-CFC refrigerant), cruise control, electronically-tuned AM/FM cassette stereo audio system with Dolby noise reduction/automatic metal tape capability/automatic program search/4 speakers, diversity antenna system, power antenna.

CODE	DESCRIPTION	DEALER	LIST

GLE (in addition to or instead of SE equipment): Electronic 4-speed auto overdrive transmission, fog lamps deleted, body-color wide protective bodyside moldings, rear spoiler and side sill extensions deleted, front sport seats deleted, adjustable lumbar support, leather-wrapped steering wheel and gear shift knob deleted, automatic temperature control, theft deterrent system, digital head-up speedometer/warning display, electronically tuned AM/FM cassette stereo audio system with CD player and Dolby noise reduction/automatic metal tape capability/automatic program search/4 active speakers/2-front-pillar dome tweeters.

Accessories

Code	Description	Dealer	List
B07	**Anti-Lock Braking System** — XE	843	995
	reqs XE option pkg		
B10	**ABS w/Viscous Limited Slip Differential** — GXE, SE, GLE	1012	1195
	GXE reqs GXE value option pkg		
S07	**Cruise Control** — XE	195	230
	reqs auto trans		
X03	**Leather Seating Surfaces** — SE, GLE	847	1000
	NA w/sports seats		
F02	**XE Option Pkg** — XE	1545	1825
	incls air cond, cruise control, AM/FM stereo radio w/cassette/4 speakers		
J01	**Power Sunroof** — GXE	699	825
	reqs GXE value option pkg w/auto trans		
F09	**GXE Value Option Pkg** — GXE	1016	1200
	incls air conditioning, cruise control, AM/FM stereo radio w/cassette/4 speakers/power antenna		
C01	**California Emissions**	128	150

MAXIMA

		Dealer	List
08414	GXE 4-Dr Sedan (auto)	19246	22199
08254	SE 4-Dr Sedan (5-spd)	20200	23299
08214	SE 4-Dr Sedan (auto)	21011	24234
	Destination Charge:	375	375

Standard Equipment

MAXIMA GXE: 3.0L SOHC V6 engine, sequential multi-point fuel injection, variable induction system, electronically controlled 4-speed automatic overdrive transmission with lock-up torque converter, power assisted rack-and-pinion steering, 4-wheel independent suspension, front and rear stabilizer bars, power assisted front vented disc/rear drum brakes, aluminum alloy wheels w/bright finish, flush-mounted halogen headlamps, flush-mounted halogen cornering lamps, semi-concealed windshield wipers, tinted glass w/dark upper windshield band, dual heated power remote-controlled outside mirrors with passenger-side convex mirror, body color bodyside moldings, single chrome-tipped exhaust finisher, reclining front bucket seats, multi-adjustable driver's seat includes seat cushion tilt/front and rear/seatback recline/3-way lumbar support/and fore/aft adjustments, fold-down rear seat center armrest, large front door map pockets, cut-pile carpeting, air conditioning with non-CFC refrigerant, power windows with driver-side auto-down, power door locks, cruise control w/steering-wheel mounted controls, tilt steering column, 2-speed variable intermittent windshield wipers/twin-stream washers, electric rear window defroster w/timer, side window defoggers, easy-glide cupholder, digital touch keyless entry system w/auto-down window/remote trunk and optional sunroof controls, theft deterrent system, remote trunk/fuel-filler door/hood releases, center console with storage area and armrest, lockable glovebox, driver and passenger-side visor vanity mirror, illuminated entry/exit fade-out system, dual overhead map lamps, interior courtesy lamps include cigarette lighter/ashtray/trunk, tachometer/coolant temperature/fuel level gauges, low fuel warning light, trip odometer, digital quartz clock, electronically tuned AM/FM stereo audio system w/auto-reverse cassette/Dolby noise reduction/4 speakers, automatic power diversity antenna system, driver side airbag (SRS), passive motorized front shoulder belt system/manual lap belt, front lap belt warning light, 3-point manual rear seatbelts in the outboard positions/center lap belt, child-safety rear door locks, energy-absorbing steering column, energy-absorbing front and rear bumpers, automatic transmission park/lock feature.

SE (in addition to or instead of GXE equipment): 3.0L DOHC V6 engine, variable induction system (5-speed only), Nissan valve timing control system (NVCS), Nissan direct ignition system (NDIS), 5-speed manual overdrive transmission, viscous limited slip differential, power-assisted 4-wheel disc front vented brakes, halogen fog lamps, dual chrome-tipped exhaust finishers, body-color rear spoiler, leather-wrapped steering wheel and shift knob, digital touch keyless entry system w/auto-down window/remote trunk/sunroof controls deleted, white-faced analog-style gauges w/reverse-to-electroluminescent lighting, Bose AM/FM cassette system w/4 amplifiers and 4 Bose speakers, automatic transmission park/lock feature deleted.

Accessories

CODE	DESCRIPTION	DEALER	LIST
V01	**Luxury Pkg** — GXE	2197	2595
	incls power sunroof, Bose audio system including CD player, leather-wrapped steering wheel and shift knob, power seats and air conditioning w/auto temp control		
X03	**GXE Leather Trim Pkg** — GXE	868	1025
	reqs luxury pkg		
B07	**Anti-Lock Braking System**	843	995
	SE reqs sunroof		
E07	**Pearlglow Paint**	297	350
C01	**California Emissions**	128	150
X03	**SE Leather Trim Pkg** — SE	1207	1425
	reqs sunroof		
J01	**Power Sunroof** — SE	741	875
H07	**CD Player** — SE	339	400
	reqs sunroof; delete dual cupholder		

NISSAN

PATHFINDER

Code	Description	Dealer	List
09254	XE 2WD 4-Dr (5-spd)	17043	19429
09214	XE 2WD 4-Dr (auto)	18113	20649
09654	XE 4WD 4-Dr (5-spd)	18508	21099
09614	XE 4WD 4-Dr (auto)	19709	22469
09754	SE 4WD 4-Dr (5-spd)	21938	25009
09714	SE 4WD 4-Dr (auto)	22903	26109
09814	LE 4WD 4-Dr (auto)	25438	28999
	Destination Charge:	375	375

Standard Equipment

PATHFINDER 2WD XE: 3.0L SOHC V6 engine, sequential multi-point electronic fuel injection, 5-speed manual overdrive transmission, power recirculating ball steering, power vented front disc/rear drum brakes, double-wishbone front suspension w/stabilizer bar, 5-link coil-spring rear suspension with stabilizer bar, rear wheel anti-lock braking system (ABS), flush-mounted halogen headlamps, tinted glass, dual outside mirrors w/passenger-side convex mirror, skid plates and tow hooks, chromed steel wheels, rear wiper/washer, reclining front bucket seats w/adjustable head restraints, split fold-down rear seats w/adjustable head restraints, reclining rear seatbacks, cloth seat trim, front and rear passenger-assist grips, front door map pockets, full carpeting, remote fuel-filler door release, tilt steering column, rear window defroster w/timer, side window defoggers, remote hood release, cargo area courtesy lamp, center console w/CD and cellular phone compartment, lockable glove box, rear cargo net, tachometer, trip odometer, digital quartz clock, coolant temperature gauge, high-output electronically-tuned AM/FM cassette stereo audio system with auto reverse/Dolby noise reduction/8-speakers, diversity antenna system, steel side-door guard beams, 3-point front seatbelt system, 3-point manual rear seatbelts in the outboard positions/center lap belt, center high mount stop lamp, child safety rear door locks, energy-absorbing bumpers, energy-absorbing steering column, front and rear outboard head restraints.

4WD XE-V6 (in addition to or instead of 2WD XE equipment): Automatic locking front hubs, integrated fender flare/mud flaps, rear heater ducts.

4WD SE-V6 (in addition to or instead of 4WD XE equipment): Exterior spare tire mount w/cover, rear quarter window privacy glass, dual heated power remote-controlled mirrors with passenger side convex mir-

NISSAN

ror, alloy wheels, rear wind deflector, step rail, fog lamps, multi-adjustable driver's seat w/2-way head restraints/seat cushion tilt/seatback recline/3-position lumbar support and fore/aft adjustments, rear-seat fold-down armrests, power windows w/driver-side one-touch auto-down feature, power door locks, cruise control, remote rear window release, 2-speed variable intermittent windshield wipers, dual illuminated visor vanity mirrors, remote vehicle security system, map lamps, flip-up/removable glass sunroof.

4WD LE-V6 (in addition to or instead of 4WD SE equipment): 4-speed automatic overdrive transmission, power 4-wheel disc brakes, rear limited slip differential, exterior spare tire mount w/cover deleted, skid plates and tow hooks deleted, integrated fender flare/mud flaps deleted, six-spoke design alloy wheels, luggage rack, rear wind deflector deleted, running board/molded splash guards, step rail deleted, reclining front bucket seats w/adjustable head restraints deleted, leather seating surfaces w/heated front seats, cloth seat trim deleted, semi-automatic air conditioning with non-CFC refrigerant, compact disc player by Nissan, SE-V6 Leather Trim Package includes: leather seating surfaces, leather-wrapped steering wheel, parking brake handle, heated front seats w/individual controls.

Accessories

CODE	DESCRIPTION	DEALER	LIST
A01	**Air Conditioning** — XE, SE.. *std on LE*	843	995
G01	**XE Convenience Pkg** — XE... *incls cruise control, power windows, power door locks, power liftgate release, intermittent windshield wipers, heated power mirrors, map lights, security system [reqs air conditioning]*	1313	1550
V01	**XE Sport Pkg** — XE.. *incls limited slip differential (4WD), fender flares, cargo net, outside spare tire carrier and cover, foglights [reqs convenience pkg]*	728	860
T06	**SE-V6 Off-Road Pkg** — SE.. *incls 4-wheel disc brakes, adjustable shock absorbers, limited slip differential, black items (bumpers, grille, mirrors, luggage rack and windshield molding [reqs air conditioning])*	635	750
X03	**Leather Trim Pkg** — SE 4WD .... *incls leather upholstery/steering wheel/brake handle/shift knob, heated seats [reqs air conditioning]*	1063	1255
E10	**Two-Tone Paint** — LE	254	300
C01	**California Emissions**..	128	150

NISSAN 2WD PICKUPS

		DEALER	LIST
33054	Standard (5-spd)	8782	9359
33554	XE Reg Cab (5-spd)	9401	10129
33514	XE Reg Cab (auto)	10622	11444
43554	Standard Long Bed V6 (5-spd)	10271	11189
53554	XE King Cab (5-spd)	10484	11679
53514	XE King Cab (auto)	11664	12994
53454	SE-V6 King Cab (5-spd)	12671	14279
53414	SE-V6 King Cab (auto)	13559	15279
	Destination Charge:	375	375

Standard Equipment

2WD STANDARD PICKUP: 2.4L SOHC 4 cylinder engine, sequential multi-point electronic fuel injection, 5-speed manual overdrive transmission, power vented front disc/rear drum brakes, independent front suspension with stabilizer bar/solid rear axle with leaf springs, double-wall cargo box with removable tailgate, tinted glass, halogen headlamps, bench seat, vinyl seat trim and floor covering, side window defoggers, steel side-door guard beams, 3-point front man seatbelt system, energy-absorbing steering column.

2WD XE PICKUP: 2.4L SOHC 4 cylinder engine, sequential multi-point electronic fuel injection, 5-speed manual overdrive transmission, power vented front disc/rear drum brakes, independent front suspension with stabilizer bar/solid rear axle with leaf springs, double-wall cargo box with removable tailgate, tinted glass, black painted rear step bumper, halogen headlamps, dual outside mirrors w/passenger-side convex mirror, styled steel wheels with trim rings, sliding rear window, cloth seat trim and full carpeting, front door map pockets, reclining front bucket seats (King Cab), bench seat (Reg Cab), side window defoggers, steel side-door guard beams, 3-point front manual seatbelt system, energy-absorbing steering column.

2WD STANDARD LONG BED: 3.0L SOHC V6 engine, sequential multi-point elec fuel injection, 5-speed man overdrive trans, power recirculating ball steering, power vented front disc/rear drum brakes, independent front suspension w/stabilizer bar/solid rear axle with leaf springs, double-wall cargo box with removable tailgate, tinted glass, halogen headlamps, dual outside mirrors with passenger-side convex mirror, bench seat, vinyl seat trim and floor covering, front door map pockets, side window defoggers, steel side-door guard beams, 3-point front man seatbelt system, energy-absorbing steering column.

NISSAN

CODE	DESCRIPTION	DEALER	LIST

2WD SE KING CAB: 3.0L SOHC V6 engine, sequential multi-point electronic fuel injection, 5-speed manual overdrive transmission, power recirculating ball steering, power vented front disc/rear drum brakes, independent front suspension with stabilizer bar/solid rear axle with leaf springs, double wall cargo box with removable tailgate, pop-up tie-down hooks, bedliner, tinted glass, chrome rear step bumper, halogen headlamps, chromed dual outside mirrors, chromed steel wheels, sliding rear window, reclining front bucket seats, multi-adjustable driver's seat with 2-way head restraints/front seat cushion tilt/seatback recline/3-position lumbar support and fore/aft adjustments, rear jump seats, cloth seat trim and full carpeting, front door map pockets, cruise control, tilt steering column, 2-speed variable intermittent windshield wipers, side window defoggers, passenger-side vanity mirror, lockable glove box, center console, map lights, tachometer, trip odometer, digital quartz clock, 100-watt (peak) electronically tuned AM/FM/cassette stereo audio system with auto reverse/diversity antenna system/Dolby noise reduction, steel-side-door guard beams, 3-point front manual seatbelt system, energy-absorbing steering column, Chrome Package (chrome grille, chrome front and rear bumpers, chrome door handles, chrome windshield moldings, chrome side marker lamp bezels, chrome dual outside mirrors, chrome wheels and body side graphics), Jump Seat Package (jump seats with seatbelts).

Accessories

CODE	DESCRIPTION	DEALER	LIST
A01	**Air Conditioning** — Standard, XE, SE-V6 King Cab	843	995
H01	**AM/FM Cassette Stereo** — Standard *std on SE-V6 King Cab*	228	500
K05	**Power Pkg** — SE-V6 King Cab *incls power windows and door locks*	423	500
S02	**Sport/Power Pkg** — SE-V6 King Cab *incls power windows and door locks, flip-up sunroof, alloy wheels*	1219	1440
P06	**Power Steering** — std on Standard Long Bed V6 & SE-V6 King Cab	266	315
E08/E09	**Metallic or Pearl Paint** — Standard	85	100
T07	**Value Truck Pkg** — XE *incls air conditioning, AM/FM cassette w/2 speakers, chrome wheels, chrome molding, chrome grille, chrome bumper, bodyside graphics, power mirrors, variable intermittent wipers, locking glove box, ashtray, cigar lighter and glove box lights, tachometer, trip odometer, digital clock, map lights (King Cab), center console (King Cab), visor vanity mirror (King Cab), 4 speakers (King Cab)*	843	995
C01	**California Emissions**	128	150
L30/L31	**Bedliner** — std on SE-V6 King Cab	128	280
G01	**Convenience Pkg** — XE Reg Cab *incls dual power outside mirrors, locking glove box/map/glove box/cigarette lighter/ashtray lamps, variable intermittent wipers, tilt steering wheel*	254	300
W04	**Chrome Pkg** — XE Reg Cab *incls chrome grille, chrome front and rear bumpers, chrome door handles, chrome windshield moldings, chrome dual outside mirrors, chrome wheels and bodyside graphics*	423	500
U03	**Jump Seat Pkg** — XE King Cab (std on SE-V6) *incls jump seats w/seatbelts*	191	225
V03	**Sport Pkg** — SE-V6 King Cab *incls flip-up sunroof, alloy wheels*	1101	1300

NISSAN 4WD PICKUPS

Code	Description	Dealer	List
33754	XE Reg Cab (5-spd)	12225	13619
53754	XE King Cab (5-spd)	13390	15089
53954	XE-V6 King Cab (5-spd)	14091	15879
53914	XE-V6 King Cab (auto)	14979	16879
53854	SE-V6 King Cab (5-spd)	14368	16379
53814	SE-V6 King Cab (auto)	15245	17379
	Destination Charge:	375	375

Standard Equipment

4WD XE PICKUP: 2.4L SOHC 12-valve 4 cylinder engine, sequential multi-point electronic fuel injection, 5-speed manual overdrive transmission, power recirculating ball steering, power vented front disc/rear drum brakes, rear-wheel anti-lock braking system (ABS), independent front suspension with stabilizer bar/solid rear axle with leaf springs, manual locking front hubs, double-wall cargo box with removable tailgate, tinted glass, black painted rear step bumper, halogen headlamps, dual outside mirrors with passenger-side convex mirror, triple skid plates and tow hook, titanium finish steel wheels, sliding rear window, bench seat (Reg Cab), reclining front bucket seats (King Cab), cloth seat trim and full carpeting, front door map pockets, side window defoggers, steel side-door guard beams, 3-point manual front seatbelt system, energy-absorbing steering column.

4WD XE-V6 KING CAB: 3.0L SOHC V6 engine, sequential multi-point electronic fuel injection, 5-speed manual overdrive transmission, power recirculating ball steering, power vented front disc/rear drum brakes, rear-wheel anti-lock braking system (ABS), independent front suspension with stabilizer bar/solid rear axle with leaf springs, automatic locking front hubs, double-wall cargo box with removable tailgate, bedliner, tinted glass, black painted rear step bumper, halogen headlamps, dual outside mirrors with passenger-side convex mirror, fender flares, triple skid plates and tow hook, titanium finish steel wheels, sliding rear window, reclining front bucket seats, rear jump seats, cloth seat trim and full carpeting, front door map pockets, side window defoggers, steel side-door guard beams, 3-point manual front seatbelt system, energy-absorbing steering column, Jump Seat Package (includes jump seats with seatbelts).

4WD SE-V6 KING CAB (in addition to or instead of 4WD XE-V6 KING CAB): Pop-up tie-down hooks, chrome rear step bumper, chromed dual outside mirrors, chromed steel wheels, multi-adjustable driver's seat w/2-way head restraints/front-seat cushion tilt/seatback recline/3-position lumbar support and fore/aft adjustments, cruise control, tilt steering column, 2-speed variable intermittent windshield wipers, passenger-side vanity mirror, lockable glove box, center console, map lamps, tachometer, trip odometer, digital quartz clock, 100-watt (peak) electronically-tuned AM/FM/cassette stereo audio system with auto reverse/diversity antenna system/Dolby noise reduction, Value Truck Package (air conditioning, AM/FM cassette w/2 speakers, chrome wheels, chrome molding, chrome grille, chrome bumper, body side graphics, power mirrors, variable intermittent wipers, locking glove box, ashtray, cigar lighter, glove box lights, tachometer, trip odometer, digital clock, fender flares, full size spare tire, map lights, center console, visor vanity mirror, 4 speakers).

Accessories

CODE	DESCRIPTION	DEALER	LIST
A01	**Air Conditioning**	843	995
L30/31	**Bedliner** — XE (std on XE-V6 & SE-V6)	128	280
W04	**Chrome Pkg** — XE Reg Cab	423	500
	incls chrome grille, chrome front and rear bumpers, chrome door handles, chrome windshield molding, chrome dual outside mirrors, fender flares and bodyside graphics		
G01	**Convenience Pkg** — XE Reg Cab	254	300
	incls dual power outside mirrors, locking glove box, map/glove box/cigar lighter/ashtray lamps, variable intermittent wipers and P235/75R15 spare tire		
V03	**Sport Pkg** — SE-V6	1587	1875
	incls flip-up sunroof, alloy wheels, limited slip differential, 31x10.5 R15 tires, P235/75R15 spare tire		
K05	**Power Pkg** — SE-V6	423	500
	incls power windows and door locks		
S02	**Sport/Power Pkg** — SE-V6	1672	1975
	incls alloy wheels, flip-up sunroof, power windows, power locks, limited slip differential, 31x10.5 R15 tires and P235/75R15 spare tire		
V03	**Jump Seat Pkg** — XE King Cab (std on XE-V6, SE-V6)	191	225
	incls jump seats w/seatbelts		
C01	**California Emissions**	128	150
T07	**Value Truck Pkg** — XE, XE-V6	843	995
	incls air conditioning, AM/FM cassette w/2 speakers, chrome wheels, chrome molding, chrome grille, chrome bumper, body side graphics, power mirrors, variable intermittent wipers, locking glove box, ashtray, cigar lighter and glove box lights, tachometer, trip odometer, digital clock, fender flares, full size spare, tilt steering wheel (XE-V6 King Cab), cruise control (XE-V6 King Cab), map lights (King Cab), center console (King Cab), visor vanity mirror (King Cab), 4 speakers (King Cab)		

QUEST

		DEALER	LIST
00314	XE 7-Passenger (auto)	16065	18529
00414	GXE (auto)	19975	23039
Destination Charge:		375	375

Standard Equipment

QUEST - XE: 3.0L SOHC V6 engine, sequential multi-point fuel injection, front wheel drive, electronically controlled 4-speed automatic overdrive transmission, power-assisted rack-and-pinion steering, power-assisted front vented disc/rear drum brakes, independent front suspension w/stabilizer bar, beam rear axle with leaf springs, full wheel covers, aerodynamic halogen headlamps, flush-mounted cornering lamps, tinted glass with upper windshield band, body-color body side moldings, sliding passenger side door, rear window wiper/washer, 7-passenger seating (2nd and 3rd row bench), 4-way reclining front bucket seats, Quest Trac flexible seating system, moquette seat trim, full carpeting, carpeted floor mats, air conditioning (non-CFC refrigerant), power-boosted ventilation system, tilt steering column, 2-speed variable intermittent windshield wipers/twin-stream washers, rear wiper with intermittent setting, electric rear window defroster, remote fuel-filler door and hood releases, center console w/cassette and CD storage, lockable glove box, entry/exit fade-out system, tabletop surfaces w/cupholders, cargo area net, tachometer, trip odometer, speedometer/coolant temperature/fuel level gauges, electronically-tuned AM/FM cassette stereo audio system/Dolby noise reduction/4 speakers, diversity antenna system, passive motorized front shoulder belt system/active lap belt, driver side airbag (SRS), 3-point manual rear seatbelts (outboard, 2nd and 3rd row/center lap belt), 5 mph energy-absorbing front/rear bumpers, steel side-door guard beams and pillar/roof reinforcement, child-safety lock on sliding side door.

GXE (in addition to or instead of XE equipment): Anti-lock braking system (ABS) includes rear disc brakes, aluminum alloy wheels, side and rear privacy glass, dual liftgate w/opening glass hatch, dual power remote-controlled outside mirrors w/passenger-side convex, roof luggage rack, 8-way power driver's seat, 4-way reclining front bucket seats deleted, velour seat trim, leather-wrapped steering wheel, rear air conditioning, rear heater controls, power front windows, power rear quarter windows, power door locks, cruise control, passenger under-seat storage bin, dual illuminated visor vanity mirrors, deluxe electronically-tuned AM/FM cassette stereo audio system/Dolby noise reduction/4 speakers/rear seat audio controls, power antenna, Power Package includes power front windows/dual power mirrors/power door locks, Convenience Package includes privacy glass/deluxe AM/FM cassette stereo audio system/cruise control/luggage rack/lockable under-seat storage/leather-wrapped steering wheel/illuminated passenger visor vanity mirror.

Accessories

CODE	DESCRIPTION	DEALER	LIST
S02	**Power Pkg** — XE	699	825
	incls power windows w/driver's side down feature, power door locks w/central locking, power mirrors [std on GXE]		
F05	**Convenience Pkg** — XE	677	800
	incls cruise control, privacy glass, lockable underseat storage, illuminated passenger side visor vanity mirror, luggage rack, leather-wrapped steering wheel, AM/FM stereo radio w/cassette [reqs power pkg]		
T02	**XE Extra Performance Pkg** — XE	805	950
	incls 215/70R15 97H tires, full-size spare tire, rear stabilizer bar, heavy-duty battery and radiator, tuned shocks and springs, 3500 lb. towing pkg		
T02	**GXE Extra Performance Pkg** — GXE	445	525
	incls 215/70R15 97H tires, full-size spare tire, rear stabilizer bar, heavy-duty battery and radiator, tuned shocks and springs, alloy wheels, 3500 lb. towing pkg		
V01	**Luxury Pkg** — GXE	677	800
	incls 2nd row captain's chairs, digital illuminated entry system, power passenger seat, automatic headlamp feature		
X03	**Leather Trim Pkg** — GXE	847	1000
	reqs luxury pkg; GXE extra performance pkg required when power sunroof and leather pkg are combined		
J01	**Power Sunroof** — GXE	699	825
	GXE extra performance pkg required when power sunroof and leather pkg are combined		
A04	**Rear Air Conditioning** — XE (std on GXE)	529	625
	reqs power pkg		
B07	**4-Wheel Anti-Lock Braking System** — XE (std on GXE)	593	700
E10	**Two-Tone Paint** — GXE	254	300
H07	**Premium Audio Pkg** — GXE	859	1015
	incls CD player (reqs luxury pkg)		
C01	**California Emissions**	127	150

SENTRA

2-DR

Code	Description	Dealer	List
22054	E 2-Dr Sedan (5-spd)	9430	10049
22041	E 2-Dr Sedan (auto)	10978	11699
22154	XE 2-Dr Sedan (5-spd)	10737	12099
22114	XE 2-Dr Sedan (auto)	11446	12899
22354	SE 2-Dr Sedan (5-spd)	11116	12599
22314	SE 2-Dr Sedan (auto)	11822	13399
22454	SE-R 2-Dr Sedan (5-spd)	12175	13799
22414	SE-R 2-Dr Sedan (auto)	12881	14599

4-DR

Code	Description	Dealer	List
42054	E 4-Dr Sedan (5-spd)	9946	10599
42014	E 4-Dr Sedan (auto)	11166	11899
42154	XE 4-Dr Sedan (5-spd)	10914	12299
42114	XE 4-Dr Sedan (auto)	11624	13099
42254	GXE 4-Dr Sedan (5-spd)	12943	14669
42214	GXE 4-Dr Sedan (auto)	13649	15469
	Destination Charge:	375	375

Standard Equipment

SENTRA E 2-DR: 1.6L DOHC 16-valve 4 cylinder engine, sequential multi-point elect fuel injection, 5-speed man overdrive trans, power vented front disc/rear drum brakes, 4-wheel independent suspension, styled-steel wheels w/half wheel covers, flush-mounted halogen headlamps, tinted glass, black body side moldings, reclining front bucket seats, tricot cloth trim, full vinyl door trim, front door map pockets, carpeting, dual cupholders, rear window defroster/side window defoggers, remote hood release, center console, trip odometer, speedometer, coolant temperature gauge, 3-point passive front shoulder belt system, 3-point manual rear seatbelts in the outboard positions, energy-absorbing bumpers and steering column.

XE 2-DR (in addition to E 2-DR equipment): Power rack-and-pinion steering, front/rear stabilizer bars, full wheel covers, dual power remote-controlled outside mirrors with passenger-side convex mirror, body-color bumpers, deluxe door trim with cloth insert, passenger-side walk-in device, air conditioning (with non-CFC refrigerant), cruise control, tilt steering column, 2-speed intermittent windshield wipers/washers, remote trunk/fuel filler door releases, lockable glove box, front and rear assist grips, digital quartz clock, electronically-tuned AM/FM cassette stereo audio system with Dolby noise reduction/auto-reverse/4 speakers, diversity antenna system.

SE 2-DR (in addition to or instead of XE 2-DR equipment): Integrated front air dam, body-color body side moldings, bright exhaust outlet, rear spoiler, front sport bucket seats, sporty velour cloth seat trim, air cond deleted, cruise control deleted, leather-wrapped steering wheel/shift knob (manual trans), tachometer, electronically tuned AM/FM cassette stereo audio system deleted, diversity antenna system deleted.

SE-R 2-DR (in addition to or instead of SE 2-DR equipment): 2.0L DOHC 16-valve 4 cylinder engine, power-assisted 4-wheel disc brakes, viscous front limited slip differential, aluminum alloy wheels, full wheel covers deleted, fog lamps.

SENTRA E 4-DR: 1.6L DOHC 16-valve 4 cylinder engine, sequential multi-point electronic fuel injection, 5-speed manual overdrive transmission, power vented front disc/rear drum brakes, 4-wheel independent suspension, styled-steel wheels with half wheel covers, flush-mounted halogen headlamps, tinted glass, black body side moldings, reclining front bucket seats, tricot cloth trim, full vinyl door trim, front door map pockets, carpeting, dual cupholders, rear window defroster/side window defoggers, remote hood release, center console, trip odometer, speedometer, coolant temperature gauge, automatic motorized front shoulder belts w/manual lap belts, 3-point manual rear seatbelts in the outboard positions, child-safety rear door locks, energy-absorbing bumpers and steering column.

XE 4-DR (in addition to or instead of E 4-DR equipment): Power rack-and-pinion steering, front/rear stabilizer bars, full wheel covers, dual power remote-controlled outside mirrors w/passenger-side convex mirror, body-color bumpers, deluxe door trim w/cloth insert, air cond (with non-CFC refrigerant), cruise control, tilt steering column, remote trunk/fuel-filler door releases, lockable glove box, front and rear assist grips, digital quartz clock, elec tuned AM/FM cassette stereo audio system with Dolby noise reduction/auto-reverse/4 speakers, diversity antenna system, 2-speed intermittent windshield wipers/washers.

GXE 4-DR (in addition to or instead of XE 4-DR equipment): Aluminum alloy wheels, body-color body side moldings, bright exhaust outlet, split fold-down rear seatbacks, velour seat trim, power windows and door locks, tachometer, driver-side airbag (SRS).

Accessories

Code	Description	Dealer	List
A01	**Air Conditioning** — E, SE, SE-R.. *std on XE and GXE*	843	995
N03	**Driver Side Air Bag** — std on GXE	487	575
F09	**SE/SE-R Value Option Pkg** — SE, SE-R........................... *incls air conditioning, cruise control and AM/FM stereo radio w/cassette*	1101	1300
J01	**Power Sunroof** — SE-R, GXE.. *NA w/ABS*	699	825
E09	**Metallic Paint** — E.. *no charge on XE, SE and GXE*	85	100
B07	**Anti-Lock Braking System** — SE-R, GXE........................ *ABS and power sunroof ar not available in combination on GXE*	593	700
S05	**Cruise Control** — SE, SE-R... *std on XE and GXE*	195	230
C01	**California Emissions**..	128	150
H01	**AM/FM Stereo Radio w/Cassette** — SE, SE-R................ *std on XE and GXE*	508	600
W01	**Fleet Pkg** — E... *incls air conditioning and AM/FM stereo radio w/cassette*	1067	1260
S02	**Power Steering Pkg** — E... *E models w/man trans require air bag*	423	500

NISSAN

240SX

		DEALER	LIST
26814	SE 2-Dr Convertible (auto)	21025	23969
	Destination Charge:	375	375

Standard Equipment

240SX SE CONVERTIBLE: 2.4L DOHC 16-valve 4 cylinder engine, sequential multi-point electronic fuel injection, electronically controlled 4-speed automatic overdrive, transmission, power assisted rack and pinion steering, independent strut type front suspension, independent multi-link rear suspension, front and rear stabilizer bars, power assisted 4-wheel disc brakes (front-vented), alloy wheels, retractable halogen headlamps, semi-concealed windshield wipers, tinted glass w/dark upper windshield band, rear spoiler, dual chrome-tipped exhaust finishers, reclining low-back front bucket seats, cloth door trim, leather-wrapped steering wheels and gear shift knob, front door map pockets, cut-pile carpeting, air conditioning (non-CFC refrigerant), power windows w/driver side one-touch auto down window control, power convertible top, power door locks, cruise control with steering wheel-mounted controls, tilt steering column, 2-speed variable intermittent windshield wipers/twin-stream washers, side window defoggers, remote trunk/hatch, fuel filler door and hood releases, center console, day/night mirror, lockable glove compartment, dual covered visor vanity mirrors, courtesy lamps, dual map lamps, driver's left footrest, tachometer, trip odometer, coolant temperature and fuel level gauges, warning lights, digital quartz clock, electronically-tuned AM/FM/cassette stereo audio system w/Dolby noise reduction and 4-speakers, automatic power diversity type antenna, energy absorbing front and rear bumpers, 195/60R15 all-season steel belted radial tires.

Accessories

		DEALER	LIST
A01	**Air Conditioning**	843	995
C01	**California Emissions**	128	150

| CODE | DESCRIPTION | DEALER | LIST |

PORSCHE

911 CARRERA 2
COUPE/TARGA/CABRIOLET & RS AMERICA

Code	Description	Dealer	List
964330	Carrera 2 2-Dr Coupe (5-spd)	54405	64990
964330	Carrera 2 2-Dr Coupe (auto)	57040	68140
964430	Carrera 2 2-Dr Targa (5-spd)	55765	66600
964430	Carrera 2 2-Dr Targa (auto)	58400	69750
964630	Carrera 2 2-Dr Cabriolet (5-spd)	62070	74190
964630	Carrera 2 2-Dr Cabriolet (auto)	64705	77340
964320	Carrera 2 RS America 2-Dr Coupe (5-spd)	45875	54800
	Destination Charge:	725	725
	Gas Guzzler Tax: Models w/auto trans	1000	1000

Standard Equipment

911 CARRERA 2 COUPE/TARGA/CABRIOLET: 3.6L, 247HP, aluminum alloy, twin spark plug, air cooled, horizontally opposed 6 cylinder engine w/partial engine encapsulation; fully integrated electronic ignition and fuel injection system, Digital Motor Electronics (DME) with dual knock-sensor system, dual-mass flywheel, five-speed manual transmission or four-speed Tiptronic dual-function transmission w/shift lock and key lock features, hydraulically activated single-disc dry clutch, rack and pinion steering w/force-sensitive power assist, MacPherson strut front suspension (aluminum alloy lower control arms w/stabilizer bar), rear coil spring suspension (aluminum alloy semi-trailing arms w/toe correction characteristics and stabilizer bar), four-wheel disc brakes w/anti-lock braking system (ABS) and asbestos free pads (power assisted, aluminum alloy four-piston fixed caliper, internally ventilated), 5-spoke pressure-cast light alloy wheels w/locks (front - 6Jx16 with 205/55ZR16 SBR tires; rear - 8Jx16 with 225/50ZR16 SBR tires), 20.3 gallon fuel tank, full-power top w/automatic latching and unlatching (Cabriolet), removable roof panel (Targa), electric sliding sunroof (Coupe), integrated fog lights into front apron, halogen headlights, welded unitized body construction (double-sided zinc-galvanized steel), speed-dependent extendable rear spoiler, heated windshield washer nozzles, electrically adjustable and heatable outside rearview mirrors, windshield antenna w/signal amplifier, rear window defroster (Coupe, Targa), all around tinted glass (windshield-graduated tint), driver and front seat passenger airbags, partial leather reclining bucket seats w/electric height adjustment, air conditioning w/automatic temperature control, leather-covered steering wheel, backlit analog instrumentation w/tachometer and gauges indicating oil pressure/oil temperature/oil level/fuel level, corresponding warning lights, trip odometer, power windows, analog quartz clock, brake pad wear indicator, mirrors in sunvisors, interior light w/delayed shut-off, cruise control, one-key central locking and alarm system, AM/FM digital display stereo cassette radio w/8 speakers and amplifier (6 speakers on Cabriolet), cassette holder, rear storage compartments (Cabriolet).

911 RS AMERICA: 3.6L, 247HP, aluminum alloy, twin spark plug, air cooled, horizontally opposed, 6 cylinder engine w/partial engine encapsulation, fully integrated electronic ignition and fuel injection system, Digital Motor electronics (DME) w/dual knock-sensor system, dual mass flywheel, 5-speed manual transmission, hydraulically activated single-disc dry clutch, rack and pinion unassisted steering, sport suspension package, MacPherson front strut suspension (aluminum alloy lower control arms w/stabilizer bar), rear suspension (performance spec. progressive coil springs, aluminum alloy semi-trailing arms with toe correction characteristic stabilizer bar), power assisted/dual circuit/4 piston aluminum alloy/fixed caliper/internally vented anti-lock braking system (ABS) and asbestos free pads, 5-spoke pressure-cast light alloy wheels w/locks (front - 7Jx17 with 205/50ZR17 SBR tires; rear - 8Jx17 with 255/40ZR17 SBR tires), 20.3 gallon fuel tank, integrated fog lights into front apron, halogen headlights, welded unitized body construction (double-sided zinc-galvanized steel), fixed plane rear spoiler, heated windshield washer nozzles, rear window defroster, all around tinted glass (windshield-graduated tint), driver and passenger airbags, 3-point inertia-reel seatbelts, rear storage compartments, corduroy sport seats with electric height adjustment, leather-covered steering wheel, 911 Carrera RS-style door panels w/straps to open doors, backlit analog instrumentation with tachometer and gauges indicating oil pressure/oil temperature/oil level/fuel level, corresponding warning lights, trip odometer, power windows, analog quartz clock, brake pad wear indicator, mirrors in sunvisors, interior light w/delayed shut-off, one-key central locking and alarm system, radio preparation (2 speakers, amplifier and windshield antenna).

Accessories

CODE	DESCRIPTION	DEALER	LIST
573	**Air Conditioning** — automatic - 911 RS America	2248	2805
288	**Headlight Washers** — 911 except RS America	210	262
X17	**Dashboard** — light rootwood - 911 except RS America	3490	4356
X18	**Dashboard** — dark rootwood - 911 except RS America	3490	4356
XF5	**Leather-Wrapped Instrument Trim Rings** — 911 except RS America	354	442
XF6	**Leather Gear Box Tunnel** — 911 except RS America	158	198
XF7	**Leather-Covered Tray** — 911 except RS America	154	193
220	**Limited Slip Differential** — 911 Carrera 2 w/man trans; RS America	732	913

PORSCHE

CODE	DESCRIPTION	DEALER	LIST
425	**Rear Window Wiper** — 911 Coupes (except RS America) & Targa	273	340
070	**Tonneau Cover** — std color - 911 Cabriolet..	900	1102
Z67	**Tonneau Cover** — special color - 911 Cabriolet..................................	NA	NA
X10	**Exclusive Pkg** — 911 except RS America..	677	845
	incls XN2 leather inside door opener, XJ3 leather door lock knobs and bezels, XP9 leather radio speaker grilles (in doors)		
X11	**Exclusive Pkg** — 911 except RS America..	1214	1516
	incls XW2 leather rear safety belt lock/housing, XF6 leather gear box tunnel, XN7 leather parking brake lever, XF7 leather-covered tray, XP6 leather seatbelt lock and housing		
X12	**Exclusive Pkg** — 911 except RS America..	1347	1682
	incls XR6 leather front backrest lock control, XV6 leather switch seat adjustment, XR3 leather seat hinges, XV5 leather seat adjust switches, XV4 leather heat adjust switches		
—	**Cellular Telephone** — portable - 911 except RS America..........................	2195	2395
	installed w/exclusive console		
S11	**Cellular Telephone** — w/installation kit and mounting bracket - 911 except RS America	1275	1425
S99	**Cellular Telephone** — w/exclusive console, color to sample - 911 except RS America	NA	NA
SPP	**Cellular Telephone** — power pack plus - 911 except RS America.............	39	45
SBE	**Cellular Telephone** — battery eliminator - 911 except RS America	77	90
SLB	**Cellular Telephone** — large std battery - 911 except RS America	43	50
SAC	**Cellular Telephone** — AC rapid charger - 911 except RS America	153	177
SUL	**Cellular Telephone** — small ultra light battery - 911 except RS America...	101	118
403	**Wheels** — 17" 5-spoke - 911 except RS America.................................	1104	1378
XD4	**Wheels** — rim cap w/Porsche crest - 911 except RS America..................	172	214
XD9	**Wheels** — rims painted in color of car - 911 except RS America	865	1079
030	**Special Chassis** — 911 Coupes except RS America	495	630
XR7	**Washers** — rear window - 911 Coupes (except RS America) & Targa........	654	817
—	**Interior Upholstery** — cloth seat inlay, leatherette trim - 911....................	NC	NC
—	**Interior Upholstery** — special leather - 911 Coupe & Targa.....................	3205	4000
	911 Cabriolet..	2221	2772
—	**Interior Upholstery** — all cloth - 911 except RS America	NC	NC
—	**Interior Upholstery** — leather seats w/leatherette beltline -		
	911 Coupe & Targa..	1181	1474
	911 Cabriolet..	928	1149
—	**Interior Upholstery** — leather interior w/leather or cloth seats - 911 Coupe & Targa......................	2860	3569
	911 Cabriolet..	1875	2340
—	**Interior Upholstery** — leather w/leatherette beltline and cloth inlays -		
	911 Coupe & Targa..	1181	1474
	911 Cabriolet..	928	1149
98	**Interior Upholstery** — leather interior in deviating current mdl year colors -		
	911 Coupe & Targa..	3039	3793
	911 Cabriolet..	2055	2565
980	**Interior Upholstery** — front/rear supple leather seats - 911 Coupe/ Targa	306	382
99	**Interior Upholstery** — leather in color to sample - 911 Coupe/Targa.........	4495	5610
	911 Cabriolet..	3761	4695
980	**Interior Upholstery** — front supple leather seats - 911 Cabriolet..............	226	282
Z37	**Carpeting** — deviating color, prior model year - 911 except RS America...	214	267

PORSCHE

CODE	DESCRIPTION	DEALER	LIST
Z85	**Carpeting** — color to sample, deviating, leather, carpet welting - 911 except RS America	1423	1776
Z07	**Carpeting** — velour-like, luggage compartment - 911 except RS America.	82	103
Z09	**Carpeting** — leather, matching interior, color to sample, carpet welting - 911 except RS America	808	1020
Z13	**Carpeting** — leatherette, current color, deviating, carpet welting - 911 except RS America	133	166
Z69	**Carpeting** — std color, deviated carpeting - 911 except RS America	52	65
Z11	**Carpeting** — current colors, leather, matching interior, carpet welting - 911 except RS America	818	1020
XN1	**Leather Power Window Switches** — three - 911 except RS America	274	342
XN2	**Leather Inside Door Openers** — two - 911 except RS America	136	169
ZN3	**Leather Fresh Air Vents** — two - 911 except RS America	531	662
ZN4	**Leather Center Fresh Air Vents** — 911 except RS America	278	347
XN7	**Leather Parking Brake Lever** — deviating color - 911 except RS America	200	249
XN8	**Leather Sunvisors** — current color - 911 Targa & Cabriolet	464	579
XN9	**Leather Sunvisors** — right illuminated visor vanity mirror - 911 except RS America	537	671
659	**On-Board Computer** — 911 except RS America	338	442
387	**Seats** — right sport w/power height adjustment - 911 except RS America.	251	314
383	**Seats** — left sport w/power height adjustment - 911 except RS America...	251	314
340	**Seats** — right heated - 911 except RS America	231	289
139	**Seats** — left heated - 911 except RS America	231	289
437	**Seats** — left, full power - 911 except RS America	430	538
438	**Seats** — right, full power - 911 except RS America	430	538
513	**Seats** — lumbar support, right - 911 except RS America	442	551
586	**Seats** — lumbar support, left - 911 except RS America	442	551
XV1	**Leather Defroster Panel** — 911 except RS America	346	432
XV2	**Leather Side Fresh Air Vent Covers** — two - 911 except RS America	17	22
XV3	**Leather Heat Adjustment/Air Conditioning Cover** — 911 ex. RS America	241	300
XV4	**Leather Heat Adjustment Switches** — two - 911 except RS America	128	159
XV5	**Leather Seat Adjustment Switches** — six - 911 except RS America	432	540
526	**Door Trim Panels** — cloth - 911 except RS America	140	174
Z43	**Door Trim Panels** — current color, leather - 911 except RS America	376	470
Z23	**Door Trim Panels** — alternate current colors, stitching - 911 except RS America	72	90
Z77	**Door Trim Panels** — leather lower door panel instead of carpeting - 911 except RS America	NA	NA
X09	**Console** — special leather, center - 911 except RS America	2115	2639
XJ3	**Leather Door Lock Rosettes & Knobs** — 911 except RS America	233	291
XJ4	**Leather Ignition Lock Plate Rosette** — 911 except RS America	47	58
XJ5	**Leather Ignition/Door Key** — 911 except RS America	125	156
XJ6	**Leather Steering Column** — 911 except RS America	226	282
XJ8	**Leather Tiptronic Selector Lever** — 911 w/auto trans	197	246
Z53	**Head Restraints** — w/stamped Porsche Crest - 911 except RS America	85	106
Z47	**Hood** — w/o Porsche Crest, front - 911 except RS America	53	66
Z19	**Seat Trim** — 911 except RS America	149	186
	incls leather front & rear seats, deviating from interior color		
Z49	**Seat Trim** — 911 except RS America	37	46
	incls cloth seat inlays, prior model year color, deviating		

CODE	DESCRIPTION	DEALER	LIST
Z71	**Seat Trim** — 911 except RS America... *incls multi-colored cloth seat inlays, deviating*	NA	NA
Z45	**Seat Trim** — 911 except RS America... *incls cloth seat inlays, current color, deviating*	36	45
Z93	**Seat Trim** — 911 except RS America... *incls leather seat inlays, deviating current color*	82	103
Z51	**Seat Trim** — 911 except RS America... *incls front & rear leather seats, color to sample*	1736	2166
419	**Storage Compartment** — rear - 911 Coupe (except RS America) & Targa.	525	656
XK7	**Leather Shift Lever Boot & Knob** — 911 (except RS America) w/man trans *color to sample*	182	227
XB3	**Leather Boot Cover** — 911 Cabriolet..	2069	2583
XP6	**Leather Seatbelt Lock & Housing** — two - 911 except RS America	374	466
XP9	**Leather Radio Speak Covers** — six - 911 except RS America	383	478
X24	**Selector Lever** — dark rootwood - 911 models w/auto trans...................	346	432
X25	**Selector Lever** — light rootwood - 911 models w/auto trans...................	346	432
XM5	**Leather Control Knobs** — four on dash - 911 except RS America.............	323	403
XM7	**Leather Glove Box Knob** — 911 except RS America	74	93
XM9	**Leather Turn Signal/Wiper Switch** — 911 except RS America.................	225	281
Z21	**Seat Stitching** — alternate current colors - 911 except RS America..........	69	86
Z27	**Leather Headliner** — current colors - 911 Coupes except RS America.....	883	1102
Z05	**Leather Headliner** — color to sample - 911 Coupes except RS America....	1089	1360
XR3	**Leather Front Seat Hinges** — four - 911 except RS America	382	476
XR6	**Leather Backrest Lock Controls** — 911 except RS America....................	382	476
XC8	**Shift Lever Knob** — light rootwood - 911 except RS America...................	289	360
XC9	**Shift Lever Knob** — dark rootwood - 911 except RS America...................	289	360

911 Carrera 2 Cabriolet

911 CARRERA 2 SPEEDSTER/TURBO 3.6
CARRERA 4 COUPE

		DEALER	LIST
964830	Carrera 2 Speedster 2-Dr Cabriolet (5-spd)	55595	66400
964830	Carrera 2 Speedster 2-Dr Cabriolet (auto)	58230	69550
964770	Carrera 2 Turbo 3.6 2-Dr Coupe (5-spd)	82870	99000
964150	Carrera 4 2-Dr Coupe (5-spd)	65695	78450
	Destination Charge:	725	725
	Gas Guzzler Tax: Carrera 2 Speedster (auto)	1000	1000

Standard Equipment

911 SPEEDSTER: 3.6L, 247HP, aluminum alloy, twin spark plug, air-cooled, horizontally opposed, 6 cylinder engine w/partial engine encapsulation, fully integrated electronic ignition and fuel injection system, Digital Motor Electronics (DME) w/dual knock-sensor system, dual-mass flywheel, 5-speed manual transmission or 4-speed Tiptronic dual-function transmission w/shift lock and key lock features, hydraulically activated single-disc dry clutch, rack and pinion steering w/force sensitive power-assist, fully independent suspension, MacPherson front strut suspension (aluminum alloy lower control arms w/stabilizer bar), rear suspension (coil springs, aluminum alloy semi-trailing arms w/toe correction characteristics; stabilizer bar), four-wheel disc brakes w/anti-lock braking system (ABS) and asbestos free pads (power-assisted, aluminum alloy four-piston fixed caliper), 5-spoke pressure-cast light alloy wheels w/locks (front - 7Jx17 with 205/50ZR17 SBR tires; rear - 8Jx17 with 255/40ZR17 SBR tires), 20.3 gallon fuel tank, folding top with rigid composite tonneau cover, integrated fog lights into front apron, halogen headlights, welded unitized body construction (double-sided zinc-galvanized steel), speed-dependent extendable rear spoiler, heated windshield washer nozzles, all around tinted glass (windshield-graduated tint), wheels painted to match body color (unpainted, silver-colored wheels w/black exterior), driver and passenger airbags, 3-point inertia-reel seatbelts, leather racing-type black or body color-keyed bucket seats, leather-covered steering wheel, 911 Carrera RS-style door panels with black or body color-keyed straps to open doors, backlit analog instrumentation with tachometer and gauges indicating oil pressure/oil temperature/oil level/fuel level, corresponding warning lights, trip odometer, power windows, analog quartz clock, brake pad wear indicator, mirrors in sun visors, interior light w/delayed shut-off, locking and alarm system w/light-emitting diodes in door lock buttons to show alarm is engaged, radio preparation (4 speakers, amplifier and windshield antenna), cassette holder.

CODE	DESCRIPTION	DEALER	LIST

911 TURBO 3.6: 3.6L, 355HP, aluminum alloy, air cooled, horizontally opposed, 6-cylinder turbocharged engine; fully integrated electronic ignition and K-Jetronic fuel injection system, turbocharger w/intercooler and separate wastegate exhaust system, dual-mass flywheel, 5-speed manual transmission with limited slip differential, hydraulically activated single-disc dry clutch, rack and pinion steering w/force-sensitive power assist, fully independent suspension, MacPherson front struts (aluminum alloy lower control arms with stabilizer bar; rear-coil springs, aluminum alloy semi-trailing arms w/toe correction characteristics, stabilizer bar), four-wheel disc brakes w/anti-lock braking system (ABS) and asbestos free pads (power assisted, aluminum alloy four-piston, fixed caliper, internally ventilated), 3-piece Cup-design pressure-cast light alloy wheels with locks (front - 8Jx18 with 225/40ZR18 SBR tires; rear - 10Jx18 with 265/35ZR18 SBR tires), 20.3 gallon fuel tank, electric sliding sunroof, integrated fog lights into front apron, halogen headlights, welded unitized body construction (double-sided zinc galvanized steel), fixed plane rear spoiler, heated windshield washer nozzles, electrically adjustable and heatable outside rearview mirrors, windshield antenna w/signal amplifier, rear window defroster, rear window wiper, headlight washers, all around tinted glass (windshield-graduated tint), metallic paint, driver and front seat passenger airbags, 3-point inertia reel front and rear seatbelts, driver and passenger full power seats, partial leather reclining bucket seats, air conditioning w/automatic temperature control, leather-covered steering wheel, backlit analog instrumentation with tachometer gauges indicating oil pressure/oil temperature/oil level/fuel level, corresponding warning lights, 6-function computerized driver-information center w/digital boost gauge, trip odometer, power windows, analog quartz clock, brake pad wear indicator, mirrors in sun visors, interior light w/delayed shut-off, one-key central locking and alarm system, AM/FM digital display stereo cassette radio w/8 speakers and amplifier, cassette holder.

911 CARRERA 4: 3.6L, 247HP, aluminum alloy, twin spark plug, air cooled, horizontally opposed, 6 cylinder engine w/partial engine encapsulation; fully integrated electronic ignition and fuel injection system, Digital Motor Electronics (DME) with dual knock-sensor system, dual-mass flywheel, 5-speed manual transmission, Porsche-designed computer-controlled full-time all-wheel-drive system w/automatic differential-clutch actuation, hydraulically activated single-disc dry clutch, rack and pinion steering w/force-sensitive power assist, MacPherson front strut suspension (aluminum alloy lower control arms w/stabilizer bar), rear coil spring suspension (aluminum alloy semi-trailing arms w/toe correction characteristics and stabilizer bar), four-wheel disc brakes w/anti lock braking system (ABS) and asbestos free pads (power assisted, aluminum-alloy four piston fixed caliper, internally ventilated), 5-spoke pressure-cast

CODE	DESCRIPTION	DEALER	LIST

light alloy wheels w/locks (front - 7Jx17 with 205/50ZR17 SBR tires; rear - 9Jx17 with 255/40ZR17 SBR tires), 20.3 gallon fuel tank, electric sliding sunroof, integrated fog lights into front apron, halogen headlights, welded unitized body construction (double-sided zinc-galvanized steel), widened rear fenders, speed-dependent extendable rear spoiler, heated windshield washer nozzles, electrically adjustable and heatable outside rearview mirrors, windshield antenna w/signal amplifier, rear window defroster, all-around tinted glass (windshield w/graduated tint), driver and front seat passenger airbags, 3-point inertia-reel front and rear seatbelts, partial leather reclining bucket seats w/electric height adjustment, air conditioning w/automatic temperature control, leather-covered steering wheel, backlit analog instrumentation with tachometer and gauges indicating oil pressure/oil temperature/oil level/fuel level, corresponding warning lights, trip odometer, power windows, analog quartz clock, brake pad wear indicator, mirrors in sunvisors, interior light with delayed shut-off, cruise control, one-key central locking and alarm system, AM/FM digital display stereo cassette radio w/8 speakers and amplifier, cassette holder.

Accessories

Code	Description	Dealer	List
Z87	**Dashboard** — leatherette (in all leather inter) - 911 Carrera 4	19	23
X17	**Dashboard** — light rootwood - 911 except Speedster	3490	4356
X18	**Dashboard** — dark rootwood - 911 except Speedster	3490	4356
XN1	**Leather Power Window Switches** — three - 911 except Speedster	274	342
XN2	**Leather Inside Door Openers** — two - 911 except Speedster	136	169
XN3	**Leather Dash Fresh Air Vents** — two - 911 except Speedster	531	662
XN4	**Leather Center Fresh Air Vents** — 911 except Speedster	278	347
XN7	**Leather Parking Brake Lever** — deviating color - 911 except Speedster	200	249
XN9	**Leather Sunvisors** — w/right illuminated visor vanity mirror - 911 except Speedster	537	671
573	**Air Conditioning** — automatic - 911 Speedster	2248	2805
Z05	**Headliner** — leather, color to sample - 911 except Speedster	1089	1360
Z27	**Headliner** — leather, current color - 911 except Speedster	883	1102
220	**Limited Slip Differential** — 911 Speedster	732	913
288	**Headlight Washers** — 911 (std Turbo 3.6)	210	262
X19	**Leather Instrument Housing** — 911 except Speedster	716	893
XX6	**Leather Shift Pattern Insert** — 911 except Speedster	55	68
XX2	**Lights** — additional interior footwell - 911 except Speedster	462	576
XX3	**Lights** — additional for door compartments - 911 except Speedster	495	618
X31	**Parking Brake Handle** — light rootwood - 911 except Speedster	428	535
X32	**Parking Brake Handle** — dark rootwood - 911 except Speedster	428	535
—	**Interior Upholstery** — leather w/leatherette beltline & cloth inlays - 911 Turbo 3.6	1181	1474
98	**Interior Upholstery** — leather interior in deviating current mdl year colors - 911 except Speedster	3039	3793
—	**Interior Upholstery** — special leather - 911 except Speedster	3205	4000
980	**Interior Upholstery** — front & rear supple leather seats - 911 except Speedster	306	382
	Turbo reqs all leather seats		
99	**Interior Upholstery** — leather in color to sample - 911 except Speedster	4495	5610
425	**Wiper** — rear window - 911 Carrera 4	273	340
XR7	**Washing System** — rear window - 911 except Speedster	654	817
XV1	**Leather Defroster Panel** — 911 except Speedster	346	432
XV2	**Leather Side Fresh Air Vent Covers** — two - 911 except Speedster	17	22
XV3	**Leather Air Conditioning/Heat Adjustment Cover** — 911 except Speedster	241	300

CODE	DESCRIPTION	DEALER	LIST
XV4	**Leather Heat Adjustment Switches** — two - 911 except Speedster	128	159
XV5	**Leather Seat Adjustment Switches** — six - 911 except Speedster	432	540
XV6	**Leather Switch/Seat Adjustor Covers** — two - 911 except Speedster	287	359
XV7	**Leather Fuel Tank Pull Knob Flap** — 911 except Speedster	53	66
XV8	**Leather Outside Mirror Control Knob** — 911 except Speedster	51	63
XV9	**Leather Seatbelt Covers** — two - 911 except Speedster	92	115
Z75	**Leather Door/Window A Pillars** — 911 except Speedster	96	120
Z79	**Leather A & B Pillars** — color to sample, matching interior - 911 except Speedster	97	121
Z07	**Carpeting** — luggage compartment, velour-like- 911 except speedster	82	103
Z09	**Carpeting** — carpet welding, leather, color to sample, matching interior - 911 except Speedster	818	1020
Z13	**Carpeting** — carpet welting, leatherette, current color, deviating - 911 except Speedster	133	166
Z37	**Carpeting** — deviating color, prior model year - 911 except Speedster	214	267
Z11	**Carpeting** — carpet welting, leather, current colors, matching interior - 911 except Speedster	818	1020
Z69	**Carpeting** — deviating carpeting, standard color - 911 except Speedster	52	65
Z85	**Carpeting** — carpet welting, leather, color to sample, deviating - 911 except Speedster	1423	1776
XK7	**Leather Shift Lever Boot & Knob** — color to sample - 911 except Speedster	182	227
659	**Computer** — on-board - 911 (std Turbo 3.6)	338	422
XM5	**Leather Control Knobs on Dash** — four - 911 except Speedster	323	403
XM7	**Leather Glove Box Knob** — 911 except Speedster	74	93
XM9	**Leather Turn Signal/Wiper Switch** — 911 except Speedster	225	281
XD4	**Wheels** — rim caps w/Porsche crest - 911	172	214
407	**Wheels** — 18" polished - four - 911 Turbo 3.6	239	299
346	**Wheels** — std Carrera 2 rims, silver - 911 Speedster	NC	NC
XD9	**Wheels** — rims painted in car's color - 911 except Speedster	865	1079
526	**Door Trim Panels** — cloth - 911 Carrera 4	140	174
	911 Turbo 3.6	NC	NC
Z43	**Door Trim Panels** — leather, current color - 911 except Speedster	376	470
Z23	**Door Trim Panels** — stitching, alternate current colors - 911 except Speedster	72	90
Z89	**Door Trim Panels** — lower door panel in deviating std color - 911 Carrera 4	39	48
Z77	**Door Trim Panels** — lower door panel in leather instead of carpeting - 911 Turbo 3.6	125	156
	911 Carrera 4	NA	NA
454	**Cruise Control** — 911 Speedster	539	672
XJ3	**Leather Door Lock Rosettes & Knobs** — two - 911 except Speedster	233	291
XJ4	**Leather Ignition Lock Plate Rosette** — 911 except Speedster	47	58
XJ5	**Leather Ignition/Door Key** — 911 except Speedster	125	156
XJ6	**Leather Steering Column** — 911 except Speedster	226	282
XJ8	**Leather Tiptronic Shift Lever** — 911 Carrera 4	197	246
Z47	**Hood** — front w/o Porsche crest - 911 except Speedster	53	66
—	**Mats** — velour floor - 911	81	125
XW1	**Leather Front Seatbelt Rosettes** — 911 except Speedster	122	153
XW2	**Leather Rear Seatbelt Lock/Housing** — 911 except Speedster	463	578
XW3	**Leather Rear Window Wiper Swatches** — 911 except Speedster	136	169

CODE	DESCRIPTION	DEALER	LIST
XW4	**Leather Light Switch** — 911 except Speedster	72	90
XW5	**Leather Wiper/Instrument Light Knobs** — 911 except Speedster	92	115
XW6	**Leather Door Locking Pin Rosettes** — 911 except Speedster	64	80
XW7	**Leather Warning Buzzer Rosette** — 911 except Speedster	41	51
XW8	**Leather-Covered Caps for Door Panels** — two - 911 except Speedster	15	18
XW9	**Leather Entrance Panel Covers** — left & right - 911 except Speedster	205	256
498	**Model Designation** — rear (delete) - 911	NC	NC
XR3	**Leather Front Seat Hinges** — four - 911 except Speedster	269	335
XR6	**Leather Front Backrest Lock Controls** — 911 except Speedster	382	476
XZ4	**Leather Glove Box Lock Frame** — 911 except Speedster	67	83
Z15	**Seat Piping** — leather front seat piping, prior model year color - 911 except Speedster	140	174
Z17	**Seat Piping** — leather front seat piping, current color - 911 except Speedster	98	123
Z25	**Seat Piping** — leatherette front seat piping, current color, deviating - 911 except Speedster	60	75
Z33	**Seat Piping** — leather piping, all seats, current color - 911 except Speedster	162	203
Z29	**Leather shift Boot/Knob** — color to sample or special leather - 911 except Speedster	37	46
Z65	**Leatherette Beltline** — in deviating std color (dash color) - 911 Turbo 3.6	52	65
Z31	**Leather Kneebar** — lower dash, current color - 911 except Speedster	332	415
Z35	**Leather Kneebar** — lower dash, deviating current color - 911 except Speedster	36	45
331	**Radio** — w/cassette player - 911 Speedster	790	986
XF5	**Leather Instrument Trim Rings** — 911 except Speedster	354	442
XR6	**Leather Gear Box Tunnel** — 911 except Speedster	158	189
XF7	**Leather-Covered Tray** — 911 except Speedster	154	193
Z53	**Head Restraints** — w/stamped Porsche crest - 911 except Speedster	85	106
X09	**Console** — center, special leather - 911 except Speedster	2115	2639
Z01	**Leather Sunvisors** — current colors - 911 except Speedster	485	606
Z03	**Leather Sunvisors** — color to sample - 911 except Speedster	552	689
—	**Paint** — metallic - 911 Turbo 3.6	NC	NC
Z41	**Paint** — pearl white metallic - 911 except Speedster	NA	NA
98	**Paint** — non-metallic to sample - 911 Turbo 3.6	1277	1594
	911 except Turbo 3.6	2002	2498
99	**Paint** — metallic to sample - 911 Turbo 3.6	1277	1594
	911 except Turbo 3.6	2002	2498
XP6	**Leather Seatbelt Lock & Housing** — two - 911 except Speedster	374	466
XP9	**Leather Radio Speaker Covers** — six - 911 except Speedster	383	478

928 GTS

CODE	DESCRIPTION	DEALER	LIST
928920	GTS 2-Dr Coupe (5-spd)	68030	82260
928920	GTS 2-Dr Coupe (auto)	68030	82260
	Destination Charge:	725	725
	Gas Guzzler Tax: Models w/manual trans	3000	3000
	Models w/auto trans	2100	2100

Standard Equipment

928 GTS: 5.4L, 345HP, aluminum alloy, double overhead cam V8 engine; four valves per cylinder, EZK ignition w/knock sensor system, LH Jetronic fuel injection with 2-stage resonance induction system, 5-speed manual or 4-speed automatic transmission w/shift lock and key lock features, "PSD" electronically-variable limited slip differential, rack and pinion steering w/force-sensitive power assist, sport shock absorbers, fully independent suspension, (front - aluminum alloy double A-arms w/coil springs, negative steering roll radius and stabilizer bar; rear - aluminum alloy multi-link "Weissach" rear axle w/self-stabilizing toe characteristics and stabilizer bar), power assisted internally ventilated disc brakes w/anti-lock braking system (ABS) and asbestos free pads (race-developed aluminum alloy, four-piston fixed caliper), five-spoke pressure-cast light alloy wheels w/locks (front - 7.5Jx17 with 225/45ZR17 SBR tires; rear - 9Jx17 with 225/40ZR17 SBR tires), 22.7 gallon fuel tank, electric sunroof (closes automatically when vehicle is locked w/key), integrated fog and driving lights in front bumper, retractable halogen headlights, welded unitized body construction (double-sided zinc-galvanized steel), lightweight aluminum front fenders/hood/doors/rear spoiler painted to match exterior color, metallic paint, heated windshield washer nozzles, rear window wiper and defroster w/two heat settings, electrically adjustable and heatable outside rearview mirrors, roof mounted antenna, all around tinted glass (windshield-graduated tint), headlight washers, driver and front seat passenger airbags, 3-point inertia-reel front and rear seatbelts, driver-information and diagnostic system monitoring 10 information functions and 22 separate warning functions in a combination backlit display; automatic climate control system w/separate rear air conditioning, AM/FM digital display stereo cassette radio w/remote CD changer or AM/FM digital display stereo radio w/CD player/10-speaker hi-fi sound system/160-watt 6 channel amplifier, front and rear leather seats, leather-covered steering wheel/gearshift lever boot, full power front seats, 3-position Positrol memory for driver's seat and outside mirrors, one-key central locking and alarm system with light-emitting diodes in door lock buttons to show the alarm is engaged, backlit analog instrumentation including tachometer and gauges indicating oil pressure/coolant temperature/fuel level/battery charge, adjustable tilt steering column and instrument cluster, power windows, electrical rear-hatch release on driver and passenger sides, cruise control, individual fold-down rear seats, fold-out front armrests, cassette holder, red warning lights and white courtesy lights in doors, interior lighting w/delayed shut-off, rear sun visors, illuminated mirrors in front sun visors.

Accessories

Code	Description	Dealer	List
S88	**Cellular Telephone** — w/mounting bracket & installation kit	1275	1425
SUL	**Cellular Telephone** — small, ultralight battery	101	118
SLB	**Cellular Telephone** — large, std battery	43	50
SAC	**Cellular Telephone** — AC rapid charger	153	177
SPP	**Cellular Telephone** — power pack plus	39	45
SBE	**Cellular Telephone** — battery eliminator	77	90
X13	**Exclusive Pkg**	1048	1308
	incls XP9 leather radio spkr covers in doors, XJ3 leather door lock knobs and bezels, XM6 leather inside door opener and handle recess plates		
X14	**Exclusive Pkg**	819	1023
	incls XZ1 leather rosette for parking brake, XW2 leather rear seatbelt lock/housing cover, XN7 leather parking brake lever, XP6 leather front seatbelt locks and housing		
X15	**Exclusive Pkg**	1503	1876
	incls XV6 leather seat adjustment switch covers, XR3 leather front seat hinges, XV4 leather heat adjustment switches, XR5 leather backrest lock control, XV5 leather seat adjustment switches		
X16	**Exclusive Pkg**	875	1092
	incls XY4 leather frame for center console, XY6 leather cover for ashtray, XY8 leather frame for switches, XJ8 leather wrapped shift lever, XY5 leather cover for auto selector lever, XY7 leather switches for rear wiper/windows/sunroof		
XJ3	**Leather Door Lock Knobs & Bezels**	233	291
XJ5	**Leather Ignition/Door Key**	125	156
XJ8	**Leather Shift Lever** — manual	221	276
Z14	**Leather Door Trim Panels** — color to sample	37	46
Z36	**Leather Luggage Compartment Cover**	500	624
418	**Bodyside Moldings**	NC	NC
538	**Seats** — seat position memory, right side	831	1038
513	**Seats** — right seat lumbar support	442	551
586	**Seats** — left seat lumbar support	442	551
383	**Seats** — power sport left	NC	NC
387	**Seats** — power sport right	NC	NC
340	**Seats** — right heated	231	289
139	**Seats** — left heated	231	289
XV1	**Leather Defroster Panel**	253	315
XV3	**Leather Air Conditioning/Heat Adjustment Cover**	241	300
XV4	**Leather Heat Adjustment Switches** — two	128	159
XV5	**Leather Seat Adjustment Switches** — six	432	540
XV6	**Leather Seat Adjustment Switch Covers** — two	287	359
570	**Air Conditioning** — increased output	NC	NC
—	**Mats** — velour floor	81	125

CODE	DESCRIPTION	DEALER	LIST
—	**Paint** — metallic	NC	NC
Z40	**Paint** — pearl white metallic	10366	12938
98	**Paint** — non-metallic to sample	2135	2664
99	**Paint** — metallic to sample	2135	2664
XY1	**Leather Console Area for Switch & Dials**	126	158
XY2	**Leather Seat Adjustor** — w/o covered memory switch	57	71
XY3	**Leather Seat Adjuster** — w/covered memory switch	93	116
XY4	**Leather Frame for Center Console**	225	281
XY5	**Leather Cover for Auto Selector Lever**	198	247
XY6	**Leather Cover for Ashtray**	72	90
XY7	**Leather Switches for Rear Wiper, Windows & Sunroof**	200	249
XY8	**Leather Frame for Switches**	57	71
498	**Model Designation** — rear (delete)	NC	NC
Z04	**Seat Trim** — all leather seats, color to sample	718	896
Z06	**Seat Trim** — leather welting, color to sample	1310	1635
Z08	**Seat Trim** — leather welting, current colors	911	1137
Z10	**Seat Trim** — leatherette welting, current colors	37	46
Z12	**Seat Trim** — leatherette piping, current colors	37	46
Z18	**Seat Trim** — seat stitching, current colors	69	86
Z30	**Seat Trim** — leather piping, current colors	153	191
Z32	**Seat Trim** — leather piping, color to sample	213	266
—	**Seat Trim** — leather seats w/cloth inlays	NC	NC
XN3	**Leather Side Instrument Panel Air Vents**	516	644
XN4	**Leather Center Instrument Panel Air Vent**	354	442
XN7	**Leather Parking Brake Lever**	293	365
XN9	**Leather Sunvisors** — w/right illuminated make-up mirror	537	671
Z31	**Door Trim Panel Stitching** — current colors	NA	NA
—	**Interior** — leather trim w/leatherette beltline	2480	3096
—	**Interior** — leather trim w/leatherette beltline & cloth inlays	2480	3096
—	**Interior** — special leather trim w/black leatherette beltline	3066	3826
980	**Interior** — supple leather seats	450	561
94	**Interior** — std leather w/leatherette beltline in deviating std color combos	2893	3610
95	**Interior** — leather in color to sample w/leatherette beltline	4855	6059
XR7	**Window Washing System** — rear	1011	1262
XC8	**Shift Lever Knob** — light rootwood - 928 w/man trans	289	360
XC9	**Shift Lever Knob** — dark rootwood - 928 w/man trans	289	360
474	**Shock Absorbers** — sport	274	342
Z44	**Porsche Crest on Hood** — delete	53	66
XZ1	**Leather Rosette for Parking Brake**	170	212
XZ2	**Leather Rosettes for Rear Seatbelts**	153	191
XZ3	**Leather Frame for Locking System Dial Area**	122	153
XZ4	**Leather Frame for Glove Box Lock**	173	216
XZ5	**Leather Cover for Interior Sensor**	35	43
XZ6	**Leather Right Fresh Air Vent**	44	55
XZ7	**Leather Frame/Knob/Rocker for Outside Mirror**	88	110
XZ8	**Leather Rosette for Luggage Compartment Cover**	161	201
XZ9	**Leather Safety Belt Tongue Frame**	106	133
Z38	**Carpeting** — deviating, prior model year colors	214	267
Z34	**Carpeting** — deviating, current colors	52	65
Z16	**Head Restraints** — w/stamped Porsche Crest, front seat	85	106
596	**Spoiler** — black rear	NC	NC

PORSCHE

CODE	DESCRIPTION	DEALER	LIST
XD4	**Wheel Rims** — rimcap w/Porsche Crest	172	214
XD9	**Wheel Rims** — rims painted in vehicle color	865	1079
XK7	**Leather Shift Lever** — (automatic)	197	246
XR3	**Leather Front Seat Hinges** — four	269	335
XR5	**Leather Backrest Lock Controls**	555	692
XX5	**Leather Cassette Holder** — left door	1232	1537
XX6	**Leather Shift Lever Knob** — (manual)	55	68
XL4	**Console/Door Trim** — light rootwood	3927	4902
XL5	**Console/Door Trim** — dark rootwood	3927	4902
XP6	**Leather Front Seatbelt Locks & Housing**	374	466
XP7	**Leather Rear Seatbelt Housing Covers**	164	204
XP9	**Leather Speaker Covers in Doors** — ten	605	755
X31	**Parking Brake Handle** — light rootwood	428	535
X32	**Parking Brake Handle** — dark rootwood	428	535
XM6	**Leather Inside Door Opener & Handle Recess Plates**	327	408
XM9	**Leather Turn Signal & Wiper Switch**	225	281
XW2	**Leather Rear Seatbelt Lock/Housing Cover**	285	355
XW6	**Leather Rosettes for Door Lock Pins**	73	91
X22	**Selector Level** — dark rootwood - 928 w/auto trans	366	457
X23	**Selector Level** — light rootwood - 928 w/auto trans	366	457

968

968110	968 2-Dr Coupe (6-spd)	32760	39950
968110	968 2-Dr Coupe (auto)	35340	43100
968310	968 2-Dr Cabriolet (6-spd)	42555	51900
968310	968 2-Dr Cabriolet (auto)	45135	55050
	Destination Charge:	725	725

Standard Equipment

968 COUPE & CABRIOLET: 3.0L, 236HP, aluminum alloy, double overhead cam 4-cylinder engine w/twin balance shafts, four valves per cylinder with Vario Cam control, fully integrated electronic ignition and fuel injection system (Digital Motor Electronics - [DME]), dual-knock-sensor system, front engine and rear transaxle, twin pipe high flow exhaust system coupled w/reduced flow loss metal-monolith catalytic converter, lightweight forged pistons (lightened, forged crankshaft and connecting rods), 911 Turbo-type dual-mass flywheel, 6-speed manual transmission or 4-speed Tiptronic dual-function transmission w/shift lock and key lock features, hydraulically activated single-patch clutch, rack and pinion steering w/force-sensitive power-assist, fully independent suspension, MacPherson front strut suspension (aluminum alloy lower control arms with stabilizer bar), rear suspension (coil springs, aluminum alloy semi-trailing arms and torsion bars w/stabilizer bar), dual-circuit internally ventilated 4-wheel disc brakes w/anti lock braking system (ABS) and asbestos free pads (race-developed aluminum alloy, four-piston fixed caliper, power assisted), 5-spoke pressure-cast light alloy wheels w/locks (front - 7Jx16 with 205/55ZR16 SBR tires; rear - 8Jx16 with 225/50ZR16 SBR tires), 19.6 gallon fuel tank, electric tilt/removable sunroof (Coupe), power top (Cabriolet), projector-type fog lights integrated into the front spoiler, pop-up variable focal point halogen headlights, new integrated design energy absorbing front and rear bumper covers, welded unitized body construction (double-sided zinc-galvanized steel), heated windshield washer nozzles, electrically adjustable and heatable outside rearview mirrors, roof-mounted antenna (Coupe), windshield antenna w/signal amplifier (Cabriolet), rear window defroster (Coupe), all around tinted glass (windshield with graduated tint), driver and front passenger airbags, 3-point front and rear inertia-reel seatbelts (Cabriolet - front only), reclining bucket seats with electric height adjustment, leatherette interior w/cloth seat inlays, split fold-down rear seatback (Coupe), air conditioning with automatic temperature control/outside Fahrenheit and Centigrade temperature display, electric release for rear hatch/Cabriolet trunk, leather covered steering wheel/gearshift lever boot, backlit analog instrumentation including tachometer and gauges indicating oil pressure/coolant temperature/fuel level/battery charge, corresponding warning lights, trip odometer, power windows, analog quartz clock, brake pad wear-indicator, mirrors in sunvisors, interior light w/delayed shut-off, cruise control, one-key central locking and alarm system, AM/FM digital display stereo cassette radio w/6 speakers and anti-theft coding, cassette holder.

Accessories

CODE	DESCRIPTION	DEALER	LIST
XJ5	**Leather Ignition/Door Key**	125	156
XJ7	**Leather Lower Dash/Steering Column**	1051	1311
XJ8	**Leather Shift Knob & Cover** — color to sample	197	246
Z13	**Carpeting** — leatherette carpet welting, deviating std color	130	163
Z69	**Carpeting** — deviating, std color	52	66
XW2	**Leather Rear Seatbelt Locks/Housings**	479	598
XW6	**Leather Rosettes for Door Locking Pins**	67	83
340	**Seats** — heated, right	230	289
139	**Seats** — heated, left	230	289
437	**Seats** — full power, left	431	538
438	**Seats** — full power, right	431	538
513	**Seats** — right seat lumbar support	442	551
586	**Seats** — left seat lumbar support	442	551
383	**Seats** — sport left w/power height	251	314
387	**Seats** — sport right w/power height	251	314
XD4	**Wheels** — rim cap w/Porsche Crest	172	214
403	**Wheels** — 17" 5-spoke	1104	1378
XD9	**Wheels** — rims painted to match exterior paint	865	1079
XN1	**Leather Power Window/Mirror Switches**	160	199
XN7	**Leather Parking Brake Lever**	293	365
XN8	**Leather Sunvisors**	499	623

CODE	DESCRIPTION	DEALER	LIST
XN9	**Leather Sunvisors** — w/right illuminated make-up mirror	537	671
XX6	**Leather Shift Lever Knob** — w/manual trans	55	68
030	**Special Chassis** — 986 Coupe	1616	2017
	incls 403 5-spoke 17" wheels		
XK7	**Leather Shift Knob & Cover**	182	227
220	**Limited Slip Differential** - w/man trans	732	913
Z15	**Seat Trim**	140	174
	incls leather piping, front seats, prior model year colors		
Z17	**Seat Trim**	98	123
	incls leather piping, front seats, current Porsche colors		
A21	**Seat Trim**	64	80
	incls seat stitching, alternate, std colors		
Z25	**Seat Trim**	60	75
	incls leatherette piping, front seats, current Porsche colors		
Z73	**Seat Trim**	1164	1453
	incls leather piping, all seats, color to sample		
S88	**Cellular Telephone** — w/mounting bracket & installation kit	1275	1425
SBE	**Cellular Telephone** — battery eliminator	77	90
SUL	**Cellular Telephone** — ultra light small battery	101	118
SLB	**Cellular Telephone** — std large battery	43	50
SAC	**Cellular Telephone** — AC rapid charger	153	177
SPP	**Cellular Telephone** — power pack plus	39	44
98	**Paint** — non-metallic to sample	2002	2498
—	**Paint** — metallic	660	823
99	**Paint** — metallic to sample	2002	2498
490	**Radio** — hi-fi sound w/amplifier	450	561
595	**Spoiler** — color-keyed, rear	170	213
288	**Headlight Washers**	210	262
—	**Mats** — velour floor	81	125
XV4	**Leather Heat Adjustment Switches** — two	128	159
XV5	**Leather Seat Adjustment Switches** — six	432	540
XV6	**Leather Switch/Seat Adjustment Covers** — two	287	359
XV9	**Leather B-Pillar Seatbelt Covers**	93	116
Z29	**Leather Shift Lever Knob** — matching interior color	37	46
—	**Upholstery** — leather seats - 968 Coupe	1807	2256
	968 Cabriolet	1561	1949
—	**Upholstery** — leather interior w/leatherette beltline		
	968 Coupe	3631	4532
	968 Cabriolet	3344	4173
—	**Upholstery** — partial leather w/leatherette trim	547	682
—	**Upholstery** — special leather - 968 Coupe	3977	4963
	968 Cabriolet	3688	4603
Z55	**Upholstery** — supple leather front seats	355	443
—	**Upholstery** — all cloth seats - 968 Coupe	172	215
	968 Cabriolet	84	105
Z19	**Upholstery** — all leather seats, deviating std color	130	163
98	**Upholstery** — std Porsche leather		
	w/leatherette beltline in deviating std color combinations - 968 Coupe	3810	4755
	968 Cabriolet	3523	4397
99	**Upholstery** — leather in color to sample w/black leatherette belt	5240	6540

CODE	DESCRIPTION	DEALER	LIST
Z23	**Door Trim Panels** — alternate stitching	39	48
526	**Door Trim Panels** — cloth	140	174
XP6	**Leather Seatbelt Locks/Housings**	406	506
XP9	**Leather Loud Speaker Covers**	140	174
Z05	**Leather Luggage Compartment Cover** — color to sample........................	1087	1356
Z31	**Leather Kneebar** — lower dash, current colors....................................	539	672
Z27	**Leather Luggage Compartment Cover** — current colors 968 Coupe	771	963
Z43	**Leather Door Trim Panels** — deviating current color	41	51
498	**Model Designation** — rear (delete)...	NC	NC
X24	**Shift Lever Knob** — dark rootwood (auto) - w/auto trans...........................	313	390
XC8	**Shift Lever Knob** — dark rootwood (man) w/man trans	289	360
XC9	**Shift Lever Knob** — dark rootwood (man) w/man trans	289	360
XM6	**Leather Door Openers & Handle Recess Plates** — two	293	365
XM9	**Leather Turn Signal/Wiper Switch**...	233	291
Z53	**Head Restraints** — stamped w/Porsche Crest	85	106
	reqs leather seats		
418	**Bodyside Moldings**	280	350
X31	**Parking Brake Lever** — light rootwood	428	535
X32	**Parking Brake Lever** — dark rootwood	428	535
XR3	**Leather Front Seat Hinges** — four	269	335
XR6	**Leather Front Backrest Lock Controls**..	346	432

Porsche 968 Cabriolet

SAAB (side tab)

900

		DEALER	LIST
—	900 S 2-Dr Convertible (5-spd)	28750	33275
—	900 Turbo 2-Dr Convertible (5-spd)	32730	38415
—	900 Turbo 2-Dr Convertible Commemorative (5-spd)	34434	40415
	Destination Charge:	460	460

Standard Equipment

900 S: AM/FM stereo radio with cassette, bodyside molding, dual heated power mirrors, dual illuminated visor vanity mirrors, central locking system, manual CFC-free air conditioning, trunk light, glove box light, alarm system, tinted glass, turbo booster gauge, temperature gauge, 18.0 gallon fuel tank, front wheel drive, fog lights, floor mats, rear window defroster, center console, anti-lock braking system, power antenna, front spoiler, dual air bag, cruise control, cloth heated bucket seats, dual power seats, folding rear seat, front and rear stabilizer bars, tilt and telescoping steering wheel, power steering, power windows, wheel covers, intermittent washer/wipers, digital trip odometer, tachometer, front MacPherson strut suspension, P195/60VR15 SBR tires, 5-speed manual transmission

900 TURBO (in addition to or instead of 900 S equipment): Leather heated bucket seats.

900 TURBO COMMEMORATIVE (in addition to or instead of 900 TURBO equipment): Trunk light and remote control release, black metallic paint, wood dash, special edition wheels.

Accessories

—	**Automatic Transmission** — 4-speed w/OD	576	705
	NA on Turbo Convertible Commemorative		
—	**Wood Dash** — Turbo Convertible	520	650

CODE	DESCRIPTION	DEALER	LIST

9000

		DEALER	LIST
—	9000 Aero 5-Dr Hatchback (5-spd)..	32654	38690
—	9000 CD 4-Dr Sedan (5-spd)...	25876	29850
—	9000 CDE 4-Dr Sedan (5-spd)	27684	32685
—	9000 CS 5-Dr Hatchback (5-spd)..	24208	27745
—	9000 CSE 4-Dr Sedan (5-spd)	27989	33045
	Destination Charge:...	460	460

Standard Equipment

9000 AERO: AM/FM stereo radio with cassette, bodyside molding, dual heated power mirrors, dual illuminated visor vanity mirrors, central locking system, manual CFC-free air conditioning, trunk/map/reading lights, glove box light, alarm system, tinted glass, turbo booster gauge, temperature gauge, 17.4 gallon fuel tank, front wheel drive, fog lights, floor mats, rear window defroster, overhead and floor consoles, anti-lock braking system, power antenna, front spoiler, dual air bag, cruise control, cloth heated bucket seats, leather heated buckets with memory, dual power seats, folding rear seat, front and rear stabilizer bars, tilt and telescoping steering wheel, power steering, power windows, intermittent washer/wipers, trip computer, tachometer, rear spoiler, P205/55ZR16 tires, 5-speed manual transmission, rear window wiper/washer, alloy wheels, power sunroof.

9000 CD/9000 CS (in addition to or instead of 9000 AERO equipment): Power antenna deleted, cloth heated bucket seats, folding rear seat deleted, rear spoiler deleted, front MacPherson strut suspension, P195/65TR15 tires, power sunroof deleted.

9000 CDE (in addition to or instead of 9000 CD/9000 CS equipment): Power antenna, leather heated buckets with memory, power sunroof, leather-wrapped steering wheel.

9000 CSE (in addition to or instead of 9000 CDE equipment): Folding rear seat, P195/65VR15 tires, leather-wrapped steering wheel deleted.

Accessories

		DEALER	LIST
—	**Automatic Transmission** — 4-speed w/OD...	773	945
—	**Leather Seats** — 9000 CD, 9000 CS	1243	1520
—	**Power Sunroof** — 9000 CD, 9000 CS...	855	980
—	**Turbo Engine** — 140 CID 4-cylinder - 9000 CSE	2497	3055

JUSTY (1993)

NOTE: 1994 Subaru Justy models were unavailable at time of publication.

		DEALER	LIST
PAA	Base 2-Dr Hatchback (5-spd)	6838	7463
PAB	GL 2-Dr Hatchback (auto)	8277	9238
PAC	GL AWD 2-Dr Hatchback (auto)	8995	10038
PAD	GL AWD 5-Dr Hatchback (5-spd)	8607	9603
PAE	GL AWD 5-Dr Hatchback (auto)	9084	10138
Destination Charge:		445	445

Standard Equipment

JUSTY - BASE: 1.2 liter 3 cylinder EFI engine, 5-speed man trans, rack and pinion steering, power vented front disc/rear drum brakes, P145/SR12 all-season SBR tires, halogen headlights, warning chimes, carpeting, inside hood release, locking fuel filler door, reclining front bucket seats, fold-down rear seat.

GL (in addition to or instead of BASE equipment): Tinted glass, tachometer, front and rear mud guards, full wheel covers, bodyside moldings, clock, electric rear window defroster, 165/65SR13 SBR all-season tires, cargo cover, AM/FM ETR stereo radio with two speakers, intermittent windshield washers/wipers, rear window wiper/washer, front and rear stabilizer bars, remote hatch release, color-keyed bumpers, split fold-down seat.

Accessories

—	**Metallic Paint**	100	120

CODE	DESCRIPTION	DEALER	LIST

LEGACY (1993)

NOTE: 1994 Subaru Legacy models were unavailable at time of publication.

Code	Description	Dealer	List
PFB	L 4-Dr Sedan (5-spd)	14405	16250
PFC	L 4-Dr Sedan (auto)	15126	17050
PFF	L AWD 4-Dr Sedan (5-spd)	15824	17850
PFG	L AWD 4-Dr Sedan (auto)	16545	18650
PHB	L 4-Dr Wagon (5-spd)	15025	16950
PHC	L 4-Dr Wagon (auto)	15746	17750
PHC	L AWD 4-Dr Wagon (5-spd)	16444	18550
PHG	L AWD 4-Dr Wagon (auto)	17165	19350
PHH	L AWD 4-Dr Wagon w/Anti-Lock Brakes (5-spd)	17317	19545
PHI	L AWD 4-Dr Wagon w/Anti-Lock Brakes (auto)	18038	20345
PFE	LS 4-Dr Sedan (auto)	16829	19150
PFI	LS AWD 4-Dr Sedan (auto)	18234	20750
PHE	LS 4-Dr Wagon (auto)	17444	19850
PHJ	LS AWD 4-Dr Wagon (auto)	18850	21450
PFL	LSi AWD 4-Dr Sedan (auto)	19026	21650
PHL	LSi AWD 4-Dr Wagon (auto)	19904	22650
PFJ	Sport AWD 4-Dr Sedan (5-spd)	18323	20850
PFK	Sport AWD 4-Dr Sedan (auto)	19044	21650
PHK	Touring AWD 4-Dr Wagon (auto)	19904	22650
	Destination Charge:	445	445

Standard Equipment

LEGACY - L: 2.2 liter 4 cylinder EFI engine, air conditioning, power steering, tinted glass, power windows, bodyside molding, power 4-wheel disc brakes, tachometer, cruise control, dual power mirrors, cloth reclining front bucket seats, 60/40 split fold-down rear seat, rear window defroster, tilt steering wheel, AM/FM radio with cassette and equalizer, power door locks, 185/70HR14 SBR all-season tires, rear seat center armrest, center console, front stabilizer bar, intermittent windshield washer/wipers, rear window wiper/washer (Wagon), remote fuel filler door, driver's side air bag.

LS (in addition to or instead of L equipment): Alloy wheels, power moonroof, power 4-wheel anti-lock disc

SUBARU

CODE	DESCRIPTION	DEALER	LIST

brakes, front and rear stabilizer bars, power antenna, dual illuminated visor vanity mirrors, leather-wrapped steering wheel, driver's seat height and lumbar support adjusters.

LSi (in addition to or instead of LS equipment): Leather upholstery and trim, CD player.

SPORT & TOURING (in addition to or instead of L equipment): Alloy wheels, power antenna, power 4-wheel anti-lock disc brakes, front and rear stabilizer bars, front air dam, 2.2 liter 4 cylinder turbo engine, sport suspension, hood scoop, analog gauges, leather-wrapped steering wheel, 195/60HR15 all-season tires, rear spoiler (Sedan), sport seats, power moonroof, suede upholstery.

Accessories

—	**Metallic Paint**..	100	120

LOYALE

RDC	5-Dr AWD Wagon (5-spd)	12046	13553
Destination Charge:	....	445	445

Standard Equipment

LOYALE: 1.8 liter SOHC EFI 4 cylinder engine, 5-speed manual transmission, air conditioning, center console, tilt steering column, tinted glass, intermittent windshield washers/wipers, rear window wiper/washer, electric rear window defroster, cargo cover, bodyside moldings, power door locks, tachometer, remote fuel filler door release, dual power mirrors, RH visor vanity mirror, power front disc/rear drum brakes, cloth reclining front bucket seats, 60/40 split fold-down rear seat, front stabilizer bar, gauges (temp, volts, oil pressure), luxury wheel covers, power windows w/driver express-down feature, AM/FM ETR stereo radio, power rack and pinion steering, 165/70SR13 SBR all-season tires, MacPherson strut front suspension.

Accessories

—	**Automatic Transmission — 3-speed**	488	550
—	**Metallic Paint**..	100	120

SUZUKI

SUZUKI

SAMURAI

JMB529R JL 2-Dr 2WD Soft Top (5 spd)	8711	9469
Destination Charge:	330	330

Standard Equipment

SAMURAI: 1.3 liter 4 cylinder in-line SOHC engine, throttle body fuel injection, 5-speed manual overdrive transmission, tinted glass, P205/70R15 all-season steel belted radial tires, 15 x 5.5JJ styled steel wheels, manual locking hubs, full-size spare tire, spare tire carrier, recirculating ball steering, power front disc/rear drum brakes, dual sport outside mirrors, front suspension (rigid axle with leaf springs and stabilizer bar), rear suspension (rigid axle with leaf springs), mud guards, windshield wipers with intermittent feature, carpeting, reclining bucket seats, trip odometer, fuel tank skid plate.

NOTE: Suzuki accessories are dealer installed. Contact a Suzuki dealer for accessory availability.

SUZUKI

SIDEKICK

Code	Description	Dealer	List
FCE623R	JS 2-Dr 2WD Soft Top (5-spd)	10762	11449
FCE624R	JS 2-Dr 2WD Soft Top (5-spd) (CA & NY)	11043	11749
FCE653R	JS 2-Dr 2WD Soft Top (auto)	11326	12049
FCE654R	JS 2-Dr 2WD Soft Top (auto) (CA & NY)	11608	12349
LTL663R	JS 4-Dr 2WD Hard Top (5-spd)	11693	12849
FAE623R	JX 2-Dr 4WD Soft Top (5-spd)	11821	12849
FAE624R	JX 2-Dr 4WD Soft Top (5-spd) (CA & NY)	12097	13149
FAE653R	JX 2-Dr 4WD Soft Top (auto)	12373	13449
FAE654R	JX 2-Dr 4WD Soft Top (auto) (CA & NY)	12649	13749
LPL663R	JX 4-Dr 4WD Hard Top (5-spd)	12531	14079
LPL693R	JX 4-Dr 4WD Hard Top (auto)	13385	15039
LPL665R	JLX 4-Dr 4WD Hard Top (5-spd)	13732	15429
LPL695R	JLX 4-Dr 4WD Hard Top (auto)	14568	16369
Destination Charge: Sidekick 2-Dr		330	330
Sidekick 4-Dr		350	350

Standard Equipment

SIDEKICK - 2 DOOR: 1.6 liter 4 cylinder in-line EFI SOHC engine (16-valve MFI engine standard on certain models - see model listing), 5-speed manual overdrive transmission or 3-speed automatic transmission, tinted glass, power front disc brakes/rear drum brakes with anti-lock, tilt steering wheel, recirculating ball steering (power steering on JX), P195/75R15 all-season steel belted radial tires (JS), P205/75R15 all-season steel belted radial tires (JX), full-size spare tire, spare tire carrier, automatic free-wheeling front hubs (JX), dual outside mirrors (power on JX), stripes, windshield wipers with intermittent feature, cloth reclining sport bucket seats, split folding rear seat, alarm system, tachometer (JX), 15 x 5.5JJ styled steel wheels, console, front suspension (MacPherson strut, separate coil springs, stabilizer bar), rear suspension (rigid axle with lower trailing arm, upper A shape arm, coil springs), carpeting.

SIDEKICK - 4 DOOR: 1.6 liter 4 cylinder 16-valve MFI SOHC engine, 5-speed manual overdrive transmission or 4-speed automatic transmission with overdrive, tinted glass, tilt steering wheel, speed control (JLX), console, alarm system, power steering delete, dual power outside mirrors, windshield wipers with intermittent feature, rear window defroster, carpeting, bodyside molding, cloth reclining sport bucket seats, split folding rear seat, spare tire carrier, (locking case on JLX), map light (JLX), power front disc brakes/rear drum brakes (anti-lock feature on JS), ET AM/FM stereo radio with cassette, P195/75R15 all-season steel belted radial tires (JS), P205/75R15 all-season steel belted radial tires (JX, JLX), full-size spare tire, front suspension (MacPherson strut, separate coil springs, stabilizer bar), rear suspension (rigid axle with lower trailing arm, upper A shape arm, coil springs), automatic free-wheeling hubs (JX, JLX), power windows (JLX), power door locks (JLX), rear window wiper/washer (JLX), chrome wheels (JLX), remote fuel filler door release (JLX).

NOTE: *Suzuki accessories are dealer installed. Contact a Suzuki dealer for accessory availability.*

SWIFT

CODE	DESCRIPTION	DEALER	LIST
HES532R	GA 3-Dr Hatchback (5-spd)	6945	7549
HES552R	GA 3-Dr Hatchback (auto)	7497	8149
SEF532R	GA 4-Dr Sedan (5-spd)	7847	8529
SEF552R	GA 4-Dr Sedan (auto)	8454	9189
SEF534R	GS 4-Dr Sedan (5-spd)	9027	10029
SEF554R	GS 4-Dr Sedan (auto)	9593	10659
HES574R	GT 3-Dr Hatchback (5-spd)	9027	10029
Destination Charge:		315	315

Standard Equipment

SWIFT - GA: Tinted glass, 5-speed manual transmission, 1.3 liter 4 cylinder SOHC EFI engine, trip odometer (Sedan), rear window defroster, power front disc/rear drum brakes, full wheel covers, trunk light (Sedan), P155/70R13 SBR all-season BW tires, carpeting, intermittent windshield washers/wipers, cloth reclining front bucket seats, folding rear seat (split fold-down on Sedan), dual foldaway OS mirrors.

GS (in addition to or instead of GA equip): Pwr steering, dual pwr mirrors, tachometer, remote fuel filler dr release, remote decklid release, AM/FM ETR stereo radio w/cass, four spkrs, map pockets, digital clock.

GT (in addition to or instead of GA equipment): Power 4-wheel disc brakes, 1.3 liter 16-valve DOHC EFI engine, halogen fog lights, P175/60R14 SBR all-season BW tires, sport wheel covers, dual power mirrors, front air dam, rear spoiler, side skirts, tachometer, rear window wiper/washer, map pockets, dual exhaust, color-keyed sport bumpers, bodyside stripe, rear mud guards, AM/FM ETR stereo radio with cassette and four speakers, sport seats, digital clock, remote fuel filler door/rear hatch release.

NOTE: *Suzuki accessories are dealer installed. Contact a Suzuki dealer for accessory availability.*

CAMRY

Code	Description	Dealer	List
2501	DX 4 Cyl 2-Dr Coupe (5-spd)	13645	16148
2502	DX 4 Cyl 2-Dr Coupe (auto)	14321	16948
2504	LE 4 Cyl 2-Dr Coupe (auto)	16003	18938
2508	LE V6 2-Dr Coupe (auto)	17929	21218
2506	SE V6 2-Dr Coupe (auto)	18791	22238
2521	DX 4 Cyl 4-Dr Sedan (5-spd)	13890	16438
2522	DX 4 Cyl 4-Dr Sedan (auto)	14566	17238
2532	LE 4 Cyl 4-Dr Sedan (auto)	16248	19228
2534	LE V6 4-Dr Sedan (auto)	18174	21508
2540	XLE 4 Cyl 4-Dr Sedan (auto)	17857	21258
2544	XLE V6 4-Dr Sedan (auto)	19806	23578
2546	SE V6 4-Dr Sedan (auto)	19036	22528
2590	DX 4 Cyl 5-Dr Wagon (auto)	15758	18648
2594	LE 4 Cyl 5-Dr Wagon (auto)	17422	20618
2596	LE V6 5-Dr Wagon (auto)	19366	22918
	Destination Charge: approximate	400	400

Standard Equipment

CAMRY - DX: Front and rear stabilizer bars, tachometer, driver and front passenger airbags, digital clock, 2.2L 4 cylinder EFI 16-valve engine, full wheel covers, front door map pockets, color-keyed bodyside moldings, tilt steering column, color-keyed bumpers, retractable assist grips, trip odometer, child-safety rear door locks (except Coupe), remote decklid release (except Wagon), full carpeting (includes trunk), diagnostic warning lights, AM/FM ETR stereo radio w/4 speakers (Wagon - 6 speakers), tinted glass, cloth upholstery, dome & trunk lights (Coupe & Sedan), cargo area lights (Wagon), rear seat center armrest, reclining front bucket seats, 60/40 split fold-down rear seat, power front disc/rear drum brakes, center console w/storage, dual black manual remote mirrors, fixed-intermittent wipers, dual rear window wipers (Wagon), cargo area cover (Wagon), variable-assist power steering, door trim panels w/cloth inserts, 195/70HR14 SBR all-season BW tires, electric rear window defroster w/timer, remote fuel-filler door release, halogen headlights w/automatic shut-off.

CODE	DESCRIPTION	DEALER	LIST

LE (in addition to or instead of DX equipment): Power antenna, cloth headliner, dual color-keyed power mirrors, cruise control, dual exhaust system (V6 Models), reclining front bucket seats w/6-way driver's seat adjuster, air conditioning, power windows w/driver's side express down, power door locks, deluxe AM/FM ETR stereo radio w/cassette and 4 speakers (Wagon - 6 speakers), power 4-wheel disc brakes (V6), 205/65HR15 tires (V6), retained accessory power, 3.0L V6 EFI 24-valve engine (V6).

XLE (in addition to or instead of LE V6 SEDAN equipment): Map light, alum alloy wheels, pwr tilt/slide moonroof w/sunshade, upgraded XLE cloth upholstery, variable intermittent wipers, illum entry sys w/ automatic fade-out, reclining front bucket seats w/7-way pwr driver seat, dual illum visor vanity mirrors.

SE (in addition to or instead of DX equipment): Power door locks, power antenna, cruise control, blackout exterior trim, sport-tuned suspension, quick-ratio power steering, reclining front bucket seats w/6-way driver seat adjuster, sport aluminum alloy wheels, dual black power mirrors, 3.0L V6 EFI 24-valve engine, power windows, leather-wrapped steering wheel, deluxe AM/FM ETR stereo radio w/cassette and 4 speakers, air conditioning, chrome-tipped tailpipes, power 4-wheel disc brakes, color-keyed rear spoiler, 205/65VR15 SBR BW tires.

Accessories

CODE	DESCRIPTION	DEALER	LIST
MG	**Black Mud Guards**	40	50
AW	**Aluminum Wheels** — LE 4 cyl	320	400
	LE V6	336	420
LS	**Leather Trim Pkg** — SE Sedan	780	975
	incls adjustable leather headrests, leather seats, leather door trim		
LP	**Leather Trim Pkg** — LE Coupe	824	1030
	incls leather door trim, adjustable leather headrests, power driver seat, leather seats, leather-wrapped parking brake lever (4 cyl), leather-wrapped steering wheel		
LA	**Leather Trim Pkg** — XLE	824	1030
	incls leather door trim, adjustable leather headrests, leather seats, leather-wrapped parking brake lever (4 cyl), leather-wrapped steering wheel		
LA	**Leather Trim Pkg** — SE Coupe	780	975
	incls leather door trim, adjustable leather headrests, leather seats		
PE	**Power Seat Pkg** — LE Coupe	272	340
AC	**Air Conditioning** — DX	780	975
PL	**Power Door Locks** — DX Coupe	176	220
	DX Sedan & Wagon	208	260
TH	**Rear-Facing Third Seat** — 4 cyl Wagon	375	465
	incls rear disc brakes, 14" temporary spare tire, cargo cover		
TH	**Rear-Facing Third Seat** — V6 Wagon	252	315
	incls cargo cover, 15" temporary spare tire		
TB	**Rear-Facing Third Seat w/Anti-Lock Brakes** — 4 cyl Wagon	1154	1415
	incls anti-lock disc brakes, cargo cover, rear-facing third seat, 14" temporary spare tire, rear disc brakes		
TB	**Rear-Facing Third Seat w/Anti-Lock Brakes** — V6 Wagon	1031	1265
	incls anti-lock disc brakes, rear-facing third seat, cargo cover, 15" temporary spare tire		
SR	**Power Glass Moonroof** — tilt/slide - LE & SE	760	950
	incls map light, sunshade		
CL	**Cruise Control** — DX	212	265
EX	**Deluxe AM/FM ETR Radio w/Cassette** — DX	127	170
	incls 4 speakers		

CODE	DESCRIPTION	DEALER	LIST
CE	**Premium AM/FM ETR Radio w/Cassette** — except DX	304	405
	incls 6 speakers, power antenna w/diversity reception, programmable equalization		
DC	**Premium 3-In-1 Combo Radio** — LE Coupe, SE, XLE	904	1205
	incls 6 speakers, power antenna w/diversity reception, programmable equalization, AM/FM ETR stereo radio w/compact disc and cassette		
AB	**Anti-Lock Brakes** — V6 Models	779	950
	4 cyl Models	902	1100
	incls rear disc brakes		

CELICA

2165	ST 2-Dr Coupe (5-spd)	13824	16168
2162	ST 2-Dr Coupe (auto)	14508	16968
2167	ST 3-Dr Liftback (5-spd)	14114	16508
2166	ST 3-Dr Liftback (auto)	14798	17308
2175	GT 2-Dr Coupe (5-spd)	15664	18428
2172	GT 2-Dr Coupe (auto)	16344	19228
2195	GT 3-Dr Liftback (5-spd)	16063	18898
2192	GT 3-Dr Liftback (auto)	16743	19698
	Destination Charge: approximate	400	400

Standard Equipment

CELICA ST: Trip odometer, cut-pile carpeting, tinted glass, map lights, full wheel covers, center console, tachometer, front and rear stabilizer bars, driver/front passenger airbags, electric rear window defroster, AM/FM ETR stereo radio w/4 speakers, color-keyed front and rear bumpers, automatic-off headlights, cloth upholstery, digital clock, remote fuel-filler door release, remote hatch release (Liftback), speed-sensitive power steering, 185/70R14 SBR all-season BW tires, power vented front disc/rear drum brakes, variable intermittent wipers, 1.8L 4 cylinder EFI 16-valve engine, reclining front bucket seats w/4-way adjustable driver's seat, 50/50 split fold-down rear seat w/lock, rear cargo cover (Liftback), remote deck-lid release (Coupe), dual color-keyed power mirrors, dual visor vanity mirrors, diagnostic warning lights.

GT (in addition to or instead of ST equipment): Power door locks, tilt steering column, power antenna, 2.2L 4 cylinder EFI 16-valve engine, engine oil cooler, power 4-wheel disc brakes, power windows w/driver side express down, deluxe AM/FM ETR radio w/cass/6 speakers, intermittent rear wiper (Liftback), electric rear window defroster w/timer, 205/55R15 SBR all-season BW tires, door trim panels w/cloth inserts.

Accessories

CODE	DESCRIPTION	DEALER	LIST
CL	**Cruise Control**	212	265
AC	**Air Conditioning**	780	975
PO	**Power Pkg** — ST	408	510
	incls power door locks, power windows w/driver side express down		
LA	**Leather Pkg** — GT	836	1045
	incls leather door trim panels, leather-trimmed seats, leather-wrapped steering wheel (Models with 5-spd man trans also include leather-wrapped shift knob [reqs cruise control])		
SX	**Fabric Sport Pkg** — GT Liftback	724	905
	incls aluminum wheels, cloth sport seats, front sport suspension, leather-wrapped steering wheel and shift knob. 205/55R15 summer tires (reqs cruise control)		
SL	**Leather Sport Pkg** — GT Liftback	1252	1565
	incls aluminum wheels, leather sport seats, front sport suspension, leather-wrapped steering wheel & shift knob, 205/55R15 summer tires (reqs cruise control)		
RW	**Rear Window Wiper** — intermittent - ST Liftback	127	155
SR	**Power Sunroof**	592	740
EX	**Deluxe AM/FM ETR Radio** — w/cassette - ST	127	170
	incls 4 speakers		
DC	**Premium 3-In-1 Combo Radio** — GT	903	1205
	incls compact disc, 8 speakers, AM/FM ETR stereo radio w/cassette, power antenna w/diversity system, programmable equalization		
CE	**Premium AM/FM ETR Radio** — w/cassette - GT	273	365
	incls power antenna w/diversity sys, 6 spkrs, programmable equalization		
CA	**California Emissions** — ST	NC	NC
	GT	130	153
TW	**Tilt Steering Column** — ST	133	155
AB	**Anti-Lock Brakes**	676	825
	incls larger temporary spare tire (ST) (reqs CL cruise control)		
AW	**Aluminum Wheels** — GT	336	420
	incls 205/55R15 all-season tires		
RF	**Rear Spoiler** — Liftback	300	375
	ST reqs RW rear intermittent wiper (std GT)		

COROLLA

CODE	DESCRIPTION	DEALER	LIST
1701	Standard 4-Dr Sedan (5-spd)	10607	11918
1700	Standard 4-Dr Sedan (auto)	11052	12418
1702	DX 4-Dr Sedan (5-spd)	11177	12998
1704	DX 4-Dr Sedan (auto)	11865	13798
1767	DX 5-Dr Wagon (5-spd)	12114	14088
1766	DX 5-Dr Wagon (auto)	12804	14888
1706	LE 4-Dr Wagon (auto)	13787	16088
	Destination Charge: approximate	400	400

Standard Equipment

COROLLA STANDARD SEDAN: Center console, trip odometer, color-keyed bumpers, driver and front passenger airbags, full wheel covers, rear stabilizer bar, dual black mirrors, tinted glass, 1.6L 4 cylinder EFI 16-valve engine, child safety rear door locks, diagnostic warning lights, automatic-off headlights, cut-pile carpeting, remote fuel-filler door release, cloth upholstery, power front disc/rear drum brakes, P175/65R14 SBR all-season BW tires, reclining front bucket seats, door trim panels w/cloth inserts.

DX SEDAN & WAGON (in addition to or instead of STANDARD SEDAN equipment): Digital clock, front and rear stabilizer bars, dual black remote mirrors, intermittent wipers, power steering, electric rear window defroster, power tailgate lock (Wagon), 60/40 split fold-down rear seat w/locks, cargo area cover (Wagon), P185/65R14 SBR all-season BW tires, remote decklid release (Sedan), wide black bodyside moldings, tachometer (manual transmission), 1.8L 4 cylinder EFI 16-valve engine.

LE SEDAN (in addition to or instead of DX SEDAN equipment): Power door locks, air conditioning, tachometer, variable intermittent wipers, color-keyed wide bodyside moldings, All-Weather Guard Pkg, tilt steering column, reclining front bucket seats w/4-way adjustable driver seat, deluxe AM/FM ETR stereo radio w/4 speakers, cruise control, power windows, dual color-keyed power mirrors.

Accessories

CODE	DESCRIPTION	DEALER	LIST
AB	**Anti-Lock Brakes**	676	825
CQ	**Convenience Pkg** — Standard	958	1180
	incls air conditioning, power steering		
RR	**Radio Prep Pkg** — (except LE)	75	100
	incls antenna, wiring harness, 2 speakers		

CODE	DESCRIPTION	DEALER	LIST
CK	**All Weather Guard Pkg**		
	Standard w/man trans	191	235
	Standard w/auto trans	199	245
	DX	55	65
	incls 4.5L washer tank, rear heater ducts, heavy-duty battery, heavy-duty windshield wiper motor, 1.4 kilowatt starter motor, luggage door trim, heavy-duty rear window defroster w/timer (std w/auto trans), heavy-duty booster ventilator and heater		
VP	**Value Pkg** — Standard	761	845
	incls power steering, air conditioning, carpeted floor mats		
VP	**Value Pkg** — DX Sedan	1454	1615
	incls tilt steering column, carpeted floor mats, air conditioning, AM/FM radio w/cassette & 4 speakers, Power Pkg		
VP	**Value Pkg** — LE	1476	1640
	incls aluminum wheels, anti-lock brakes, carpeted floor mats, AM/FM stereo radio w/cassette and 4 speakers, sunroof		
AC	**Air Conditioning** — (std LE)	736	920
PO	**Power Pkg** — DX	496	620
	incls power door locks, power windows w/driver side express down		
TA	**Tachometer** — DX w/man trans	52	65
MG	**Black Mud Guards** — DX	40	50
PS	**Power Steering** — Standard	222	260
CL	**Cruise Control** — DX	212	265
	incls variable intermittent wipers w/timer		
RW	**Rear Window Wiper** — Wagon	143	175
CA	**California Emissions**	130	153
AW	**Aluminum Wheels** — LE	320	400
	incls P185/65R14 SBR all-season tires, alloy wheels caps		
ER	**Deluxe AM/FM ETR Stereo Radio** — (std LE)	289	385
	incls 4 speakers		
EX	**Deluxe AM/FM ETR Stereo Radio** — w/cassette		
	LE	127	170
	Standard, DX	416	555
	incls 4 speakers		
SR	**Power Steel Sliding Sunroof** — DX & LE Sedans	464	580
DE	**Rear Window Defroster** — Standard	136	170
TW	**Tilt Steering Column** — DX	133	155

TOYOTA

LAND CRUISER

6154	5-Dr 4WD Wagon (auto)	28614	34268
	Destination Charge: approximate	400	400

Standard Equipment

LAND CRUISER: Tilt steering column, heavy-duty battery, cruise control, rear heater, cloth upholstery, rear mud guards, front and rear stabilizer bars, front and rear carpeting, fender flares, tow harness, styled steel wheels, door map pockets, tachometer, trip odometer, variable intermittent wipers, rear window intermittent wipers, heavy-duty cooling system, locking center differential, tinted glass, heavy-duty transmission oil cooler, air conditioning, digital clock, door trim panels w/cloth inserts, reclining front bucket seats, rear fold-down bench seats, power steering, ignition key light, electric rear window defroster, diagnostic warning lights, power diversity antenna system, center console w/storage, soft urethane steering wheel, power front disc/rear drum brakes, remote fuel-filler door release, power windows w/driver side express down, P275/70R16 SBR BW tires, full-size spare tire, 4.5L 6 cylinder EFI 24-valve engine, power door locks, child-safety rear door locks, 4-speed ECT automatic overdrive transmission, dual color-keyed power mirrors, right illuminated visor vanity mirror, premium AM/FM ETR stereo radio w/cassette, programmable equalizer, rear woofer and 9 speakers; transfer case/fuel tank skid plates.

Accessories

CODE	DESCRIPTION	DEALER	LIST
TX	**Two-Tone Pkg**	208	260
AW	**Aluminum Wheels**	412	515
	incls five P275/70R16 tires, five aluminum wheels		
FE	**50-State Emissions**	NC	NC
SR	**Power Moonroof**	920	1150
AB	**Anti-Lock Brakes**	968	1180
	incls full floating axle, transfer case, power anti-lock 4-wheel disc brakes		
LA	**Leather Trim Pkg**	3224	4030
	incls leather-wrapped steering wheel, leather seating, dual power front seats, leather headrests, leather-wrapped transmission lever and transfer		

case knob, door panels w/leather inserts, leather-covered center console, third rear seat (reqs premium 3-in-1 Combo Radio)

| DL | **Differential Locks** | 1568 | 1930 |

incls transfer case, anti-lock 4-wheel disc brakes, lockable front and rear differentials, full-floating axle

| TH | **Third Rear Seat** | 1116 | 1395 |

incls rear 3-point seatbelts, split-fold-down rear third seat, rear assist grips, rear quarter sliding windows, privacy glass, cloth headrests, child-safety locking rear hatch

| DC | **Premium 3-In-1 Combo Radio** | 600 | 800 |

incls compact disc player, 9 speakers, premium AM/FM ETR stereo radio w/cassette, programmable equalization

MR2 (1993)

NOTE: 1994 Toyota MR2 models were unavailable at time of publication.

3088	Base 2-Dr Coupe (5-spd)	16011	18948
3087	Base 2-Dr Coupe (auto)	16687	19748
3098	Base 2-Dr Coupe w/T-Bar Roof (5-spd)	17608	20838
3085	Turbo 2-Dr Coupe w/T-Bar Roof (5-spd)	20895	24728
	Destination Charge:	325	325

Standard Equipment

MR2 - BASE: 2.2 liter 4-cylinder EFI engine, tinted glass, carpeting, tilt steering column, intermittent wipers, cloth reclining sport bucket seats, tachometer, digital clock, color-keyed bumpers, driver side air bag, electric rear window defroster, dual color-keyed power mirrors, trip odometer, front and rear stabilizer bars, power 4-wheel disc brakes, AM/FM ETR stereo radio with cassette and six speakers, aluminum alloy wheels, remote decklid release, air conditioning (T-Bar models), retractable headlights, map pockets, bodyside moldings, remote fuel filler door release, 195/55R15 83V SBR BW tires (front), 225/50R15 91V SBR BW tires (rear).

TOYOTA

CODE	DESCRIPTION	DEALER	LIST

TURBO (in addition to or instead of BASE equipment): Power windows, cruise control, color-keyed rear spoiler, intermittent wipers, fog lights, color-keyed bodyside moldings, front air dam, power door locks, reclining sport bucket seats with 7-way adjustment, AM/FM ETR stereo radio with cassette, programmable equalization and eight speakers; center console, 2.0 liter 4-cylinder turbo-charged engine with intercooler, illuminated entry system, leather-wrapped steering wheel, courtesy lights, turbo boost gauge.

Accessories

CA	**California Emissions**	85	100
SR	**Power Sunroof** — NA w/T-Bar	304	380
PS	**Power Steering**	513	600
AC	**Air Conditioning** — NA w/T-Bar	732	915
CL	**Cruise Control** — std on Turbo	212	265
RF	**Rear Spoiler** — std on Turbo	240	300
PN	**Anti-Theft System**	132	165
AB	**Anti-Lock Brakes**	845	1030
LD	**Limited Slip Differential** — Turbo	320	400
CE	**AM/FM ETR Radio w/Cassette** — models w/o T-Bar	386	515
	models w/T-Bar	337	450
DC	**Premium 3-In-1 Combo** — models w/o T-Bar	911	1215
	models w/T-Bar	862	1150
	Turbo model	525	700

incls AM/FM ETR radio w/cassette and compact disc player, 8 speakers

PASEO

1525	2-Dr Coupe (5-spd)	10847	12468
1526	2-Dr Coupe (auto)	11543	13268
	Destination Charge: approximate	400	400

Standard Equipment

PASEO: Tinted glass, digital clock, front and rear stabilizer bars, trip odometer, diagnostic warning lights, dual black remote mirrors, tachometer, driver side airbag, electric rear window defroster, 1.5L 4 cylinder EFI 16-valve engine, variable intermittent wipers, AM/FM ETR stereo radio w/2 speakers, color-keyed front and rear bumpers, trunk light, full wheel covers, cloth upholstery, power steering, black bodyside moldings, remote fuel-filler door release, headlights-on warning buzzer, sport-tuned suspension, power front disc/rear drum brakes, full carpeting, door map pockets, rear quarter door map pockets, sport high-back front reclining bucket seats, fold-down rear seats, remote decklid release, door trim panels w/sport cloth inserts, 185/60R14 SBR all-season tires.

Accessories

AW	**Aluminum Wheels**..	320	400
	incls center wheel ornament, 4 aluminum alloy wheels, four 185/60R14 SBR all-season tires		
AC	**Air Conditioning**	720	900
EX	**Deluxe AM/FM ETR Radio - w/Cassette**	236	315
	incls 4 speakers		
CL	**Cruise Control**	212	265
RF	**Rear Spoiler**	300	375
AB	**Anti-Lock Brakes**..	676	825
CK	**All-Weather Guard Pkg**..	54	65
	incls heavy-duty rear defroster, heavy-duty battery, heavy-duty heater		
SR	**Pop-Up Moonroof — removable**	320	400
CA	**California Emissions**...	130	153

TOYOTA PICKUPS

2WD

8100	Standard 4 Cyl Reg Cab (5-spd)..	8836	9818
8113	DX 4 Cyl Reg Cab (5-spd)	9654	10908
8104	DX 4 Cyl Reg Cab (auto)...	10291	11628
8116	DX 4 Cyl Xtracab (5-spd)	10838	12458
8123	DX 4 Cyl Xtracab (auto)..	11465	13178
8154	DX V6 Xtracab (5-spd)..	11839	13608
8153	DX V6 Xtracab (auto)..	12674	14568

CODE	DESCRIPTION	DEALER	LIST
8157	SR5 V6 Xtracab (5-spd)	13302	15558
8158	SR5 V6 Xtracab (auto)	14123	16518
4WD			
8503	DX 4 Cyl Reg Cab (5-spd)	12642	14448
8504	DX 4 Cyl Reg Cab (auto)	13429	15348
8524	DX 4 Cyl Xtracab (5-spd)	13750	15988
8513	DX V6 Reg Cab (5-spd)	13736	15698
8554	DX V6 Xtracab (5-spd)	14807	17218
8553	DX V6 Xtracab (auto)	15865	18448
8557	SR5 V6 Xtracab (5-spd)	16180	19148
8558	SR5 V6 Xtracab (auto)	17211	20368
Destination Charge:		400	400

Standard Equipment

PICKUP - STANDARD REGULAR CAB: Vinyl upholstery, power front disc/rear drum brakes, cargo tie-down hooks, vinyl floor mats, intermittent wipers, tilt forward bench seat, double-wall cargo bed, one-touch tailgate release, styled steel wheels, 2.4L 4 cylinder EFI engine, left black mirror, front stabilizer bar, P195/75R14 SBR all-season BW tires, full-size spare tire.

DX REGULAR CAB (in addition to or instead of STANDARD REGULAR CAB equipment): Cloth upholstery, passenger assist grip, door trim panels w/cloth inserts, skid plates (4WD), P225/75R15 SBR mud & snow tires (4WD), tinted windshield, dual black mirrors (right convex), day/night rearview mirror, full wheel covers (2WD), cut-pile carpeting, manual locking front hubs (4WD), front and rear mud guards (4WD), 3.0L V6 EFI engine (V6), power steering (V6).

DX XTRACAB (in addition to or instead of DX REGULAR CAB equipment): Reclining front bucket seats, flip-out rear quarter windows, front and rear mud guards (4WD), rear mudguards (2WD), P205/75R14 SBR all-season BW tires (2WD), P225/75R15 SBR mud & snow tires (4WD), dual rear quarter storage.

SR5 (in addition to or instead of DX XTRACAB equipment): Digital clock, halogen headlights, lower door trim panel carpeting, trip odometer, tilt steering column, manual locking front hubs (4WD) deleted, 60/40 split fold-down front bench seats, dual forward-facing rear jump seats, right visor vanity mirror, door map pockets, tachometer, power front disc/anti-lock rear drum brakes, variable intermittent wipers, AM/FM ETR stereo radio w/2 speakers.

Accessories

PX	**Metallic Paint** — Standard	76	120
	Pickup except Standard	NC	NC
SX	**Sports Pkg** — SR5	248	310
	incls 7-way adjustable cloth sport seats, gray privacy glass on quarter windows, rear storage console (reqs Chrome Pkg or Value Pkg)		
VP	**Value Pkg** — (DX w/4 cyl engine)		
	2WD Reg Cab	373	414
	4WD Reg Cab	418	464
	Xtracab Models	481	534
	incls power steering, sliding rear window, chrome rear bumper, carpeted floor mats, exterior stripes, AM/FM ETR radio w/2 spkrs, Chrome Pkg (Xtracab also incls rear jump seats w/seatbelts, 60/40 split frt bench seat)		
VP	**Value Pkg** — (DX w/V6 engine)		
	4WD Reg Cab	202	244
	Xtracab Models	310	344
	incls chrome rear bumper, sliding rear window, carpeted floor mats,		

CODE	DESCRIPTION	DEALER	LIST
	AM/FM ETR stereo radio w/2 spkrs, Chrome Pkg, exterior stripes (Xtracab also includes rear jump seats w/seatbelts, 60/40 split front bench seat)		
VP	**Value Pkg** — SR5	365	405
	incls chrome rear bumper, sliding rear window, carpeted floor mats, deluxe AM/FM ETR stereo radio w/cassette & 4 speakers, Chrome Pkg		
BG	**Cloth Pkg** — 2WD Standard	84	105
	incls cut-pile carpeting, cloth bench seat, cigarette lighter, day/night rearview mirror		
PW	**Window Pkg**	160	200
	incls sliding rear window, front vent windows		
CK	**All Weather Guard Pkg**	55	65
	incls large windshield washer, heavy-duty starter, front and rear mud guards. (4 cylinder models also incl distributor & coil cover) (V6 models also incl heavy-duty battery) (Standard also incls heavy-duty heater)		
TP	**Touring Pkg** — (DX w/man trans)		
	2WD, 4WD V6 models	92	115
	4WD 4 cyl models	124	155
	incls trip odometer, halogen headlights, tachometer. (4WD DX w/4 cyl also incls front and rear gas shock absorbers)		
CM	**Comfort Pkg** — DX Xtracab	216	270
	incls rear jump seats w/seatbelts, 60/40 split fold-down front bench seat		
PO	**Power Pkg** — SR5	588	735
	incls power door locks, power antenna, power windows w/driver side express down, dual chrome power mirrors (req's Cruise Control Pkg)		
TO	**Towing Pkg** — (2WD w/auto trans)		
	w/4-cyl engine	40	50
	w/V6 engine	52	65
	incls larger radiator		
CH	**Chrome Pkg** — 2WD DX, 4WD	144	180
	2WD SR5	128	160
	incls chrome grille/front bumper/door handles/windshield moldings		
CL	**Cruise Control Pkg** — SR5	308	385
	incls intermittent windshield wipers w/timer, cruise control, leather-wrapped steering wheel		
CL	**Cruise Control Pkg** — DX except 2WD w/4 cyl engine	212	265
	incls 3-spoke urethane-wrapped steering wheel, cruise control, intermittent windshield wipers		
CA	**California Emissions**	130	153
PS	**Power Steering** — std V6 models	246	290
RA	**AM/FM ETR Radio** — std SR5	180	240
	incls 2 speakers		
EX	**Deluxe AM/FM ETR Radio** — w/cassette		
	Standard & DX Reg Cab	341	455
	DX Xtracab	416	555
	SR5 Xtracab	236	315
	incls 2 speakers (Reg Cab), 4 speakers (Xtracab)		
CE	**Premium AM/FM ETR Radio w/Cassette** — SR5	472	630
	incls 4 speakers		
SV	**Styled Steel Wheels** — DX Regular Cab 4WD V6	464	580
	incls five 10.5 R15 tires, wheel opening moldings, five silver steel wheels		
AW	**Aluminum Wheels** — 2WD SR5	612	765

CODE	DESCRIPTION	DEALER	LIST
	incls aluminum wheels w/center caps, chrome wheel opening moldings, P215/65R15 tires (reqs Value Pkg or Chrome Pkg)		
AW	**Aluminum Wheels** — 4WD SR5...	708	885
	incls aluminum wheels, 10.5 R15 tires, large wheel opening moldings (reqs Valve Pkg or Chrome Pkg)		
LK	**Anti-Lock Rear Brakes** — std SR5......................................	255	300
	models w/4 cyl engine req Power Steering or Value Pkg		
SR	**Pop-Up Moonroof** — SR5..	304	380
	4WD models req Value Pkg or Chrome Pkg		
VW	**Front Vent Windows**...	52	65
FD	**Four-Wheel On Demand System** — DX 4WD V6...............	178	210
TW	**Tilt Steering Column** — DX..	132	155
	incls intermittent wipers w/timer		

T100 PICKUPS

8713	DX Half-Ton 2WD (5-spd)..	12787	14698
8712	DX Half-Ton 2WD (auto)...	13570	15598
8813	DX Half-Ton 4WD (5-spd)..	15624	18168
8812	DX Half-Ton 4WD (auto)...	16398	19068
8717	DX One-Ton 2WD (5-spd)..	13431	15438
8716	DX One-Ton 2WD (auto)..	14214	16338
8715	SR5 Half-Ton 2WD (5-spd)..	14504	16768
8714	SR5 Half-Ton 2WD (auto)..	15283	17668
8815	SR5 Half-Ton 4WD (5-spd)..	17252	20178
8814	SR5 Half-Ton 4WD (auto)..	18022	21078
	Destination Charge:approximate...	400	400

Standard Equipment

T100 - DX: Power steering, driver side airbag, double-wall cargo bed, cloth upholstery, tinted glass, full carpeting, P215/75R15 all-season SBR tires (2WD Half-Ton), P235/75R15 mud & snow SBR tires (One-Ton & 4WD Half-Ton), front and rear mud guards, skid plates (4WD), styled steel wheels (4WD), digital clock, center armrest, cargo tie-down hooks, full wheel covers (2WD), door map pockets, front stabilizer

CODE	DESCRIPTION	DEALER	LIST

bar (heavy-duty on One-Ton), 3.0L V6 EFI engine, dual black mirrors (right convex), intermittent wipers, 3-passenger bench seat, power front disc/rear drum brakes (heavy-duty on One-Ton).

SR5 (in addition to or instead on DX equipment): Trip odometer, center armrest w/storage, chrome front bumper, 60/40 split bench seat, right visor vanity mirror, tachometer, chrome grille, variable intermittent wipers, tool storage and cover, power brakes w/anti-lock rear, overhead map lights, tilt steering column, sliding rear window, P235/75R15 SBR mud & snow tires, door trim panels w/cloth inserts, deluxe AM/FM ETR radio w/5 speakers.

Accessories

CODE	DESCRIPTION	DEALER	LIST
CQ	**Convenience Pkg** — DX	367	445
	incls sliding rear window, tilt steering column, oil pressure and voltmeter gauges, tachometer, variable intermittent wipers		
QL	**Convenience Pkg** — DX	595	730
	incls sliding rear window, tilt steering column, oil pressure and voltmeter gauges, tachometer, variable intermittent wipers, cruise control		
RR	**Radio Prep Pkg** — DX	37	50
	incls antenna, wiring harness		
CH	**Chrome Pkg** — DX..	120	150
	incls chrome grille, door handles and front bumper		
PO	**Power Pkg** — SR5	588	735
	incls power antenna, power door locks, power windows w/driver side express down, dual chrome power mirrors (reqs Cruise Control Pkg, VP Value Pkg or VK Value Pkg/Two-Tone)		
VP	**Value Pkg** — DX Half-Ton 2WD..	298	331
	incls Chrome Pkg, bodyside moldings, carpeted floor mats, chrome rear bumper, P235/75R15 tires		
VP	**Value Pkg** — DX One-Ton; DX Half-Ton 4WD....................	185	206
	incls Chrome Pkg, bodyside moldings, carpeted floor mats, chrome rear bumper		
VP	**Value Pkg** — SR5	1261	1401
	incls bodyside moldings, carpeted floor mats, chrome rear bumper, cruise control, Power Pkg, air conditioning, variable intermittent wipers, upgraded 5-speed shift knob (manual trans only), leather-wrapped steering wheel		
CL	**Cruise Control Pkg** — DX..	279	345
	incls 3-spoke urethane-wrapped steering wheel, upgraded 5-spd shift knob (man trans only), cruise control, variable intermittent wipers		
CL	**Cruise Control Pkg** — SR5..	288	360
	incls leather-wrapped steering wheel, upgraded 5-spd shift knob (man trans), variable intermittent wipers, cruise control		
HT	**Chrome Pkg/Two-Tone** — DX	384	480
	incls two-tone paint, Chrome Pkg		
VK	**Value Pkg/Two-Tone** — DX Half-Ton 2WD........................	505	561
	DX Half-Ton 4WD, DX One-Ton..	392	436
	SR5	1468	1631
	incls VP Value Pkg and two-tone paint; bodyside moldings deleted		
WR	**Sliding Rear Window** — DX 4WD	108	135
CA	**California Emissions**...	130	153
RA	**AM/FM ETR Radio** - DX..	180	240
	incls 2 speakers		
EX	Deluxe AM/FM ETR Radio w/Cassette — DX	461	615

CODE	DESCRIPTION	DEALER	LIST
	incls 3 speakers		
EX	Deluxe AM/FM ETR Radio w/Cassette — SR5	127	170
	incls 5 speakers		
CE	Premium AM/FM ETR Radio w/Cassette — SR5	394	525
	incls programmable equalization, 7 speakers		
DC	Premium 3-In-1 Combo Radio — SR5	994	1325
	incls 7 speakers, programmable equalization, premium AM/FM ETR stereo w/cassette, compact disc		
PX	**Metallic Paint**	NC	NC
TT	**Two-Tone Paint** — DX	320	400
	incls chrome front bumper		
TU	**Tire Upgrade** — DX Half-Ton	100	125
	incls P235/75R15 tires		
LK	**Rear Brakes** — anti-lock - DX	255	300
ST	**Styled Steel Wheels** — DX 4WD	212	265
	incls 31-10.5 tires, styled steel wheels		
AW	**Aluminum Wheels** — SR5 2WD	472	590
	incls chrome wheel opening moldings, aluminum wheels, P235/75R15 tires, aluminum wheel ornament		
AW	**Aluminum Wheels** — SR5 4WD	588	735
	incls chrome wheel opening moldings, aluminum wheels, 31-10.5 tires, aluminum wheel ornament		

PREVIA

		DEALER	LIST
5122	DX (auto)	18937	22148
5142	DX All-Trac (auto)	21580	25388
5132	LE (auto)	21928	25798
5152	LE All-Trac (auto)	24521	28848
	Destination Charge: approximate	400	400

CODE	DESCRIPTION	DEALER	LIST

Standard Equipment

PREVIA DX: Full wheel covers, front and rear assist grips, rear heater ducts, trip odometer, digital clock, diagnostic warning lights, front stabilizer bar, tilt steering column, sliding side door, engine oil auto-feeder, power front disc/rear drum brakes, power steering, cloth upholstery, driver and front passenger airbags, swing-out side windows, full carpeting (includes cargo area), door trim panels w/cloth inserts, P215/65R15 SBR all-season BW tires, full-size spare tire, electric rear window defroster, reclining front bucket seats, 2-passenger removable second row bench seat, 3-passenger split fold-down third-row bench seat, headlights with automatic off, dual manual remote mirrors, right visor vanity mirror, remote fuel-filler door release, glove box/ashtray lights, key-in-ignition warning chime, variable intermittent front wipers, fixed intermittent rear window wiper/washer, 2.4L 4 cylinder EFI 16-valve engine, protective lower bodyside cladding, 4-speed ECT automatic transmission, child-safety sliding side door locks, deluxe AM/FM ETR stereo radio w/6 speakers.

LE (in addition to or instead of DX equipment): Cruise control, power windows, dual air conditioning, power 4-wheel disc brakes, front seatback map pockets, deluxe AM/FM ETR stereo radio w/cassette and 6 speakers, adjustable front armrests, power door locks w/anti lockout feature, dual power mirrors, illuminated right visor vanity mirror.

Accessories

Code	Description	Dealer	List
AC	**Air Conditioning** — DX	1348	1685
PO	**Power Pkg** — DX	596	745
	incls power windows w/driver side express down, power door locks, dual power mirrors		
CC	**Seats** — captain's chairs - LE	632	790
CL	**Cruise Control** — DX	220	275
EX	**Deluxe AM/FM ETR Radio** — w/cassette - DX	127	170
	incls 6 speakers		
CE	**Premium AM/FM ETR Radio** — w/cassette - LE	326	435
	incls programmable equalization, 7 speakers (reqs privacy glass		
DC	**Premium 3-In-1 Combo Radio** — 956 1275		
	incls 9 speakers, programmable equalization, AM/FM ETR stereo radio w/cassette and compact disc, antenna w/diversity reception (reqs privacy glass)		
PN	**Security Pkg** — DX	756	945
	incls Power Pkg, anti-theft device		
PN	**Security Pkg** — LE	160	200
	incls anti-theft device		
CA	**California Emissions**	130	153
SR	**Dual Moonroofs** — LE 2WD	1240	1550
	incls rear power sliding moonroof, front pop-up moonroof, rear spoiler, sunshade		
AB	**Anti-Lock Power Brakes** — 4-wheel disc - DX	889	1100
	LE	779	950
	incls rear disc brakes (std on LE), anti-lock brakes (reqs cruise control)		
PG	**Privacy Glass** — LE	308	385
AW	**Aluminum Wheels** — LE	336	420
	incls P215/65R15 all-season tires, aluminum wheels		

TOYOTA

SUPRA

Code	Description	Dealer	List
2398	Base 2-Dr Liftback (5-spd)	29356	35800
2396	Base 2-Dr Liftback (auto)	30094	36700
2393	Base 2-Dr Liftback w/Sport Roof (5-spd)	30258	36900
2394	Base 2-Dr Liftback w/Sport Roof (auto)	30996	37800
2381	Turbo 2-Dr Liftback (6-spd)	35096	42800
2383	Turbo 2-Dr Liftback w/Sport Roof (6-spd)	35998	43900
2387	Turbo 2-Dr Liftback w/Sport Roof (auto)	35096	42800
	Destination Charge: approximate	400	400

Standard Equipment

SUPRA - BASE: Tachometer, front and rear stabilizer bars, aluminum alloy wheels, tinted glass, power door locks, power windows, driver and front passenger airbags, cargo area cover, front spoiler, cold kit, digital clock, front fog lights, digital trip odometer, diagnostic master warning lights, premium AM/FM ETR stereo w/cassette/6 speakers/theft deterrent system, power antenna w/diversity reception, front and rear color-keyed bumpers, leather-wrapped steering wheel, cruise control, tilt steering column, illuminated entry system w/automatic fade-out, halogen retractable headlights w/automatic-off system, dual color-keyed heated power mirrors, right visor vanity mirror, 3-way adjustable sport seats w/power slide and recline, driver's seat height adjustment, 2-way manual adjustable passenger seat, fold-down rear seat, automatic air conditioning, speed-sensitive power steering, anti-lock power 4-wheel disc brakes, heavy-duty electric rear window defroster w/timer, remote hatch release, variable intermittent wipers, 3.0L 6 cylinder EFI DOHC 24-valve engine, rear window intermittent wipers, remote fuel-filler door release, 225/50ZR16 SBR high-performance front tires, 245/50ZR16 SBR high-performance rear tires, full cut-pile carpeting (including cargo area), lights include door/luggage area/glove box/ignition, cloth upholstery.

TURBO (in addition to or instead of BASE equipment): Engine oil cooler, sport-tuned suspension, Torsen limited slip differential, 235/45ZR17 SBR high-performance front tires, 255/40ZR17 SBR high-performance rear tires, 3.0L 6 cylinder EFI 24-valve twin turbocharged engine w/intercooler, traction control system w/indicator light.

Accessories

Code	Description	Dealer	List
LD	**Limited Slip Differential** — Base	368	460

CODE	DESCRIPTION	DEALER	LIST
LA	**Leather Trim Pkg**	880	1100
	incls leather trimmed armrests and seats		
DC	**Premium Radio** — 3-in-1 combo	652	870
	incls AM/FM ETR stereo radio w/cassette, programmable equalization and logic control, compact disc, power antenna w/diversity system, 7 speakers (includes subwoofer)		
FE	**50-State Emissions** — Turbo	NC	NC
CA	**California Emissions** — Base	130	153
RF	**Rear Spoiler** — Turbo	336	420

TERCEL

1301	Standard 2-Dr Sedan (4-spd)	7958	8698
1315	DX 2-Dr Sedan (5-spd)	9133	10148
1316	DX 2-Dr Sedan (auto)	9583	10648
1325	DX 4-Dr Sedan (5-spd)	9223	10248
1326	DX 4-Dr Sedan (auto)	9673	10748
	Destination Charge: approximate	400	400

Standard Equipment

TERCEL - STANDARD: Rear stabilizer bar, diagnostic warning lights, driver side airbag, gray bumpers, left black mirror, full carpeting, vinyl upholstery, rear quarter area storage pockets, reclining highback front bucket seats, power front disc/rear drum brakes, 145/80R13 SBR BW tires, 1.5L 4 cylinder EFI 12-valve engine, warning chimes for seatbelt/door-ajar/headlights on/key-in-ignition, 4-spd manual transmission.

DX (in addition to or instead of STANDARD equipment): Dome light, tinted glass, trip odometer, dual black mirrors, full wheel covers (2-Dr), assist grips, child safety-rear door locks (4-Dr), 155/80SR13 SBR all-season tires, color-keyed bumpers, color-keyed grille, styled steel wheels w/black center caps, cloth upholstery, 5-spd manual transmission.

Accessories

AC	**Air Conditioning**	720	900

CODE	DESCRIPTION	DEALER	LIST
AK	**Appearance Pkg** — DX..	104	130
	incls bodyside moldings, color-keyed bumpers		
PS	**Power Steering** — DX...	222	260
CA	**California Emissions**...	130	153
VP	**Value Pkg** — DX..	1346	1495
	incls power steering, dual manual mirrors, air conditioning, AM/FM stereo radio w/cassette and 4 speakers, digital clock, remote fuel-filler door release, intermittent wipers, split fold-down rear seat, remote decklid release		
RA	**AM/FM ETR Stereo Radio**	180	240
	incls 2 speakers		
ER	**Deluxe AM/FM ETR Stereo Radio** — DX	289	385
	incls 4 speakers		
EX	**Deluxe AM/FM ETR Stereo Radio w/Cassette** — DX	416	555
	incls 4 speakers		
DE	**Rear Window Defroster**..	144	170
AB	**Anti-Lock Brakes** — including larger temporary spare tire........	676	825
CQ	**Convenience Pkg** — DX	264	330
	incls split fold-down rear seat, dual manual remote mirrors, remote decklid release, digital clock, intermittent wipers, remote fuel-filler door release		
CK	**All Weather Guard Pkg**..	201	235
	incls heavy-duty heater, heavy-duty electric rear window defroster, heavy-duty battery		

4RUNNER

8642	SR5 V6 2WD 4-Dr (auto)..	17769	21028
8657	SR5 4WD 4-Dr (5-spd)...	16998	19998
8665	SR5 V6 4WD 4-Dr (5-spd)...	18538	21938
8664	SR5 V6 4WD 4-Dr (auto)...	19425	22988
	Destination Charge: approximate...	400	400

Standard Equipment

4RUNNER SR5 4-CYLINDER: Power steering, passenger assist grips, cloth upholstery, tinted glass, power rear window, 2.4L 4 cylinder EFI engine, digital clock, tachometer, front center console w/storage, front and rear mud guards, trip odometer, cut-pile carpeting (including cargo area), front and rear stabilizer bars, rear window wiper/washer, remote fuel-filler door release, dual rear storage compartments, dual black outside mirrors, power front disc/rear drum brakes, P225/75R15 mud & snow SBR BW tires, full-size spare tire, styled-steel wheels, reclining front bucket seats, split fold-down rear bench seat, child-safety rear door locks, skid plates (suspension, fuel tank, transfer case).

SR5 V6 (in addition to or instead of SR4 4-CYLINDER equipment): Sport stripes, electric rear window defroster, transfer case skid plate deleted (2WD), AM/FM ETR stereo radio w/4 speakers, tilt steering column, 3.0L V6 EFI engine, variable intermittent front wipers, power front disc/rear anti-lock drum brakes.

Accessories

CODE	DESCRIPTION	DEALER	LIST
BR	**Bronze Tinted Glass** — V6	128	160
TW	**Tilt Steering Column** — 4-Cylinder	183	215
AC	**Air Conditioning**	764	955
VP	**Value Pkg 1** — 4-Cylinder models	1792	1991
	incls cruise control, Chrome Pkg, intermittent wipers w/timer, air conditioning, carpeted floor mats, leather-wrapped steering wheel, Power Pkg, deluxe AM/FM radio w/cassette & 4 speakers		
VP	**Value Pkg 1** — V6 models	1292	1436
	incls Chrome Pkg, cruise control, air conditioning, carpeted floor mats, intermittent wipers w/timer, Power Pkg		
VF	**Value Pkg 2** — V6 4WD models	2053	2281
	incls Value Pkg 1, chrome bumper (accommodating wider tire), alum whls		
VQ	**Value Pkg 3** — V6 4WD models	3227	3586
	incls Value Pkg 2, Leather Trim Pkg (reqs bronze tinted glass)		
CH	**Chrome Pkg**	196	245
	incls chrome windshield molding/grille/front & rear bumpers/outside door handles (4-Cyl models also include small chrome wheel opening moldings)		
SX	**Sports Pkg** — gray glass	360	450
	incls adjustable fore/aft sport headrests, cloth front sport seats, rr window gray privacy glass (req's Chrome Pkg or Value Pkg or aluminum wheels)		
SY	**Sports Pkg** — bronze glass - V6 models	232	290
	incls adjustable fore/aft sport headrests, cloth front sport seats, rr window bronze privacy glass (reqs Chrome Pkg, bronze tinted glass or Value Pkg)		
LA	**Leather Trim Pkg** — V6 4WD models	1344	1680
	incls leather-wrapped steering wheels, leather-trimmed sport seats, cruise control, rear window privacy glass, door trim panels w/leather inserts, 4-way adjustable headrests, intermittent wipers w/timer (reqs Power Pkg)		
CK	**All Weather Guard Pkg** — 4-Cylinder models	191	235
	V6 models	55	65
	incls rear window defroster (std V6), heavy-duty battery (V6 models), heavy-duty specifications for windshield wiper motor/starter motor/distributor cover		
PO	**Power Pkg**	632	790
	incls power door locks, power windows w/driver side express down, dual chrome power mirrors (reqs cruise control and Chrome Pkg or aluminum wheels; or cruise control or Leather Trim Pkg)		

CODE	DESCRIPTION	DEALER	LIST
LK	**Anti-Lock Rear Brakes** — 4-cylinder	255	300
AB	**4-Wheel Anti-Lock Brakes** — V6	541	660
CA	**California Emissions**	130	153
PX	**Metallic Paint**	NC	NC
AW	**Aluminum Wheels** — V6 4WD	872	1090
	incls center wheel cap ornament, Chrome Pkg, large wheel opening arch moldings, five 31-10.5 R15 tires		
AY	**Aluminum Wheels** — w/P225 tires - V6	376	470
	incls center wheel cap ornament, P225/75R15 tires, small wheel opening moldings (reqs Value Pkg 1 or Chrome Pkg)		
CL	**Cruise Control**	300	375
	incls intermittent wipers w/timer, cruise control, headlights-on warning buzzer (V6 models), urethane-wrapped steering wheel (4-Cylinder models req tilt steering column, Power Pkg)		
EX	**Deluxe AM/FM ETR Radio w/Cassette** — 4-Cylinder	416	555
	incls 4 speakers		
EX	**Deluxe AM/FM ETR Radio w/Cassette** — V6	207	270
	incls power antenna, 4 speakers		
CE	**Premium AM/FM ETR Radio w/Cassette** — V6	506	675
	incls power antenna w/diversity reception, 6 speakers		
DC	**Premium 3-In-1 Combo Radio** — V6	1106	1475
	incls 6 speakers, AM/FM ETR stereo radio w/cassette and compact disc, power antenna w/diversity reception		
RH	**Rear Heater**	128	160
	incls large rear console box (req's All-Weather Guard Pkg)		
SR	**Power Moonroof** — V6	648	810

VOLKSWAGEN

GOLF III

		DEALER	LIST
1H13P4	GL 4-Dr Hatchback (5-spd)	10953	11900
	Destination Charge:	390	390

Standard Equipment

GOLF III: 2.0L 4 cylinder 115HP engine, manual 5-speed transmission, power rack and pinion steering, independent coil spring strut front suspension, independent track correcting torsion beam axle rear suspension, power assist 4-wheel disc front vented brakes, 14" all season tires, space saver spare tire, steel wheels, anti-theft vehicle alarm system w/warning LED, illuminated front ashtray, electric rear window defroster, molded door trim w/cloth inserts and integrated armrests, front carpeted floor mats, tinted glass, RF assist handles and rear w/coat hooks, instrumentation displays; speedometer, odometer trip odometer, tachometer, fuel and temperature gauges, digital clock, service interval indicator, cigarette lighter, interior light, luggage compartment light, child safety locks on rear doors (4 door), power locking system including trunk/fuel filler, passenger side visor vanity mirror, 8 speaker sound system prep, driver and passenger airbag (SRS), fully reclining front seats w/adjustable height and angle headrests, driver's seat height adjustment, folding rear seat, 4-spoke padded steering wheel, front door storage pockets w/beverage holder, rear door storage pockets, front seatback magazine/storage pockets, center console w/front and center storage bins, front illuminated ashtray, covered luggage compartment, power remote hatch/trunk release, velour seat trim, 2-speed windshield wipers w/intermittent wipe, rear wiper w/intermittent feature, chrome telescoping antenna, body color bumpers w/black lower section, factory 26-step paint/corrosion protection, tinted glass, body color grille, dual horns, Eurostyle oval halogen headlights, driver/pass side remote mirrors (convex-passenger side), black side molding, body color license surround panel (rear), small black front spoiler, black rear spoiler w/integrated stoplamp), 14" full wheelcover.

Accessories

Code	Description	DEALER	LIST
—	Automatic Transmission — 4-speed	856	875
9AB	Air Conditioning	742	850
B0W	California/New York Emissions	98	100
3FE	Power Sunroof	502	575
—	Clearcoat Metallic Paint	153	175
8YS	AM/FM ETR Stereo Radio w/Cassette	291	350

CODE	DESCRIPTION	DEALER	LIST

JETTA III

		DEALER	LIST
1H23P4 GL 4-Dr Sedan (5-spd)...		11866	13125
Destination Charge:..		435	435

Standard Equipment

JETTA III GL: 2.0L 4 cylinder 115HP 5-speed engine, power rack-and-pinion steering, power assisted vented front 4-wheel disc brakes, heavy duty cooling, dual horns, anti-theft vehicle alarm system w/warning LED, space saver spare tire, tinted glass, assist handles, electric rear window defroster, locking and illuminated glove box, remote trunk release in glovebox, instrumentation includes: speedometer, odometer, trip odometer, tachometer, fuel and temperature gauges, digital clock, warning lights, service interval indicator; interior light with time delay, automatic safety belt system w/supplemental manual front lap belts, 3-point outboard and center lap rear seatbelts, fully reclining front seats with adjustable height/angle headrest, rear seat headrests, velour seat trim, molded door trim with cloth inserts and integrated armrests, driver's seat height adjustment, lockable one-piece folding rear seatback, front/rear door storage pockets, driver and passenger illuminated vanity mirrors, height adjustable steering column, 4-spoke padded steering wheel, center console w/storage compartment, illuminated front and rear ashtrays, cigarette lighter, power locking system includes trunk/fuel filler, 8-speaker sound system prep, full carpeting, carpeted luggage compartment, luggage compartment light, child safety locks on rear doors (4 Dr), 2-speed variable intermittent windshield wipers, driver and passenger side remote mirrors (convex-passenger), front carpeted floor mats, body color bumpers, small black front spoiler, black body side molding, bright telescoping antenna, full 14" wheelcover, black license plate surround panel, black mirror housings, body color 2-bar grille.

Accessories

		DEALER	LIST
—	**Automatic Transmission** — 4-speed	856	875
9AB	**Air Conditioning**	742	850
—	**Clearcoat Metallic Paint**	153	175
3FE	**Power Sunroof**	502	575
B0W	**California/New York Emissions**	98	100
8YS	**AM/FM ETR Stereo Radio w/Cassette**	291	350

VOLKSWAGEN

850

Code	Description	Dealer	List
854GTO	850 Level I 4-Dr Sedan (5-spd)	22100	24300
854GTA	850 Level I 4-Dr Sedan (auto)	23000	25200
854GTOS	850 Level II 4-Dr Sedan (5-spd)	23495	26695
854GTAS	850 Level II 4-Dr Sedan (auto)	24395	27595
855GTOS	850 Level II 5-Dr Wagon (5-spd)	24495	27695
855GTAS	850 Level II 5-Dr Wagon (auto)	25395	28595
854T	850 Turbo 4-Dr Sedan (auto)	25785	29985
855T	850 Turbo 5-Dr Wagon (auto)	26785	30985
Destination Charge:		425	425

Standard Equipment

850 LEVEL I: Cruise control, power windows, tilt/telescopic steering column, driver and front passenger air bags, front and rear floor mats, power antenna, AM/FM stereo radio w/cassette/8 speakers/anti-theft device, front and rear stabilizer bars, velour upholstery, air conditioning, power door locks with central locking system, on-call road assistance, power steering, power anti-lock 4-wheel disc brakes, 195/60R15 SBR Michelin tires, dual heated power mirrors, front bucket seats w/8-way adjustable driver seat, 2.4L 5 cylinder EFI 20-valve engine.

850 LEVEL II (also has in addition to or instead of 850 LEVEL I equipment): Security system, power glass sunroof, power antenna deleted (Wagon), retractable cargo net (Wagon), 24-spoke alloy wheels, 8-way power driver seat with 3-position memory, 60/40 split fold-down rear seat with trunk pass through (Wagon), front passenger fold-down seat (Wagon), rear stabilizer bar deleted (Wagon), remote keyless entry system, rear window wiper/washer (Wagon).

850 TURBO (also has in addition to or instead of 850 LEVEL II equipment): Trip computer, 5-spoke alloy wheels, automatic air conditioning w/dual controls, outside temperature display, 205/50R16 SBR high performance tires, split leather upholstery, 2.3L 5 cylinder EFI 20 valve turbocharged engine w/intercooler, leather-wrapped steering wheel, burled wood instrument panel trim.

Accessories

Code	Description	Dealer	List
000200	**Decklid Spoiler** — 850 Sedans	260	325
002000	**Alloy Wheels** — 6-spoke - 850 Level I	320	400

VOLVO

CODE	DESCRIPTION	DEALER	LIST
	850 Level II...	NC	NC
004000	**Alloy Wheels** — 24-spoke - 850 Level I................................	320	400
000005	**Nordic Pkg**	360	450
	incls outside temperature gauge, heated front seats, headlight wipers/washers		
—	**Leather Upholstery**	795	995
500000	**Sport Suspension** — 850 Sedans....................................	120	150
500000	**Self-Leveling Rear Suspension** — 850 Wagons	320	400
—	**Metallic Paint**..	NC	NC
400000	**Automatic Air Conditioning** — 850 Level II.........................	280	350
010000	**Traction Control System**...	305	385
003000	**Instrument Panel Wood Trim** — 850 Series except Level I.........	480	600
020000	**Trip Computer** — 850 Level II..	220	275
—	**California Emissions**...	NC	NC
000040	**Power Driver Seat** — 850 Level I...................................	395	495
	incls memory		
000050	**Power Passenger Seat** — 850 Series except Level I...............	395	495
	incls memory		
000003	**Heated Rear Seat** — 850 Wagons	320	400

940/960

944	940 Level I 4-Dr Sedan (auto)...................................	21700	22900
945	940 Level I 5-Dr Wagon (auto)..................................	22800	24000
944TG	940 Level II 4-Dr Sedan (auto)...............................	24095	26295
945TG	940 Level II 5-Dr Wagon (auto)..............................	25095	27295
964NS	960 Level I 4-Dr Sedan (auto)...............................	26750	28950
964	960 Level II 4-Dr Sedan w/Sunroof (auto)	29250	33450
964MR	960 Level II 4-Dr Sedan w/Moonroof (auto)	29750	33950
965	960 Level II 5-Dr Wagon w/Sunroof (auto)	30250	34450
965MR	965 Level II 5-Dr Wagon w/Moonroof (auto).................	30750	34950
Destination Charge:...		425	425

Standard Equipment

940 LEVEL I: front and rear stabilizer bars, driver and front passenger airbags, power windows, cruise control, dual power mirrors, power steering, on-call road assistance, air conditioning, 2.3L 4 cylinder EFI engine, tricot upholstery, 185/65R15 SBR all-season tires, floor mats, automatic locking differential, power antenna (Sedan), full wheel covers, power door locks with central locking system, 4-speed automatic transmission, reclining front bucket seats, anti-lock power 4-wheel disc brakes, AM/FM stereo radio w/cassette/6 speakers/anti-theft device.

940 LEVEL II (also has in addition to or instead of 940 LEVEL I equipment): Leather upholstery, front foglights, power sliding sunroof, 10-spoke alloy wheels, 2.3L 4 cylinder EFI turbocharged engine w/intercooler, 195/65R15 SBR all-season tires, AM/FM stereo radio cassette/6 speakers/anti-theft device (CD compatible), reclining front bucket seats with 8-way power driver seat with 3-position memory.

960 LEVEL I (also has in addition to or instead of 940 LEVEL I equipment): Tilt steering column, full wheel covers deleted, front foglights, automatic air conditioning, 195/65VR15 SBR all-season tires, AM/FM stereo with cassette/6 speakers/anti-theft device (CD compatible), 4-speed ECT automatic transmission, 2.9L 6 cylinder EFI engine, velour upholstery, reclining front bucket seats w/8-way power driver seat w/3-position memory.

960 LEVEL II (also has in addition to or instead of 960 LEVEL I equipment): Leather upholstery, burled-elm instrument panel trim, leather-wrapped steering wheel, 15-spoke alloy wheels, dual 8-way power reclining front bucket seats w/driver seat 3-position memory.

Accessories

CODE	DESCRIPTION	DEALER	LIST
PS	**Power Sunroof** — 940 Level I	635	980
001000	**20-Spoke 15" Alloy Wheels** — Level I	320	495
	960 Level II	NC	NC
004000	**10-Spoke 15" Alloy Wheels** — Level I	320	495
	960 Level II	NC	NC
002000	**5-Spoke 16" Alloy Wheels** — 940 Level II	240	370
—	**Leather Upholstery** — Level I	795	1225
—	**California Emissions**	NC	NC
100000	**Nordic Pkg**	280	435
	incls dual heated mirrors, outside temperature gauge, heated front seats		
000400	**8-Way Power Driver Seat** — 940 Level I	395	610
	incls 3-position memory		
000004	**Dual 8-Way Power Front Seat** — 940 Level I	720	1110
	incls driver seat 3-position memory		
000004	**8-Way Power Passenger** — 940 Level II	325	500
	960 Level I	325	500
—	**Metallic Paint**	NC	NC
000002	**Roof Rails** — Wagons	195	300

Edmund's wants your
success stories!

Edmund's wants to publish your own personal accounts of how you were able to use the information in our Consumer Price Guides to save money when purchasing/leasing a vehicle. Tell us what vehicle and model you acquired, how you negotiated with the dealer/seller, what you paid, and how much you saved by taking advantage of Edmund's price information. Write us your story in as few words as possible, and if you want, include a photograph of yourself standing in front of your new vehicle.

Success stories, to be published in future editions of Edmund's books, will be selected by a panel of experts including Dr. Burke Leon, author of the *The Insider's Guide to Buying a New or Used Car*. If your smart auto-buying story is selected, it will be published together with your name, city, state, and photo (if submitted). No compensation will be paid for use of your story or photo.

To enter your money-saving success story for Edmund's consideration, please send it with the order form below to: *EDMUND'S PUBLISHING CORPORATION*
300 N Sepulveda, Suite 2050, Los Angeles, CA 90245
Attn: Success Stories

OFFICIAL ENTRY FORM / EDMUND'S SUCCESS STORIES

NAME

ADDRESS

CITY, STATE, ZIP

By submitting story/photo, entrant consents to publication without compensation

SIGNATURE   DATE

Specifications
and EPA
Mileage Ratings

contents

Porsche 911 Speedster

Specifications and EPA Mileage Ratings

ACURA

	INTEGRA GS-R 2DR CPE	INTEGRA LS 2DR CPE	INTEGRA RS 2DR CPE	INTEGRA LS 4DR SDN	INTEGRA RS 4DR SDN	LEGEND L 2DR CPE	LEGEND LS 2DR CPE	LEGEND GS 4DR SDN	LEGEND L 4DR SDN	LEGEND LS 4DR SDN	NSX 2DR CPE	VIGOR GS 4DR SDN
Length (in.)	172.4	172.4	172.4	178.1	178.1	192.5	192.5	194.9	194.9	194.9	174.2	190.4
Width (in.)	67.3	67.3	67.3	67.3	67.3	71.3	71.3	71.3	71.3	71.3	71.3	70.1
Height (in.)	50.8	50.8	50.8	52.1	52.1	53.7	53.7	55.1	55.1	55.1	46.1	52.0
Curb Weight (lbs.)	2667	2643	2529	2703	2628	NA	NA	NA	NA	NA	3020	3208
Wheelbase (in.)	101.2	101.2	101.2	103.1	103.1	111.4	111.4	114.6	114.6	114.6	99.6	110.4
Track, front (in.)	58.1	58.1	58.1	58.1	58.1	61.0	61.0	61.0	61.0	61.0	59.4	59.8
Track, rear (in.)	57.8	57.8	57.8	57.8	57.8	60.6	60.6	60.6	60.6	60.6	60.2	59.4
Head Room, front (in.)	38.6	38.6	38.6	38.9	38.9	37.3	37.3	38.5	38.5	38.5	36.3	38.8
Head Room, rear (in.)	35.0	35.0	35.0	36.0	36.0	35.9	35.9	36.5	36.5	36.5	NA	36.2
Shoulder Room, front (in.)	51.7	51.7	51.7	51.5	51.5	56.3	56.3	56.3	56.3	56.3	52.5	53.5
Shoulder Room, rear (in.)	48.8	48.8	48.8	50.3	50.3	54.9	54.9	56.4	56.4	56.4	NA	53.0
Hip Room, front (in.)	50.3	50.3	50.3	50.8	50.8	53.5	53.5	53.6	53.6	53.6	53.8	51.4
Hip Room, rear (in.)	44.1	44.1	44.1	49.9	49.9	50.1	50.1	56.0	56.0	56.0	NA	52.1
Leg Room, front (in.)	42.7	42.7	42.7	42.2	42.2	42.9	42.9	42.7	42.7	42.7	44.3	43.7
Leg Room, rear (in.)	28.1	28.1	28.1	32.7	32.7	28.7	28.7	33.5	33.5	33.5	NA	30.8
Luggage Capacity (cu. ft.)	13.3	13.3	13.3	12.3	12.3	14.1	14.1	14.8	14.8	14.8	5.0	14.2
Engine Type	L4	L4	L4	L4	L4	V6	V6	V6	V6	V6	V6	L5
Displacement (cu. in.)	109.0	112.0	112.0	112.0	112.0	196.0	196.0	196.0	196.0	196.0	181.0	150.0
Fuel System	FI	FI	FI	FI	FI	FI	FI	FI	FI	FI	FI	PGM FI
Compression Ratio	10.0:1	9.2:1	9.2:1	9.2:1	9.2:1	9.6:1	9.6:1	9.6:1	9.6:1	9.6:1	10.2:1	9.0:1
BHP @ RPM (net)	170@7600	142@6300	142@6300	142@6300	142@6300	230@6200	230@6200	230@6200	200@5500	200@5500	270@7100	176@6300
Torque @ RPM (net)	128@6200	127@5200	127@5200	127@5200	127@5200	206@5000	206@5000	206@5000	210@4500	210@4500	210@5300	170@3900
Fuel Capacity (gals.)	13.2	13.2	13.2	13.2	13.2	18.0	18.0	18.0	18.0	18.0	18.5	17.2
EPA City/Hwy (mpg) —manual	25/31	25/31	25/31	25/31	25/31	18/26	18/26	18/26	18/25	18/25	19/24	20/27
EPA City/Hwy (mpg) —auto	NA	24/31	24/31	24/31	24/31	18/23	18/23	18/23	19/24	19/24	18/23	20/26

Specifications and EPA Mileage Ratings

	VIGOR LS 4DR SDN	ALFA ROMEO 164 LS 4DR SDN	ALFA ROMEO 164 Q 4DR SDN	AUDI 90 S 4DR SDN	AUDI 90 CS 4DR SDN	AUDI 90 CS QUATTRO 4DR SPT SDN	AUDI 100 S 4DR SDN	AUDI 100 S 4DR WGN	AUDI 100 CS 4DR SDN	AUDI 100 CS QUATTRO 4DR SDN	AUDI 100 CS QUATTRO 4DR WGN
Length (in.)	190.4	183.7	179.5	180.3	180.3	180.3	192.6	192.6	192.6	192.6	192.6
Width (in.)	70.1	69.3	69.3	66.7	66.7	66.7	70.0	70.0	70.0	70.0	70.0
Height (in.)	52.0	54.7	54.7	54.3	54.3	54.7	56.3	56.3	56.3	56.6	57.0
Curb Weight (lbs.)	3142	3413	3406	3197	3241	3462	3363	3628	3473	3605	3870
Wheelbase (in.)	110.4	104.7	104.7	102.8	102.8	102.2	105.8	105.8	105.8	106.0	106.0
Track, front (in.)	59.8	59.6	59.6	57.2	57.2	57.0	60.1	60.1	60.1	60.1	60.1
Track, rear (in.)	59.4	58.6	58.6	57.9	57.9	58.1	60.0	60.0	60.0	60.1	60.1
Head Room, front (in.)	38.8	38.2	38.2	37.8	37.8	37.8	38.3	38.3	38.3	38.3	38.4
Head Room, rear (in.)	36.2	36.6	36.6	37.2	37.2	37.2	37.6	37.6	37.6	37.6	39.1
Shoulder Room, front (in.)	53.5	56.4	56.4	53.3	53.3	53.3	56.5	56.5	56.5	56.5	56.5
Shoulder Room, rear (in.)	53.0	56.6	56.6	52.6	52.6	52.6	56.2	56.2	56.2	56.2	56.3
Hip Room, front (in.)	51.4	57.5	57.5	NA	NA	NA	NA	NA	NA	NA	NA
Hip Room, rear (in.)	52.1	57.5	57.5	NA	NA	NA	NA	NA	NA	NA	NA
Leg Room, front (in.)	43.7	39.3	39.3	42.2	42.2	42.2	42.4	42.4	42.4	42.4	42.4
Leg Room, rear (in.)	30.8	33.9	33.9	32.5	32.5	32.5	34.8	34.8	34.8	34.8	34.2
Luggage Capacity (cu. ft.)	14.2	17.8	17.8	14.0	14.0	14.0	16.8	16.8	16.8	16.4	33.9/65.5
Engine Type	L5	V6	V6	V6	V6	V6	V6	V6	V6	V6	V6
Displacement (cu. in.)	150.0	180.6	180.6	169.0	169.0	169.0	169.0	169.0	169.0	169.0	169.0
Fuel System	PGM FI	MPFI	MPFI	SPFI	SPFI	SPFI	SPFI	SPFI	SPFI	SPFI	SPFI
Compression Ratio	9.0:1	10.0:1	10.0:1	10.3:1	10.3:1	10.3:1	10.3:1	10.3:1	10.3:1	10.3:1	10.3:1
BHP @ RPM (net)	176 @ 6300	210 @ 6300	230 @ 6300	172 @ 5500	172 @ 5500	172 @ 5500	172 @ 5500	172 @ 5500	172 @ 5500	172 @ 5500	172 @ 5500
Torque @ RPM (net)	170 @ 3900	198 @ 5000	202 @ 5000	184 @ 3000	184 @ 3000	184 @ 3000	184 @ 3000	184 @ 3000	184 @ 3000	184 @ 3000	184 @ 3000
Fuel Capacity (gals.)	17.2	17.2	17.2	17.4	17.4	16.9	21.1	21.1	21.1	21.1	21.1
EPA City/Hwy (mpg) —manual	20/27	17/24	NA	20/26	20/26	19/24	19/24	19/24	19/24	18/24	18/24
EPA City/Hwy (mpg) —auto	20/26	15/22	NA	18/26	18/26	NA	18/24	18/24	18/24	18/23	18/23

Specifications and EPA Mileage Ratings

	CABRIOLET 2DR	S4 4DR SDN	V8 QUATTRO 4DR SDN	BMW 325i 2DR CVT	BMW 530i 4DR SDN	BMW 530i TOURING WGN	BMW 540i 4DR SDN	COLT 2DR	COLT 4DR	COLT VISTA FWD WGN	COLT VISTA SE FWD WGN
Length (in.)	176.0	192.6	191.9	174.5	185.8	185.8	185.8	171.1	174.0	168.5	168.5
Width (in.)	67.6	71.0	71.4	67.3	68.9	68.9	68.9	66.1	66.1	66.7	66.7
Height (in.)	54.3	56.5	60.0	53.1	55.6	55.8	55.6	51.4	51.4	62.1	62.1
Curb Weight (lbs.)	3494	3825	3991	3352	3627	3881	3804	2085	2195	2734	2734
Wheelbase (in.)	100.6	106.0	106.4	106.3	108.7	108.7	108.7	96.1	98.4	99.2	99.2
Track, front (in.)	57.2	61.5	59.6	55.4	57.9	57.9	57.9	57.1	57.1	57.5	57.5
Track, rear (in.)	57.0	60.1	60.3	55.9	58.9	58.9	58.9	57.5	57.5	57.5	57.5
Head Room, front (in.)	38.3	38.3	38.1	38.1	36.9	36.8	36.9	38.6	38.6	40.0	40.0
Head Room, rear (in.)	36.4	37.6	37.7	36.3	36.4	37.7	36.4	36.4	36.2	38.6	38.6
Shoulder Room, front (in.)	51.7	56.5	56.7	53.2	54.3	54.3	54.3	53.9	53.9	55.1	55.1
Shoulder Room, rear (in.)	43.0	56.2	55.4	43.6	55.2	55.2	55.2	54.1	53.5	55.1	55.1
Hip Room, front (in.)	NA	NA	NA	NA	NA	NA	NA	54.9	54.9	50.2	50.2
Hip Room, rear (in.)	NA	NA	NA	NA	NA	NA	NA	53.7	52.0	52.6	52.6
Leg Room, front (in.)	40.7	42.4	42.6	41.2	41.6	41.6	41.6	42.9	42.9	40.8	40.8
Leg Room, rear (in.)	26.5	34.8	34.6	28.1	34.2	34.2	34.2	31.1	33.5	36.1	36.1
Luggage Capacity (cu. ft.)	6.6	16.4	15.7	9.0	16.2	31.0/51.2	16.2	10.5	10.5	34.6/79.0	34.6/79.0
Engine Type	V6	L5	V8	L6	V8	V8	V8	L4	L4	L4	L4
Displacement (cu. in.)	169.0	136.0	254.0	152.0	183.0	183.0	243.0	89.6	111.9	111.9	143.0
Fuel System	SPFI	SFI	SFI	EFI	EFI	EFI	EFI	SMPI	SMPI	SMPI	SMPI
Compression Ratio	10.3:1	9.3:1	10.6:1	10.5:1	10.5:1	10.5:1	10.0:1	9.2:1	9.5:1	9.5:1	9.5:1
BHP @ RPM (net)	172 @ 5500	227 @ 5900	276 @ 5800	189 @ 5900	215 @ 5800	215 @ 5800	282 @ 5800	93 @ 6000	113 @ 6000	113 @ 6000	136 @ 5500
Torque @ RPM (net)	184 @ 3000	258 @ 1950	295 @ 4000	181 @ 4200	214 @ 4500	214 @ 4500	295 @ 4500	92 @ 3000	116 @ 4500	116 @ 4500	145 @ 4250
Fuel Capacity (gals.)	17.4	21.1	21.1	17.2	21.1	21.1	21.1	13.2	13.2	14.5	14.5
EPA City/Hwy (mpg) —manual	NA	18/23	NA	19/27	16/23	16/25	NA	32/40	27/34	21/28	19/24
EPA City/Hwy (mpg) —auto	18/26	NA	14/20	18/26	16/25	16/25	16/23	29/33	27/34	20/26	19/23

Specifications and EPA Mileage Ratings	COLT VISTA AWD WGN	GEO METRO XFI CPE	GEO METRO CPE	GEO METRO SDN	GEO PRIZM SDN	GEO PRIZM LSI SDN	GEO TRACKER 2WD CVT	GEO TRACKER 4WD CVT	GEO TRACKER 4WD HT	HONDA ACCORD DX 2DR CPE	HONDA ACCORD EX 2DR CPE
Length (in.)	168.5	147.4	147.4	151.4	172.64	172.64	142.5	142.5	142.5	184.0	184.0
Width (in.)	66.7	62.7	62.7	62.7	66.34	66.34	64.2	64.2	64.2	70.1	70.1
Height (in.)	62.6	52.4	52.4	53.5	52.76	52.76	65.6	65.6	65.6	54.7	54.7
Curb Weight (lbs.)	3064	1621	1650	1694	2348	2359	2125	2301	2323	2756	2954
Wheelbase (in.)	99.2	89.2	89.2	93.1	97.05	97.05	86.6	86.6	86.6	106.9	106.9
Track, front (in.)	57.3	53.7	53.7	53.7	57.48	57.48	54.9	54.9	54.9	59.6	59.6
Track, rear (in.)	57.5	52.8	52.8	52.8	56.50	56.50	55.1	55.1	55.1	59.1	59.1
Head Room, front (in.)	40.0	37.8	37.8	38.0	38.82	38.82	39.5	39.5	40.0	39.4	38.4
Head Room, rear (in.)	38.6	36.5	36.5	38.0	37.09	37.09	38.3	38.3	38.1	36.4	36.2
Shoulder Room, front (in.)	55.1	51.6	51.6	51.6	53.78	53.78	52.2	52.2	52.2	56.0	56.0
Shoulder Room, rear (in.)	55.1	50.5	50.5	50.6	53.27	53.27	50.2	50.2	50.2	53.5	53.5
Hip Room, front (in.)	50.2	51.1	51.1	51.1	51.3	51.3	51.8	51.8	51.8	51.6	51.6
Hip Room, rear (in.)	52.6	42.5	42.5	42.7	54.3	54.3	41.9	41.9	41.9	47.6	47.6
Leg Room, front (in.)	40.8	42.5	42.5	42.5	42.44	42.44	42.1	42.1	42.1	42.9	42.9
Leg Room, rear (in.)	36.1	29.8	29.8	32.6	32.99	32.99	31.6	31.6	31.6	31.3	31.3
Luggage Capacity (cu. ft.)	34.6/79.0	10.3	10.3	10.5	12.66	12.66	8.9	8.9	8.7	13.0	13.0
Engine Type	L4	L3	L3	L3	L4	L4	L4	L4	L4	L4	L4
Displacement (cu. in.)	143.0	61.0	61.0	61.0	97.0	97.0	97.0	97.0	97.0	131.6	131.6
Fuel System	SMPI	EFI	EFI	EFI	MFI	MFI	EFI	EFI	EFI	MPFI	MPFI
Compression Ratio	9.5:1	9.5:1	9.5:1	9.5:1	9.5:1	9.5:1	8.9:1	8.9:1	8.9:1	8.8:1	8.8:1
BHP @ RPM (net)	136 @ 5500	49 @ 4700	52 @ 5700	52 @ 5700	105 @ 5800	105 @ 5800	80 @ 5400	80 @ 5400	80 @ 5400	130 @ 5300	145 @ 5500
Torque @ RPM (net)	145 @ 4250	58 @ 3300	58 @ 3300	58 @ 3300	100 @ 4800	100 @ 4800	94 @ 3000	94 @ 3000	94 @ 3000	139 @ 4200	147 @ 4500
Fuel Capacity (gals.)	14.5	10.6	10.6	10.6	13.2	13.2	11.1	11.1	11.1	17.0	17.0
EPA City/Hwy (mpg) —manual	19/24	NA	NA	NA	NA	NA	NA	NA	NA	25/31	25/31
EPA City/Hwy (mpg) —auto	19/23	NA	NA	NA	NA	NA	NA	NA	NA	23/29	23/30

Specifications and EPA Mileage Ratings

	CIVIC DX 4DR SDN	CIVIC VX HB	CIVIC SI HB	CIVIC DX HB	CIVIC CX HB	CIVIC EX 2DR CPE	CIVIC DX 2DR CPE	ACCORD LX 4DR WGN	ACCORD EX 4DR WGN	ACCORD LX 4DR SDN	ACCORD EX 4DR SDN	ACCORD DX 4DR SDN	ACCORD LX 2DR CPE
Length (in.)	173.0	160.2	160.2	160.2	160.2	172.8	172.8	187.8	187.8	184.0	184.0	184.0	184.0
Width (in.)	66.9	66.9	66.9	66.9	66.9	66.9	66.9	70.1	70.1	70.1	70.1	70.1	70.1
Height (in.)	51.7	50.7	50.7	50.7	50.7	50.9	50.9	55.9	55.9	55.1	55.1	55.1	54.7
Curb Weight (lbs.)	2313	2094	2390	2178	2108	2443	2231	NA	NA	2877	3009	2800	2822
Wheelbase (in.)	103.2	101.3	101.3	101.3	101.3	103.2	103.2	106.9	106.9	106.9	106.9	106.9	106.9
Track, front (in.)	58.1	58.1	58.1	58.1	58.1	58.1	58.1	59.6	59.6	59.6	59.6	59.6	59.6
Track, rear (in.)	57.7	57.7	57.7	57.7	57.7	57.7	57.7	59.1	59.1	59.1	59.1	59.1	59.1
Head Room, front (in.)	39.1	38.6	38.1	38.6	38.6	37.3	38.5	39.8	38.4	39.4	38.4	39.4	39.4
Head Room, rear (in.)	37.2	36.6	36.3	36.6	36.6	34.9	34.9	39.0	36.4	37.6	36.7	37.6	36.4
Shoulder Room, front (in.)	53.7	53.4	53.4	53.4	53.4	53.4	53.4	55.7	55.7	55.7	55.7	55.7	56.0
Shoulder Room, rear (in.)	53.3	52.1	52.1	52.1	52.1	52.8	52.8	54.3	54.3	54.3	54.3	54.3	53.5
Hip Room, front (in.)	51.0	49.8	49.8	49.8	49.8	49.8	49.8	52.6	52.6	52.6	52.6	52.6	51.6
Hip Room, rear (in.)	51.3	44.6	44.6	44.6	44.6	48.9	48.9	51.4	51.4	51.4	51.4	51.4	47.6
Leg Room, front (in.)	42.5	42.5	42.5	42.5	42.5	42.5	42.5	42.7	42.7	42.7	42.7	42.7	42.9
Leg Room, rear (in.)	32.8	30.5	30.5	30.5	30.5	31.1	31.1	34.1	34.1	34.3	34.3	34.3	31.3
Luggage Capacity (cu. ft.)	12.4	13.3	13.3	13.3	13.3	11.8	11.8	25.7	25.7	13.0	13.0	13.0	13.0
Engine Type	L4	L4	L4	L4	L4	L4	L4	L4	L4	L4	L4	L4	L4
Displacement (cu. in.)	91.1	91.1	97.0	91.1	91.1	97.0	91.1	131.6	131.6	131.6	131.6	131.6	131.6
Fuel System	MPFI	MPFI	MPFI	MPFI	MPFI	MPFI	MPFI	MPFI	MPFI	MPFI	MPFI	MPFI	MPFI
Compression Ratio	9.2:1	9.3:1	9.2:1	9.2:1	9.1:1	9.2:1	9.2:1	8.8:1	8.8:1	8.8:1	8.8:1	8.8:1	8.8:1
BHP @ RPM (net)	102 @ 5900	92 @ 5500	125 @ 6600	102 @ 5900	70 @ 5000	125 @ 6600	102 @ 5900	130 @ 5300	145 @ 5500	130 @ 5300	145 @ 5500	130 @ 5300	130 @ 5300
Torque @ RPM (net)	98 @ 5000	97 @ 4500	106 @ 5200	98 @ 5000	91 @ 2000	106 @ 5200	98 @ 5000	139 @ 4200	147 @ 4500	139 @ 4200	147 @ 4500	139 @ 4200	139 @ 4200
Fuel Capacity (gals.)	11.9	10.0	11.9	11.9	10.0	11.9	11.9	17.0	17.0	17.0	17.0	17.0	17.0
EPA City/Hwy (mpg) —manual	34/40	47/56	29/35	34/40	42/46	29/35	34/40			25/31	25/31	25/31	25/31
EPA City/Hwy (mpg) —auto	29/36	NA	NA	29/36	NA	26/33	29/36			23/29	23/30	23/29	23/29

Specifications and EPA Mileage Ratings	CIVIC EX 4DR SDN	CIVIC LX 4DR SDN	DEL SOL S 2DR	DEL SOL SI 2DR	DEL SOL VTEC 2DR	PRELUDE S 2DR CPE	PRELUDE SI 2DR CPE	PRELUDE 4WS 2DR CPE	PRELUDE VTEC 2DR CPE	ELANTRA BASE 4DR SDN	ELANTRA GLS 4DR SDN	EXCEL BASE 3DR HBK
Length (in.)	173.0	173.0	157.3	157.3	157.3	174.8	174.8	174.8	174.8	172.8	172.8	161.4
Width (in.)	66.9	66.9	66.7	66.7	66.7	69.5	69.5	69.5	69.5	66.1	66.1	63.3
Height (in.)	51.7	51.7	49.4	49.4	49.4	50.8	50.8	50.8	50.8	52.0	52.0	54.5
Curb Weight (lbs.)	2522	2403	2301	2414	2491	2765	2866	2932	2932	2500	2582	2147
Wheelbase (in.)	103.2	103.2	93.3	93.3	93.3	100.4	100.4	100.4	100.4	98.4	98.4	93.8
Track, front (in.)	58.1	58.1	58.1	58.1	58.1	60.0	60.0	60.0	60.0	56.9	56.9	54.7
Track, rear (in.)	57.7	57.7	57.7	57.7	57.7	59.6	59.6	59.6	59.6	56.3	56.3	52.8
Head Room, front (in.)	38.1	39.1	37.5	37.5	37.5	38.0	38.0	38.0	38.0	38.4	38.4	37.8
Head Room, rear (in.)	36.3	37.2	NA	NA	NA	35.1	35.1	35.1	35.1	37.6	37.6	37.6
Shoulder Room, front (in.)	53.7	53.7	52.9	52.9	52.9	54.0	54.0	54.0	54.0	54.3	54.3	52.3
Shoulder Room, rear (in.)	53.3	53.0	NA	NA	NA	50.6	50.6	50.6	50.6	53.4	53.4	52.3
Hip Room, front (in.)	51.0	51.0	49.3	49.3	49.3	52.2	52.2	52.2	52.2	50.9	50.9	52.3
Hip Room, rear (in.)	51.3	51.3	NA	NA	NA	41.4	41.4	41.4	41.4	54.7	54.7	52.3
Leg Room, front (in.)	42.5	42.5	40.3	40.3	40.3	44.2	44.2	44.2	44.2	42.6	42.6	41.7
Leg Room, rear (in.)	32.8	32.8	NA	NA	NA	28.1	28.1	28.1	28.1	33.4	33.4	33.1
Luggage Capacity (cu. ft.)	12.4	12.4	10.5	10.5	10.5	7.9	7.9	7.9	7.9	11.76	11.76	11.4
Engine Type	L4	L4	L4	L4	L4	L4	L4	L4	L4	L4	L4	L4
Displacement (cu. in.)	97.0	91.1	91.1	97.0	97.3	131.6	137.9	137.9	131.6	97.4	109.6	89.6
Fuel System	MPFI	MPFI	MPFI	MPFI	MPFI	MPFI	MPFI	MPFI	MPFI	MPFI	MPFI	MPFI
Compression Ratio	9.2:1	9.2:1	9.2:1	9.2:1	10.2:1	8.8:1	9.8:1	9.8:1	10.0:1	9.2:1	9.2:1	9.4:1
BHP @ RPM (net)	125 @ 6600	102 @ 5900	102 @ 5900	125 @ 6600	160 @ 7600	135 @ 5200	160 @ 5800	160 @ 5800	190 @ 6800	113 @ 6000	124 @ 6000	81 @ 5500
Torque @ RPM (net)	106 @ 5200	98 @ 5000	98 @ 5000	106 @ 5200	111 @ 7000	142 @ 4000	156 @ 4500	156 @ 4500	158 @ 5500	102 @ 5000	116 @ 4500	91 @ 3000
Fuel Capacity (gals.)	11.9	11.9	11.9	11.9	11.9	15.9	15.9	15.9	15.9	13.7	13.7	11.9
EPA City/Hwy (mpg) —manual	29/35	34/40	35/41	29/35	26/30	23/29	22/26	22/26	22/26	22/29	21/28	28/36
EPA City/Hwy (mpg) —auto	26/33	29/36	29/36	26/33	NA	23/28	22/27	22/27	NA	NA	23/28	27/35

HYUNDAI

Specifications and EPA Mileage Ratings

Specification	EXCEL GS 4 DR SDN	EXCEL GL 4DR SDN	SCOUPE BASE 2DR CPE	SCOUPE LS 2DR CPE	SCOUPE TURBO 2DR CPE	SONATA BASE 4DR SDN	SONATA 2.0 GLS 4DR SDN	SONATA 3.0 GLS 4DR SDN	G20 4DR SDN (INFINITI)	J30 4DR SDN (INFINITI)	Q45 4DR SDN (INFINITI)
Length (in.)	161.4	168.3	165.9	165.9	165.9	184.3	184.3	184.3	174.8	191.3	199.8
Width (in.)	63.3	63.3	63.9	63.9	63.9	68.9	68.9	68.9	66.7	69.7	71.9
Height (in.)	54.5	54.5	50.0	50.0	50.0	55.4	55.4	55.4	54.7	54.7	56.5
Curb Weight (lbs.)	2185	2224	2176	2266	2240	2813	2934	2967	2877	3527	4039
Wheelbase (in.)	93.8	93.8	93.8	93.8	93.8	104.3	104.3	104.3	100.4	108.7	113.2
Track, front (in.)	54.7	54.7	54.7	54.7	54.7	58.3	58.3	58.3	57.9	59.1	61.8
Track, rear (in.)	52.8	52.8	52.8	52.8	52.8	57.5	57.5	57.5	57.5	59.1	61.8
Head Room, front (in.)	37.8	37.8	38.1	38.1	38.1	38.5	38.5	38.5	38.8	37.7	38.2
Head Room, rear (in.)	37.6	37.6	34.3	34.3	34.3	37.4	37.4	37.4	37.3	36.7	36.3
Shoulder Room, front (in.)	52.3	52.3	52.4	52.4	52.4	56.1	56.1	56.1	54.9	55.9	58.3
Shoulder Room, rear (in.)	52.3	52.3	52.1	52.1	52.1	56.5	56.5	56.5	54.9	56.5	57.5
Hip Room, front (in.)	52.3	52.3	51.4	51.4	51.4	58.0	58.0	58.0	52.1	54.1	55.2
Hip Room, rear (in.)	52.3	52.3	42.8	42.8	42.8	57.6	57.6	57.6	54.2	54.1	56.4
Leg Room, front (in.)	41.7	41.7	42.8	42.8	42.8	42.9	42.9	42.9	42.0	41.3	43.9
Leg Room, rear (in.)	33.1	33.1	29.4	29.4	29.4	37.3	37.3	37.3	32.2	30.5	32.0
Luggage Capacity (cu. ft.)	11.4	11.4	9.3	9.3	9.3	14.0	14.0	14.0	14.2	10.1	14.8
Engine Type	L4	L4	L4	L4	L4	L4	L4	V6	L4	V6	V8
Displacement (cu. in.)	89.6	89.6	91.3	91.3	91.3	121.9	121.9	181.4	122.0	180.6	274.2
Fuel System	MPFI	MPFI	MPFI	MPFI	MPFI	MPFI	MPFI	MPFI	SPFI	SPFI	SPFI
Compression Ratio	9.4:1	9.4:1	10.0:1	10.0:1	7.5:1	9.0:1	9.0:1	8.9:1	9.5:1	10.5:1	10.2:1
BHP @ RPM (net)	81 @ 5500	81 @ 5500	92 @ 5500	92 @ 5500	115 @ 5500	128 @ 6000	128 @ 6000	142 @ 5000	140 @ 6400	210 @ 6400	278 @ 6000
Torque @ RPM (net)	91 @ 3000	91 @ 3000	97 @ 4500	97 @ 4500	123 @ 4000	120.7 @ 5000	120.7 @ 5000	168 @ 2500	132 @ 4800	193 @ 4800	292 @ 4000
Fuel Capacity (gals.)	11.9	11.9	11.9	11.9	11.9	17.2	17.2	17.2	15.9	19.0	22.5
EPA City/Hwy (mpg) —manual	28/36	28/36	26/33	26/33	26/31	20/27	20/27	NA	24/32	NA	NA
EPA City/Hwy (mpg) —auto	27/35	27/35	26/33	26/33	NA	20/27	20/27	18/24	22/29	18/23	17/22

ISUZU

Specifications and EPA Mileage Ratings

Specifications and EPA Mileage Ratings	AMIGO 2WD	AMIGO 4WD	PICKUP 2WD SWB	PICKUP 2WD LWB	PICKUP 2WD SPACECAB	PICKUP 4WD SWB	PICKUP 4WD SWB V6	RODEO 2WD	RODEO 2WD V6	RODEO 4WD V6	TROOPER 2DR SWB	TROOPER 4DR LWB
Length (in.)	168.1	168.1	177.3	193.8	193.8	177.3	177.3	183.9	183.9	183.9	166.5	183.5
Width (in.)	70.1	70.1	66.6	66.6	66.6	66.6	66.6	66.5	66.4	66.5	68.7	68.7
Height (in.)	69.9	69.9	64.2	64.2	64.2	68.5	68.5	65.4	65.4	65.4	72.8	72.8
Curb Weight (lbs.)	3390	3615	2830	2940	3110	3355	3475	3345	3775	3995	4060	4210
Wheelbase (in.)	91.7	91.7	105.6	119.2	119.2	105.6	105.6	183.9	183.9	183.9	91.7	108.7
Track, front (in.)	57.7	57.7	56.9	56.9	56.9	56.7	56.7	56.7	56.7	56.7	57.3	57.3
Track, rear (in.)	58.1	58.1	55.9	55.9	55.9	56.9	56.9	56.9	56.9	56.9	57.5	57.5
Head Room, front (in.)	38.0	38.0	38.2	38.2	38.2	38.2	38.2	38.2	38.2	38.2	39.8	39.8
Head Room, rear (in.)	32.0	32.0	NA	NA	NA	NA	NA	37.8	37.8	37.8	39.8	39.8
Shoulder Room, front (in.)	55.5	55.5	55.5	55.5	55.5	55.5	55.5	55.5	55.5	55.5	57.3	57.3
Shoulder Room, rear (in.)	57.0	57.0	NA	NA	NA	NA	NA	55.5	55.5	55.5	57.3	57.3
Hip Room, front (in.)	55.5	55.5	51.7	51.7	51.7	51.7	51.7	55.5	55.5	55.5	53.7	53.7
Hip Room, rear (in.)	40.5	40.5	NA	NA	NA	NA	NA	42.5	42.5	42.5	51.2	53.5
Leg Room, front (in.)	42.5	42.5	42.5	42.5	42.5	42.5	42.5	42.5	42.5	42.5	40.8	40.8
Leg Room, rear (in.)	19.5	19.5	NA	NA	NA	NA	NA	36.1	36.1	36.1	32.2	39.1
Luggage Capacity (cu. ft.)	NA	NA	NA	NA	NA	NA	NA	35.0/74.9	35.0/74.9	35.0/74.9	30.5/68.3	47.3/90.2
Engine Type	L4	L4	L4	L4	L4	L4	V6	L4	V6	V6	V6	V6
Displacement (cu. in.)	156.2	156.2	137.5	137.5	156.2	156.2	191.0	156.2	193.2	193.2	193.2	193.2
Fuel System	MPFI	MPFI	2 bbl.	2 bbl.	MPFI	MPFI	TBI	MPFI	MPFI	MPFI	MPFI	MPFI
Compression Ratio	8.6:1	8.6:1	8.3:1	8.3:1	8.6:1	8.6:1	8.5:1	8.6:1	9.3:1	9.3:1	9.3:1	9.3:1
BHP @ RPM (net)	120 @ 4600	120 @ 4600	96 @ 4600	96 @ 4600	120 @ 4600	120 @ 4600	120 @ 4400	120 @ 4600	175 @ 5200	175 @ 5200	175 @ 5200	175 @ 5200
Torque @ RPM (net)	150 @ 2600	150 @ 2600	123 @ 2600	123 @ 2600	150 @ 2600	150 @ 2600	165 @ 2800	150 @ 2600	188 @ 4000	188 @ 4000	188 @ 4000	188 @ 4000
Fuel Capacity (gals.)	21.9	21.9	14.0	19.8	19.8	14.0	14.0	21.9	21.9	21.9	22.5	22.5
EPA City/Hwy (mpg) —manual	16/20	16/20	21/25	21/25	19/23	17/20	15/18	16/20	16/19	16/19	16/18	16/18
EPA City/Hwy (mpg) —auto	NA	NA	NA	NA	NA	NA	NA	NA	16/19	15/18	15/18	15/18

Specifications and EPA Mileage Ratings	XJ6 4DR SDN	VANDEN PLAS 4DR SDN	XJ12 4DR SDN	XJS 6.0L 2DR CPE	XJS 6.0L 2DR CVT	XJS 4.0L 2DR CPE	XJS 4.0L 2DR CVT	RANGE ROVER COUNTY	RANGE ROVER COUNTY LWB	DEFENDER 90
	JAGUAR							LAND ROVER		
Length (in.)	196.4	196.4	196.4	191.2	191.2	191.2	191.2	175.0	183.0	160.5
Width (in.)	78.9	78.9	79.3	70.6	70.6	70.6	70.6	71.4	71.4	70.5
Height (in.)	54.3	54.3	53.1	48.6	48.6	48.7	48.7	70.8	70.8	70.8
Curb Weight (lbs.)	4075	4105	4445	4053	4306	3805	3980	4401	4574	3560
Wheelbase (in.)	113.0	113.0	113.0	102.0	102.0	102.0	102.0	100.0	108.0	92.9
Track, front (in.)	59.1	59.1	59.1	59.6	59.6	58.6	58.6	58.5	58.5	58.5
Track, rear (in.)	59.0	59.0	59.0	58.7	58.7	59.2	59.2	58.5	58.5	58.5
Head Room, front (in.)	36.6	36.6	NA	NA	NA	36.1	36.1	38.4	38.4	57.0
Head Room, rear (in.)	36.5	36.5	NA	NA	NA	33.4	NA	37.3	37.3	NA
Shoulder Room, front (in.)	57.5	57.5	NA	NA	NA	NA	NA	NA	NA	NA
Shoulder Room, rear (in.)	57.6	57.6	NA	NA	NA	NA	NA	NA	NA	NA
Hip Room, front (in.)	NA	NA	NA	NA	NA	NA	NA	58.3	58.3	55.1
Hip Room, rear (in.)	NA	NA	NA	NA	NA	NA	NA	59.0	59.0	NA
Leg Room, front (in.)	41.7	41.7	NA	NA	NA	42.95	42.95	41.0	41.0	NA
Leg Room, rear (in.)	33.1	33.1	NA	NA	NA	23.4	NA	32.7	39.7	NA
Luggage Capacity (cu. ft.)	12.2	12.2	NA	8.9	8.9	8.9	8.9	36.2	36.2	NA
Engine Type	L6	L6	V12	V12	V12	L6	L6	V8	V8	V8
Displacement (cu. in.)	242.9	242.9	365.9	365.9	365.9	242.9	242.9	241.0	261.2	241.0
Fuel System	FI	FI	FI	FI	FI	FI	FI	MPFI	MPFI	MPFI
Compression Ratio	9.5:1	9.5:1	11.0:1	11.0:1	11.0:1	9.5:1	9.5:1	9.35:1	8.95:1	9.35:1
BHP @ RPM (net)	223 @ 4750	223 @ 4750	301 @ 5350	278 @ 5400	278 @ 5400	219 @ 4750	219 @ 4750	182 @ 4750	200 @ 4750	182 @ 4750
Torque @ RPM (net)	278 @ 3650	278 @ 3650	336 @ 3750	334 @ 2800	334 @ 2800	273 @ 3950	273 @ 3950	232 @ 3100	251 @ 3250	232 @ 3100
Fuel Capacity (gals.)	23.2	23.2	NA	23.6	20.7	24.0	20.7	23.4	23.4	15.6
EPA City/Hwy (mpg) —manual	NA	NA	NA	NA	NA	NA	NA	NA	NA	13/16
EPA City/Hwy (mpg) —auto	17/24	17/24	13/21	12/16	12/16	17/23	17/23	12/15	13/16	NA

Specifications and EPA Mileage Ratings

	LEXUS ES 300 4DR SDN	LEXUS GS 300 4DR SDN	LEXUS LS 400 4DR SDN	LEXUS SC 300 2DR CPE	LEXUS SC 400 2DR CPE	MAZDA MX-3 BASE 2DR CPE	MAZDA MX-3 GS 2DR CPE	MAZDA MX-5 2DR CVT	MAZDA MX-6 BASE 2DR CPE	MAZDA MX-6 LS 2DR CPE	MAZDA MPV 5-PASS 2WD WGN/VAN
Length (in.)	187.8	194.9	196.7	191.1	191.1	165.7	165.7	155.4	181.5	181.5	175.8
Width (in.)	70.0	70.7	72.0	70.5	70.5	66.7	66.7	65.9	68.9	68.9	71.9
Height (in.)	53.9	55.1	55.7	52.4	52.6	51.6	51.6	48.2	51.6	51.6	68.1
Curb Weight (lbs.)	3374	3660	3859	3506	3616	2443	2599	2293	2625	2800	3595
Wheelbase (in.)	103.1	109.4	110.8	105.9	105.9	96.3	96.3	89.2	102.8	102.8	110.4
Track, front (in.)	61.0	60.6	61.6	59.8	59.8	57.5	57.5	55.5	59.1	59.1	60.0
Track, rear (in.)	59.1	60.2	61.6	59.8	60.0	57.7	57.7	56.2	59.1	59.1	60.6
Head Room, front (in.)	37.8	38.3	38.6	38.3	38.3	38.2	38.2	37.1	38.1	38.1	40.0
Head Room, rear (in.)	36.6	36.8	36.8	36.1	36.1	33.9	33.9	NA	34.7	34.7	37.7
Shoulder Room, front (in.)	56.1	57.3	57.1	56.0	56.0	52.2	52.2	50.4	53.5	53.5	57.5
Shoulder Room, rear (in.)	55.1	57.3	56.3	52.7	52.7	48.2	48.2	NA	50.9	50.9	56.9
Hip Room, front (in.)	55.9	NA	57.5	55.1	55.1	NA	NA	51.7	NA	NA	NA
Hip Room, rear (in.)	54.3	NA	57.4	39.2	39.2	NA	NA	NA	NA	NA	NA
Leg Room, front (in.)	43.5	44.0	43.8	44.1	44.1	42.6	42.6	42.7	44.0	44.0	40.6
Leg Room, rear (in.)	33.1	33.8	34.3	27.2	27.2	31.1	31.1	NA	27.7	27.7	36.1
Luggage Capacity (cu. ft.)	14.3	13.0	13.4	9.3	9.3	15.4	15.4	3.6	12.4	12.4	11.1
Engine Type	V6	L6	V8	L6	V8	L4	V6	L4	L4	V6	L4
Displacement (cu. in.)	181.0	183.0	242.0	183.0	242.0	98.0	113.0	112.0	122.0	153.0	159.0
Fuel System	MPFI	SPFI	MPFI	MPFI	MPFI	EFI	EFI	MPFI	MPFI	MPFI	EFI
Compression Ratio	10.5:1	10.0:1	10.0:1	10.0:1	10.0:1	9.0:1	9.2:1	9.0:1	9.0:1	9.2:1	8.4:1
BHP @ RPM (net)	188 @ 5200	220 @ 5800	250 @ 5600	225 @ 6000	250 @ 5600	105 @ 6200	130 @ 6500	128 @ 6500	118 @ 5500	164 @ 5600	121 @ 4600
Torque @ RPM (net)	203 @ 4400	210 @ 4800	260 @ 4400	210 @ 4800	260 @ 4400	100 @ 3600	115 @ 4500	110 @ 5000	127 @ 4500	160 @ 4800	149 @ 3500
Fuel System	18.5	21.1	22.5	20.6	20.6	13.2	13.2	12.7	15.5	15.5	19.6
EPA City/Hwy (mpg) —manual	NA	NA	NA	18/23	NA	29/37	23/29	22/27	26/34	21/26	NA
EPA City/Hwy (mpg) —auto	18/24	18/23	18/23	17/23	18/23	25/34	20/27	23/28	23/31	20/26	18/24

Specifications and EPA Mileage Ratings	MPV 7-PASS 2WD WGN	MPV 7-PASS 4WD V6 WGN	NAVAJO DX 2WD	NAVAJO LX 2WD	NAVAJO DX 4WD	NAVAJO LX 4WD	B2300 2WD PU BASE SB	B2300 2WD PU SE SB	B2300 2WD PU BASE CAB PLUS	B3000 2WD PU SE LB	B3000 2WD PU SE CAB PLUS	B4000 2WD PU SE LB	B4000 2WD PU LE CAB PLUS
Length (in.)	175.8	175.8	175.3	175.3	175.3	175.3	184.5	184.5	202.7	197.5	202.7	197.5	202.7
Width (in.)	71.9	72.3	70.2	70.2	70.2	70.2	69.4	69.4	69.4	69.4	69.4	69.4	69.4
Height (in.)	68.1	70.8	68.1	68.1	68.1	68.1	64.0	64.0	64.0	64.0	64.0	69.4	69.4
Curb Weight (lbs.)	3745	4040	3785	3870	3980	4065	2918	2918	3208	2955	3275	3031	3418
Wheelbase (in.)	110.4	110.4	102.1	102.1	102.1	102.1	107.9	107.9	125.0	113.9	125.0	113.9	125.0
Track, front (in.)	60.0	60.8	58.3	58.3	58.3	58.3	56.7	56.7	56.7	56.7	56.7	56.7	56.7
Track, rear (in.)	60.6	60.6	58.3	58.3	58.3	58.3	57.3	57.3	57.3	57.3	57.3	57.3	57.3
Head Room, front (in.)	40.0	40.0	39.9	39.9	39.9	39.9	39.1	39.1	39.4	39.1	39.4	39.1	39.4
Head Room, rear (in.)	37.7	37.7	39.1	39.1	39.1	39.1	NA	NA	NA	NA	NA	NA	NA
Shoulder Room, front (in.)	57.5	57.5	57.1	57.1	57.1	57.1	54.6	54.6	54.6	54.6	54.6	54.6	54.6
Shoulder Room, rear (in.)	56.9	56.9	57.9	57.9	57.9	57.9	NA	NA	NA	NA	NA	NA	NA
Hip Room, front (in.)	NA	NA	NA	NA	NA	NA	NA	NA	NA	NA	NA	NA	NA
Hip Room, rear (in.)	NA	NA	NA	NA	NA	NA	NA	NA	NA	NA	NA	NA	NA
Leg Room, front (in.)	40.6	40.6	42.4	42.4	42.4	42.4	42.4	42.4	43.4	42.4	43.4	42.4	43.4
Leg Room, rear (in.)	36.1	36.1	36.6	36.6	36.6	36.6	NA	NA	NA	NA	NA	NA	NA
Luggage Capacity (cu. ft.)	11.1	11.1	32.6/69.5	32.6/69.5	32.6/69.5	32.6/69.5	NA	NA	NA	NA	NA	NA	NA
Engine Type	L4	V6	V6	V6	V6	V6	L4	L4	L4	V6	V6	V6	V6
Displacement (cu. in.)	159.0	180.0	245.0	245.0	245.0	245.0	140.0	140.0	140.0	182.0	182.0	245.0	245.0
Fuel System	EFI	EFI	MPFI	MPFI	MPFI	MPFI	EFI	EFI	EFI	EFI	EFI	EFI	EFI
Compression Ratio	8.4:1	8.5:1	9.0:1	9.0:1	9.0:1	9.0:1	9.2:1	9.2:1	9.2:1	9.3:1	9.3:1	9.1:1	9.1:1
BHP @ RPM (net)	121 @ 4600	155 @ 5000	160 @ 4500	160 @ 4500	160 @ 4500	160 @ 4500	98 @ 4600	98 @ 4600	98 @ 4600	140 @ 4800	140 @ 4800	160 @ 4000	160 @ 4000
Torque @ RPM (net)	149 @ 3500	169 @ 4000	220 @ 2500	220 @ 2500	220 @ 2500	220 @ 2500	130 @ 2600	130 @ 2600	130 @ 2600	160 @ 3000	160 @ 3000	225 @ 2500	220 @ 2800
Fuel Capacity (gals.)	19.6	19.8	19.3	19.3	19.3	19.3	16.3	16.3	19.6	19.6	19.6	19.6	19.6
EPA City/Hwy (mpg) —manual	NA	NA	18/23	18/23	17/22	17/22	22/26	22/26	22/26	19/24	19/24	18/24	NA
EPA City/Hwy (mpg) —auto	18/24	15/19	NA	16/21	NA	15/19	NA	NA	NA	19/24	NA	NA	17/23

Specifications and EPA Mileage Ratings

	B4000 4WD PU SE SB	B4000 4WD PU SE CAB PLUS	B4000 4WD PU LE CAB PLUS	PROTEGE BASE 4DR SDN	PROTEGE DX 4DR SDN	PROTEGE LX 4DR SDN	RX-7 2DR CPE	323 3DR HB	626 DX 4DR SDN	626 LX 4DR SDN	626 LX V6 4 DR SDN	626 ES 4DR SDN	929 4DR SDN
Length (in.)	184.5	202.7	202.7	171.5	171.5	171.5	168.5	163.6	184.4	184.4	184.4	184.4	193.7
Width (in.)	69.4	69.4	69.4	65.9	65.9	65.9	68.9	65.7	68.9	68.9	68.9	68.9	70.7
Height (in.)	67.5	67.5	67.5	54.1	54.1	54.1	48.4	54.3	55.1	55.1	55.1	55.1	54.9
Curb Weight (lbs.)	3258	3516	3516	2388	2388	2487	2826	2238	2606	2672	2804	2906	3627
Wheelbase (in.)	107.9	125.0	125.0	98.4	98.4	98.4	95.5	96.5	102.8	102.8	102.8	102.8	112.2
Track, front (in.)	58.3	58.3	58.3	56.3	56.3	56.3	57.5	56.3	59.1	59.1	59.1	59.1	59.4
Track, rear (in.)	57.3	57.3	57.3	56.5	56.5	56.5	57.5	56.5	59.1	59.1	59.1	59.1	59.8
Head Room, front (in.)	39.1	39.4	39.4	38.4	38.4	38.4	37.6	38.6	39.2	39.2	39.2	39.2	37.4
Head Room, rear (in.)	NA	NA	NA	37.1	37.1	37.1	NA	37.6	37.8	37.8	37.8	37.8	37.4
Shoulder Room, front (in.)	54.6	54.6	54.6	53.4	53.4	53.4	51.8	53.6	55.1	55.1	55.1	55.1	56.8
Shoulder Room, rear (in.)	NA	NA	NA	53.7	53.7	53.7	NA	53.4	54.7	54.7	54.7	54.7	55.3
Hip Room, front (in.)	NA	NA	NA	NA	NA	NA	NA	NA	NA	NA	NA	NA	NA
Hip Room, rear (in.)	NA	NA	NA	NA	NA	NA	NA	NA	NA	NA	NA	NA	NA
Leg Room, front (in.)	42.4	43.4	43.4	42.2	42.2	42.2	44.1	42.2	43.5	43.5	43.5	43.5	43.4
Leg Room, rear (in.)	NA	NA	NA	34.6	34.6	34.6	NA	34.2	35.8	35.8	35.8	35.8	37.0
Luggage Capacity (cu. ft.)	NA	NA	NA	13.1	13.1	13.1	17.0	15.7	13.8	13.8	13.8	13.8	12.4
Engine Type	V6	V6	V6	L4	L4	L4	RTRY	L4	L4	L4	V6	V6	V6
Displacement (cu. in.)	245.0	245.0	245.0	112.0	112.0	112.0	80.0	98.0	122.0	122.0	153.0	153.0	180.0
Fuel System	EFI	EFI	EFI	MPFI	MPFI	MPFI	EFI	MPFI	MPFI	MPFI	MPFI	MPFI	MPFI
Compression Ratio	9.1:1	9.1:1	9.1:1	8.9:1	8.9:1	9.0:1	9.0:1	9.3:1	9.0:1	9.0:1	9.2:1	9.2:1	9.2:1
BHP @ RPM (net)	160 @ 4000	160 @ 4000	160 @ 4000	103 @ 5500	103 @ 5500	125 @ 6500	255 @ 6500	82 @ 5000	118 @ 5500	118 @ 5500	164 @ 5600	164 @ 5600	193 @ 5750
Torque @ RPM (net)	225 @ 2500	225 @ 2500	220 @ 2800	111 @ 4000	111 @ 4000	114 @ 4500	217 @ 5000	92 @ 2500	127 @ 4500	127 @ 4500	160 @ 4800	160 @ 4800	200 @ 3500
Fuel Capacity (gals.)	16.3	19.6	19.6	14.5	14.5	14.5	20.0	13.2	15.5	15.5	15.5	15.5	18.5
EPA City/Hwy (mpg) —manual	18/22	18/22	NA	28/36	28/36	24/30	17/25	29/36	26/34	26/34	21/26	21/26	NA
EPA City/Hwy (mpg) —auto	NA	NA	16/21	24/31	24/31	23/29	18/24	26/33	23/31	23/31	20/26	20/26	19/24

MERCEDES-BENZ

Specifications and EPA Mileage Ratings

	C220 4DR SDN	C280 4DR SDN	E320 4DR SDN	E320 4DR WGN	E320 2DR CPE	E320 2DR CABRIOLET	E420 4DR SDN	E500 4DR SDN	S350 TD 4DR SDN	S320 4DR SDN	S420 4DR SDN	S500 4DR SDN
Length (in.)	177.4	177.4	187.2	188.2	183.9	183.9	187.2	187.2	201.3	201.3	205.2	205.2
Width (in.)	67.7	67.7	68.5	68.5	68.5	68.5	68.5	70.7	74.3	74.3	74.3	74.3
Height (in.)	56.1	56.1	56.3	59.8	54.9	54.8	56.3	55.4	58.7	58.7	58.9	58.9
Curb Weight (lbs.)	3173	3293	3525	3750	3525	4025	3745	3855	4610	4630	4760	4830
Wheelbase (in.)	105.9	105.9	110.2	110.2	106.9	106.9	110.2	110.2	119.7	119.7	123.6	123.6
Track, front (in.)	58.8	58.8	59.1	58.9	59.1	59.1	59.1	60.6	63.1	63.1	63.1	63.1
Track, rear (in.)	57.6	57.6	58.7	58.6	58.7	58.7	58.7	60.2	62.0	62.0	62.0	62.0
Head Room, front (in.)	37.2	37.2	36.9	37.4	36.0	37.6	36.9	37.5	38.0	38.0	38.0	38.0
Head Room, rear (in.)	37.0	37.0	36.9	36.8	36.8	35.5	36.8	36.9	37.8	37.8	38.5	38.5
Shoulder Room, front (in.)	54.6	54.6	55.9	55.9	55.7	55.7	55.9	55.9	61.7	61.7	61.7	61.7
Shoulder Room, rear (in.)	53.9	53.9	55.7	55.6	50.5	48.7	55.7	55.7	61.4	61.4	61.4	61.4
Hip Room, front (in.)	52.8	52.8	53.0	53.0	53.4	56.8	53.0	53.0	58.0	58.0	58.0	58.0
Hip Room, rear (in.)	53.9	53.9	55.4	55.3	52.4	51.0	55.4	55.4	57.6	57.6	57.6	57.6
Leg Room, front (in.)	41.5	41.5	41.7	41.7	41.9	41.9	41.7	41.5	41.3	41.3	41.3	41.3
Leg Room, rear (in.)	32.8	32.8	33.5	33.9	29.6	24.8	33.5	33.5	36.1	36.1	39.6	39.6
Luggage Capacity (cu. ft.)	13.7	13.7	14.6	42.3	14.4	10.5	14.6	13.8	15.6	15.6	15.6	15.6
Engine Type	L4	L6	L6	L6	L6	L6	V8	V8	L6	L6	V8	V8
Displacement (cu. in.)	NA	NA	195.3	195.3	195.3	195.3	256.2	256.2	210.0	195.0	256.0	303.0
Fuel System	EFI	EFI	FI	FI	FI	EFI	EFI	EFI	FI	FI	EFI	EFI
Compression Ratio	10.0:1	10.0:1	10.0:1	10.0:1	10.0:1	10.0:1	11.0:1	10.0:1	22.0:1	10.0:1	11.0:1	10.0:1
BHP @ RPM (net)	147 @ 5500	194 @ 5500	217 @ 5500	217 @ 5500	217 @ 5500	217 @ 5500	275 @ 5700	315 @ 5600	148 @ 4000	228 @ 5600	275 @ 5700	315 @ 5600
Torque @ RPM (net)	155 @ 4000	199 @ 3750	229 @ 3750	229 @ 3750	229 @ 3750	229 @ 3750	295 @ 3900	347 @ 3900	229 @ 2200	232 @ 3750	295 @ 3900	345 @ 3900
Fuel Capacity (gals.)	16.4	16.4	18.5	19.0	18.5	18.5	18.5	23.8	26.4	26.4	26.4	26.4
EPA City/Hwy (mpg) —manual	NA	NA	NA	NA	NA	NA	NA	NA	NA	NA	NA	NA
EPA City/Hwy (mpg) —auto	21/28	20/25	19/25	18/24	19/25	18/23	18/24	16/19	21/28	17/24	15/20	14/19

Specifications and EPA Mileage Ratings	300GT BASE 2DR CPE	300GT SL 2DR CPE	300GT VR4 2DR CPE	DIAMANTE ES 4DR SDN	DIAMANTE LS 4DR SDN	DIAMANTE 4DR WGN	SL 320 2DR CPE/RDSTR	SL500 2DR CPE/RDSTR	SL600 2DR CPE/RDSTR	S500 2DR CPE	S600 2DR CPE	S600 4DR SDN
Length (in.)	179.7	179.7	179.7	190.2	190.2	192.4	176.0	176.0	178.0	199.4	199.4	205.2
Width (in.)	172.4	172.4	172.4	69.9	69.9	69.9	71.3	71.3	71.3	74.6	74.6	74.3
Height (in.)	49.0	49.0	49.3	52.6	52.6	57.9	51.3	51.3	51.3	57.1	57.1	58.7
Curb Weight (lbs.)	3197	3351	3803	3483	3605	3610	4090	4165	4455	4785	5075	5095
Wheelbase (in.)	97.2	97.2	97.2	107.1	107.1	107.2	99.0	99.0	99.0	115.9	115.9	123.6
Track, front (in.)	61.4	61.4	61.4	60.4	60.4	60.4	60.4	60.4	60.4	63.1	63.1	63.1
Track, rear (in.)	62.2	62.2	62.2	60.2	60.2	59.3	60.0	60.0	60.0	62.0	62.0	62.0
Head Room, front (in.)	37.1	37.1	37.1	38.6	38.6	39.2	37.1	37.1	37.1	36.5	36.5	38.0
Head Room, rear (in.)	34.1	34.1	34.1	36.9	36.9	38.4	NA	NA	NA	37.2	37.2	38.5
Shoulder Room, front (in.)	55.9	55.9	55.9	54.7	54.7	54.7	55.4	55.4	55.4	61.7	61.7	61.7
Shoulder Room, rear (in.)	52.0	52.0	52.0	55.4	55.4	55.2	NA	NA	NA	56.5	56.5	61.4
Hip Room, front (in.)	56.7	56.7	56.7	54.2	54.2	54.2	53.2	53.2	53.2	56.7	56.7	58.0
Hip Room, rear (in.)	46.9	46.9	46.9	53.5	53.5	53.9	NA	NA	NA	53.1	53.1	57.6
Leg Room, front (in.)	44.2	44.2	44.2	43.9	43.9	43.9	42.4	42.4	42.4	41.7	41.7	41.3
Leg Room, rear (in.)	28.5	28.5	28.5	34.2	34.2	36.0	NA	NA	NA	31.5	31.5	39.6
Luggage Capacity (cu. ft.)	11.1	11.1	11.1	13.6	13.6	37.4/72.1	7.9	7.9	7.9	14.2	14.2	15.6
Engine Type	V6	V6	V6	V6	V6	V6	L6	V8	V12	V8	V12	V12
Displacement (cu. in.)	181.0	181.0	181.0	181.3	181.3	181.3	195.2	303.5	365.4	303.5	365.4	365.0
Fuel System	MPFI	MPFI	MPFI	MPFI	MPFI	MPFI	FI	EFI	EFI	EFI	EFI	EFI
Compression Ratio	10.0:1	10.0:1	8.0:1	10.0:1	10.0:1	10.0:1	10.0:1	10.0:1	10.0:1	10.0:1	10.0:1	10.0:1
BHP @ RPM (net)	222 @ 6000	222 @ 6000	320 @ 6000	175 @ 5500	202 @ 6000	175 @ 5500	228 @ 5500	315 @ 5600	389 @ 5200	315 @ 5600	389 @ 5200	389 @ 5200
Torque @ RPM (net)	205 @ 4500	205 @ 4500	315 @ 2500	185 @ 3000	201 @ 3500	185 @ 3000	232 @ 3750	347 @ 3900	420 @ 3800	347 @ 3900	420 @ 3800	421 @ 3800
Fuel Capacity (gals.)	19.8	19.8	19.8	19.0	19.0	18.8	21.3	21.3	21.3	26.4	26.4	26.4
EPA City/Hwy (mpg) —manual	19/25	19/25	18/24	NA	NA	NA	NA	NA	NA	NA	NA	NA
EPA City/Hwy (mpg) —auto	18/24	18/24	NA	18/24	18/24	19/25	17/24	16/20	13/17	14/20	13/17	12/16

Specifications and EPA Mileage Ratings

	ECLIPSE BASE 2DR CPE	ECLIPSE GS 2DR CPE	ECLIPSE GS DOHC 2DR CPE	ECLIPSE GS TURBO 2DR CPE	ECLIPSE GSX 2DR CPE	EXPO BASE WGN	EXPO LRV WGN	EXPO LRV SPORT WGN	EXPO AWD WGN	GALANT ES 4DR SDN	GALANT GS 4DR SDN	GALANT LS 4DR SDN	GALANT S 4DR SDN
Length (in.)	172.8	172.8	172.8	172.8	172.8	177.0	168.5	168.5	177.4	187.0	187.0	187.0	187.0
Width (in.)	66.7	66.7	66.7	66.7	66.7	66.7	66.7	66.7	66.7	68.1	68.1	68.1	68.1
Height (in.)	51.4	51.4	51.4	51.4	52.0	62.6	62.1	62.1	62.6	53.1	53.1	53.1	53.1
Curb Weight (lbs.)	2542	2590	2690	2778	3093	3020	2745	2888	3219	2866	2954	2976	2755
Wheelbase (in.)	97.2	97.2	97.2	97.2	97.2	107.1	99.2	99.2	107.1	103.7	103.7	103.7	103.7
Track, front (in.)	57.7	57.7	57.7	57.7	57.7	57.5	57.5	57.5	57.5	59.4	59.4	59.4	59.4
Track, rear (in.)	57.1	57.1	57.1	57.1	57.1	57.5	57.5	57.5	57.5	59.3	59.3	59.3	59.3
Head Room, front (in.)	37.9	37.9	37.9	37.9	37.9	39.3	40.0	40.0	39.3	39.4	37.3	37.3	39.4
Head Room, rear (in.)	34.1	34.1	34.1	34.1	34.1	36.9	38.6	38.6	36.9	37.5	37.5	37.5	37.5
Shoulder Room, front (in.)	53.9	53.9	53.9	53.9	53.9	55.1	55.1	55.1	55.1	55.7	55.7	55.7	55.7
Shoulder Room, rear (in.)	52.4	52.4	52.4	52.4	52.4	55.3	55.1	55.1	55.3	55.7	53.5	53.5	55.7
Hip Room, front (in.)	55.1	55.1	55.1	55.1	55.1	50.4	50.2	50.2	50.4	57.3	52.6	52.6	57.3
Hip Room, rear (in.)	45.7	45.7	45.7	45.7	45.7	38.9	52.6	52.6	38.9	57.1	52.6	52.6	57.1
Leg Room, front (in.)	43.9	43.9	43.9	43.9	43.9	40.5	40.8	40.8	40.5	43.3	43.3	43.3	43.3
Leg Room, rear (in.)	28.5	28.5	28.5	28.5	28.5	28.7	36.1	36.1	28.7	35.0	35.0	35.0	35.0
Luggage Capacity (cu. ft.)	10.2	10.2	10.2	10.2	6.9	38.0	29.5	29.5	38.0	12.5	12.5	12.5	12.5
Engine Type	L4	L4	L4	L4	L4	L4	L4	L4	L4	L4	L4	L4	L4
Displacement (cu. in.)	107.0	107.0	107.0	122.0	122.0	144.0	112.0	144.0	144.0	143.4	143.4	143.4	143.4
Fuel System	MPFI	MPFI	MPFI	MPFI	MPFI	MPFI	MPFI	MPFI	MPFI	MPFI	MPFI	MPFI	MPFI
Compression Ratio	9.0:1	9.0:1	9.0:1	7.8:1	7.8:1	9.5:1	9.5:1	9.5:1	9.5:1	9.5:1	10.0:1	9.5:1	9.5:1
BHP @ RPM (net)	92 @ 5000	92 @ 5000	92 @ 5000	195 @ 6000	195 @ 6000	136 @ 5500	113 @ 6000	136 @ 5500	136 @ 5500	141 @ 5500	160 @ 6000	141 @ 5500	141 @ 5500
Torque @ RPM (net)	105 @ 3500	105 @ 3500	105 @ 3500	203 @ 3000	203 @ 3000	145 @ 4250	116 @ 4500	145 @ 4250	145 @ 4250	148 @ 3000	160 @ 4250	148 @ 3000	148 @ 3000
Fuel Capacity (gals.)	15.9	15.9	15.9	15.9	15.9	15.8	14.5	14.5	15.8	16.9	16.9	16.9	16.9
EPA City/Hwy (mpg) —manual	23/32	23/32	22/29	21/28	20/25	22/27	24/29	22/27	20/24	NA	22/29	NA	23/30
EPA City/Hwy (mpg) —auto	23/30	23/30	22/27	19/23	19/21	20/26	NA	20/26	19/23	22/28	20/26	22/28	22/28

Specifications and EPA Mileage Ratings	MIRAGE ES 2DR CPE	MIRAGE LS 2DR CPE	MIRAGE S 2DR CPE	MIRAGE ES 4DR SDN	MIRAGE LS 4DR SDN	MIRAGE S 4DR SDN	MIGHTY MAX 2WD TRUCK	MIGHTY MAX 4WD TRUCK	MIGHTY MAX MACROCAB	MONTERO LS 4WD 4DR	MONTERO SR 4WD 4DR	ALTIMA GLE 4DR SDN
Length (in.)	171.1	171.1	171.1	172.2	172.2	172.2	177.2	177.2	188.2	185.2	186.6	180.5
Width (in.)	66.5	66.5	66.5	66.5	66.5	66.5	65.2	65.9	65.2	66.7	70.3	67.1
Height (in.)	51.6	51.6	51.6	52.2	52.2	52.2	58.3	64.4	59.6	73.4	75.2	55.9
Curb Weight (lbs.)	2105	2125	2085	2250	2335	2195	2600	3205	2780	4190	4440	2990
Wheelbase (in.)	96.1	96.1	96.1	98.4	98.4	98.4	105.1	105.1	116.1	107.3	107.3	103.1
Track, front (in.)	57.1	57.1	57.1	57.1	57.1	57.1	55.1	54.9	54.7	55.9	57.7	57.7
Track, rear (in.)	57.5	57.5	57.5	57.5	57.5	57.5	55.7	55.7	55.3	56.5	58.3	57.3
Head Room, front (in.)	38.6	38.6	38.6	39.2	39.2	39.2	38.8	38.8	38.9	40.9	40.9	39.3
Head Room, rear (in.)	36.4	36.4	36.4	37.2	37.2	37.2	NA	NA	NA	34.8	34.8	37.6
Shoulder Room, front (in.)	53.9	53.9	53.9	53.9	53.9	53.9	55.5	55.5	55.5	55.5	55.5	54.8
Shoulder Room, rear (in.)	54.1	54.1	54.1	53.5	53.5	53.5	NA	NA	NA	56.5	56.5	54.0
Hip Room, front (in.)	54.9	54.9	54.9	55.0	55.0	55.0	NA	NA	NA	53.5	53.5	52.8
Hip Room, rear (in.)	53.7	53.7	53.7	52.0	52.0	52.0	NA	NA	NA	56.5	56.5	52.4
Leg Room, front (in.)	42.9	42.9	42.9	42.9	42.9	42.9	41.9	41.9	43.4	40.3	40.3	42.6
Leg Room, rear (in.)	31.1	31.1	31.1	33.5	33.5	33.5	NA	NA	NA	15.7	15.7	34.7
Luggage Capacity (cu. ft.)	10.7	10.7	10.7	10.5	10.5	10.5	NA	NA	NA	9.2/72.7	9.2/72.7	14.0
Engine Type	L4	L4	L4	L4	L4	L4	L4	V6	L4	V6	V6	L4
Displacement (cu. in.)	89.5	111.8	89.5	111.8	111.8	89.5	143.5	181.0	143.5	181.0	213.3	145.8
Fuel System	MPFI	MPFI	MPFI	MPFI	MPFI	MPFI	MPFI	MPFI	MPFI	MPFI	MPFI	MPFI
Compression Ratio	9.2:1	9.5:1	9.2:1	9.5:1	9.5:1	9.2:1	8.5:1	8.9:1	8.5:1	8.9:1	9.5:1	9.2:1
BHP @ RPM (net)	92 @ 6000	113 @ 6000	92 @ 6000	113 @ 6000	113 @ 6000	92 @ 6000	116 @ 5000	151 @ 5000	116 @ 5000	151 @ 5000	215 @ 5500	150 @ 5600
Torque @ RPM (net)	93 @ 3000	116 @ 4500	93 @ 3000	116 @ 4500	116 @ 4500	93 @ 3000	136 @ 3500	174 @ 4000	136 @ 3500	174 @ 4000	228 @ 3000	154 @ 4400
Fuel Capacity (gals.)	13.2	13.2	13.2	13.2	13.2	13.2	13.7	15.7	18.2	24.3	24.3	15.9
EPA City/Hwy (mpg) —manual	32/39	26/33	32/39	26/33	NA	32/39	21/25	17/22	21/25	15/18	NA	NA
EPA City/Hwy (mpg) —auto	28/32	26/33	NA	26/33	26/33	28/32	19/23	NA	19/23	15/18	14/17	21/29

NISSAN

Specifications and EPA Mileage Ratings

	ALTIMA GXE 4DR SDN	ALTIMA SE 4DR SDN	ALTIMA XE 4DR SDN	MAXIMA GXE 4DR SDN	MAXIMA SE 4DR SDN	PATHFINDER XE 2WD	PATHFINDER XE 4WD	PATHFINDER SE 4WD	PATHFINDER LE 4WD	QUEST GXE VAN	QUEST XE VAN	SENTRA E 2DR	SENTRA E 4DR
Length (in.)	180.5	180.5	180.5	187.6	187.6	171.9	171.9	171.9	171.9	189.9	189.9	170.3	170.3
Width (in.)	67.1	67.1	67.1	69.3	69.3	66.5	66.5	66.5	66.5	73.7	73.7	65.6	65.6
Height (in.)	55.9	55.9	55.9	55.1	55.1	65.7	65.7	66.7	66.1	68.0	65.6	53.9	53.9
Curb Weight (lbs.)	2898	2902	2829	3139	3165	NA	3885	3955	NA	3970	3783	2324	2346
Wheelbase (in.)	103.1	103.1	103.1	104.3	104.3	104.3	104.3	104.3	104.3	112.2	112.2	95.7	95.7
Track, front (in.)	57.7	57.7	57.7	59.4	59.4	56.1	56.1	57.3	56.9	63.4	63.4	56.9	56.9
Track, rear (in.)	57.3	57.3	57.3	58.7	58.7	55.5	55.5	56.7	56.3	63.4	63.4	56.3	56.3
Head Room, front (in.)	39.3	39.3	39.3	39.5	39.5	39.3	39.3	39.3	39.3	39.4	37.3	38.5	38.5
Head Room, rear (in.)	37.6	37.6	37.6	36.9	36.9	36.8	36.8	36.8	36.8	39.4	37.3	36.6	36.6
Shoulder Room, front (in.)	54.8	54.8	54.8	56.8	56.8	54.4	54.4	54.4	54.4	62.1	62.1	52.6	52.6
Shoulder Room, rear (in.)	54.0	54.0	54.0	56.1	56.1	55.1	55.1	55.1	55.1	63.3	63.3	52.6	52.6
Hip Room, front (in.)	52.8	52.8	52.8	54.3	54.3	55.1	55.1	55.1	55.1	56.8	56.8	51.2	51.2
Hip Room, rear (in.)	52.4	52.4	52.4	48.8	48.8	55.1	55.1	55.1	55.1	49.6	49.6	53.4	53.4
Leg Room, front (in.)	42.6	42.6	42.6	43.7	43.7	42.6	42.6	42.6	42.6	39.9	39.9	41.9	41.9
Leg Room, rear (in.)	34.7	34.7	34.7	33.2	33.2	33.1	33.1	33.1	33.1	36.7	36.7	30.9	30.9
Luggage Capacity (cu. ft.)	14.0	14.0	14.0	14.5	14.5	31.4	31.4	31.4/80.2	31.4/80.2	14.1	14.1	11.7	11.7
Engine Type	L4	L4	L4	V6	V6	V6	V6	V6	V6	V6	V6	L4	L4
Displacement (cu. in.)	145.8	145.8	145.8	180.7	180.7	180.7	180.7	180.7	180.7	180.7	180.7	97.5	97.5
Fuel System	MPFI	MPFI	MPFI	MPFI	MPFI	MPFI	MPFI	MPFI	MPFI	MPFI	MPFI	MPFI	MPFI
Compression Ratio	9.2:1	9.2:1	9.2:1	9.0:1	10.0:1	9.0:1	9.0:1	9.0:1	9.0:1	9.0:1	9.0:1	9.5:1	9.5:1
BHP @ RPM (net)	150 @ 5600	150 @ 5600	150 @ 5600	160 @ 5200	190 @ 5600	153 @ 4800	153 @ 4800	153 @ 4800	153 @ 4800	151 @ 4800	151 @ 4800	110 @ 6000	110 @ 6000
Torque @ RPM (net)	154 @ 4400	154 @ 4400	154 @ 4400	182 @ 2800	190 @ 4000	180 @ 4000	180 @ 4000	180 @ 4000	180 @ 4000	174 @ 4400	174 @ 4400	108 @ 4000	108 @ 4000
Fuel Capacity (gals.)	15.9	15.9	15.9	18.5	18.5	20.4	20.4	20.4	20.4	20.0	20.0	13.2	13.2
EPA City/Hwy (mpg) —manual	24/30	24/30	24/30	NA	21/26	15/18	15/18	15/18	NA	NA	NA	29/38	29/38
EPA City/Hwy (mpg) —auto	19/23	21/29	21/29	19/26	19/25	15/19	15/19	15/18	15/18	17/23	17/23	26/35	26/35

Specifications and EPA Mileage Ratings

	SENTRA XE 2DR	SENTRA XE 4DR	SENTRA GXE 4DR	SENTRA SE-R 2DR	SENTRA SE 2DR	2WD TRUCK STD LB	2WD TRUCK SE KING CAB	2WD TRUCK STD REG CAB	2WD TRUCK XE REG CAB	2WD TRUCK XE KING CAB	4WD TRUCK XE REG CAB	4WD TRUCK XE KING CAB	4WD TRUCK XE KING CAB
Length (in.)	170.3	170.3	170.3	170.3	170.3	190.0	195.5	174.6	180.1	190.0	180.1	195.5	195.5
Width (in.)	65.6	65.6	65.6	65.6	65.6	65.0	65.0	65.0	65.0	65.0	66.5	66.7	66.5
Height (in.)	53.9	53.9	53.9	53.9	53.9	62.0	62.0	62.0	62.0	62.0	66.7	66.7	67.1
Curb Weight (lbs.)	2346	2368	2438	2467	2346	3115	3235	2970	2970	2885	3390	3525	3765
Wheelbase (in.)	95.7	95.7	95.7	95.7	95.7	116.1	116.1	104.3	104.3	116.1	104.3	116.1	116.1
Track, front (in.)	56.9	56.9	56.9	56.9	56.9	54.9	55.7	54.9	54.9	54.9	56.1	56.1	56.9
Track, rear (in.)	56.3	56.3	56.3	56.3	56.3	55.5	56.3	54.5	54.5	55.5	54.5	54.5	56.3
Head Room, front (in.)	38.5	38.5	38.5	38.5	38.5	39.3	39.3	39.3	39.3	39.3	39.3	39.3	39.3
Head Room, rear (in.)	36.6	36.6	36.6	36.6	36.6	NA	NA	NA	NA	NA	NA	NA	NA
Shoulder Room, front (in.)	52.6	52.6	52.6	52.6	52.6	54.4	54.4	54.4	54.4	54.4	54.4	54.4	54.4
Shoulder Room, rear (in.)	52.6	52.6	52.6	52.6	52.6	NA	NA	NA	NA	NA	NA	NA	NA
Hip Room, front (in.)	51.2	51.2	51.2	51.2	51.2	55.1	52.2	55.1	55.1	52.2	55.1	52.2	52.2
Hip Room, rear (in.)	53.4	53.4	53.4	53.4	53.4	NA	NA	NA	NA	NA	NA	NA	NA
Leg Room, front (in.)	41.9	41.9	41.9	41.9	41.9	42.2	42.6	42.2	42.2	42.6	42.2	42.6	42.6
Leg Room, rear (in.)	30.9	30.9	30.9	30.9	30.9	NA	NA	NA	NA	NA	NA	NA	NA
Luggage Capacity (cu. ft.)	11.7	11.7	11.7	11.7	11.7	14.4	14.4	14.4	14.4	14.4	14.4	14.4	14.4
Engine Type	L4	L4	L4	L4	L4	V6	V6	L4	L4	L4	L4	L4	V6
Displacement (cu. in.)	97.5	97.5	97.5	121.9	97.5	180.7	180.7	145.8	145.8	145.8	145.8	145.8	180.7
Fuel System	MPFI	MPFI	MPFI	MPFI	MPFI	MPFI	MPFI	MPFI	MPFI	MPFI	MPFI	MPFI	MPFI
Compression Ratio	9.5:1	9.5:1	9.5:1	9.5:1	9.5:1	9.0:1	9.0:1	8.6:1	8.6:1	8.6:1	8.6:1	8.6:1	9.0:1
BHP @ RPM (net)	110 @ 6000	110 @ 6000	110 @ 6000	140 @ 6400	110 @ 6000	153 @ 4800	153 @ 4800	134 @ 5200	134 @ 5200	134 @ 5200	134 @ 5200	134 @ 5200	153 @ 4800
Torque @ RPM (net)	108 @ 4000	108 @ 4000	108 @ 4000	132 @ 4800	108 @ 4000	180 @ 4000	180 @ 4000	154 @ 3600	154 @ 3600	154 @ 3600	154 @ 3600	154 @ 3600	180 @ 4000
Fuel Capacity (gals.)	13.2	13.2	13.2	13.2	13.2	21.1	15.9	15.9	15.9	15.9	15.9	15.9	21.1
EPA City/Hwy (mpg) —manual	29/38	29/38	29/38	23/31	29/38	19/23	19/23	23/27	23/27	23/27	18/22	18/22	15/19
EPA City/Hwy (mpg) —auto	26/35	26/35	26/35	NA	26/35	NA	18/24	NA	21/26	21/26	NA	NA	16/19

Specifications and EPA Mileage Ratings

PORSCHE

	4WD TRUCK SE KING CAB	240 SX SE 2DR CVT	300 ZX 2DR CVT	300 ZX 2-SEATER	300 ZX 2+2	300 ZX TURBO	911 CARRERA 2 2DR CPE	911 CARRERA 2 2DR TARGA	911 CARRERA 2 2DR CABRIOLET	911 CARRERA 4 2DR CPE	911RS AMERICA 2DR CPE	911 SPEEDSTER 2DR
Length (in.)	195.5	178.0	169.5	169.5	178.0	169.5	168.3	168.3	168.3	168.3	168.3	168.3
Width (in.)	66.5	66.5	70.5	70.5	70.9	70.5	65.0	65.0	65.0	69.9	65.0	65.0
Height (in.)	67.1	50.8	49.5	48.3	48.1	48.4	51.6	51.6	51.6	51.6	51.6	50.4
Curb Weight (lbs.)	3855	2870	3446	3299	3413	3517	3031	3031	3031	3340	2954	3031
Wheelbase (in.)	116.1	97.4	96.5	96.5	101.2	96.5	89.4	89.4	89.4	89.4	89.4	89.4
Track, front (in.)	56.9	57.7	58.9	58.9	58.9	58.9	54.3	54.3	54.3	56.5	54.1	54.1
Track, rear (in.)	56.3	57.5	60.4	60.4	60.4	61.2	54.1	54.1	54.1	58.8	54.1	54.1
Head Room, front (in.)	39.3	38.3	37.1	36.8	37.1	36.8	NA	NA	NA	NA	NA	NA
Head Room, rear (in.)	NA	35.5	NA	NA	34.4	NA	NA	NA	NA	NA	NA	NA
Shoulder Room, front (in.)	54.4	48.4	56.7	56.7	56.7	56.7	NA	NA	NA	NA	NA	NA
Shoulder Room, rear (in.)	NA	38.0	NA	NA	55.2	NA	NA	NA	NA	NA	NA	NA
Hip Room, front (in.)	52.2	51.0	53.5	53.5	53.5	53.5	NA	NA	NA	NA	NA	NA
Hip Room, rear (in.)	NA	38.5	NA	NA	41.2	NA	NA	NA	NA	NA	NA	NA
Leg Room, front (in.)	42.6	41.0	43.0	43.0	43.0	43.0	NA	NA	NA	NA	NA	NA
Leg Room, rear (in.)	NA	25.4	NA	NA	22.7	NA	NA	NA	NA	NA	NA	NA
Luggage Capacity (cu. ft.)	14.4	5.1	5.8	23.7	11.5	23.7	NA	NA	NA	NA	NA	NA
Engine Type	V6	L4	V6	V6	V6	V6	H6	H6	H6	H6	H6	H6
Displacement (cu. in.)	180.7	145.8	180.7	180.7	180.7	180.7	220.0	220.0	220.0	220.0	220.0	220.0
Fuel System	MPFI	MPFI	MPFI	MPFI	MPFI	MPFI	DME FI	DME FI	DME FI	DME FI	DME FI	DME FI
Compression Ratio	9.0:1	8.6:1	10.5:1	10.5:1	10.5:1	8.5:1	11.3:1	11.3:1	11.3:1	11.3:1	11.3:1	11.3:1
BHP @ RPM (net)	153 @ 4800	155 @ 5600	222 @ 6400	222 @ 6400	222 @ 6400	300 @ 6400	247 @ 6100	247 @ 6100	247 @ 6100	247 @ 6100	247 @ 6100	247 @ 6100
Torque @ RPM (net)	180 @ 4000	160 @ 4400	198 @ 4800	198 @ 4800	198 @ 4800	283 @ 3600	228 @ 4800	228 @ 4800	228 @ 4800	228 @ 4800	228 @ 4800	228 @ 4800
Fuel Capacity (gals.)	21.1	15.9	18.2	18.7	18.7	18.7	20.3	20.3	20.3	20.3	20.3	20.3
EPA City/Hwy (mpg) —manual	15/19	NA	18/24	18/24	18/24	NA	17/25	17/25	17/25	16/23	17/25	17/25
EPA City/Hwy (mpg) —auto	16/19	21/26	18/23	18/23	18/23	NA	16/23	16/23	16/23	NA	NA	16/23

Specifications and EPA Mileage Ratings

	911 TURBO 3.6 2DR CPE	928 GTS 2DR CPE	968 2DR CPE	968 2DR CABRIOLET	SAAB 900S 5DR HB	900S 2DR CVT	900SE 5DR HB	9000CS 5DR HB	9000 TURBO CS 5DR HB	9000CSE 5DR HBK	9000 TURBO CSE 5DR HBK	9000 TURBO CDE 4DR SDN
Length (in.)	168.3	178.1	170.9	170.9	182.6	182.6	182.6	187.4	187.4	187.4	187.4	188.2
Width (in.)	69.9	74.4	68.3	68.3	67.4	67.4	67.4	69.4	69.4	69.4	69.4	69.4
Height (in.)	51.6	50.5	50.2	50.2	56.5	56.5	56.5	55.9	55.9	55.9	55.9	55.9
Curb Weight (lbs.)	3274	3593	3086	3240	2950	2950	2950	3110	3110	3190	3190	3210
Wheelbase (in.)	89.4	98.4	94.5	94.5	102.4	102.4	102.4	105.2	105.2	105.2	105.2	105.2
Track, front (in.)	56.8	61.1	58.2	58.2	56.9	56.9	56.9	59.9	59.9	59.9	59.9	59.9
Track, rear (in.)	58.6	63.6	57.1	57.1	56.8	56.8	56.8	58.7	58.7	58.7	58.7	58.7
Head Room, front (in.)	NA	NA	NA	NA	NA	NA	NA	NA	NA	NA	NA	NA
Head Room, rear (in.)	NA	NA	NA	NA	NA	NA	NA	NA	NA	NA	NA	NA
Shoulder Room, front (in.)	NA	NA	NA	NA	NA	NA	NA	NA	NA	NA	NA	NA
Shoulder Room, rear (in.)	NA	NA	NA	NA	NA	NA	NA	NA	NA	NA	NA	NA
Hip Room, front (in.)	NA	NA	NA	NA	NA	NA	NA	NA	NA	NA	NA	NA
Hip Room, rear (in.)	NA	NA	NA	NA	NA	NA	NA	NA	NA	NA	NA	NA
Leg Room, front (in.)	NA	NA	NA	NA	NA	NA	NA	NA	NA	NA	NA	NA
Leg Room, rear (in.)	NA	NA	NA	NA	NA	NA	NA	NA	NA	NA	NA	NA
Luggage Capacity (cu. ft.)	NA	NA	NA	NA	24.0/49.8	24.0/49.8	24.0/49.8	23.5	23.5	23.5	23.5	17.8
Engine Type	H6	V8	L4	L4	L4	L4	V6	L4	L4	L4	L4	L4
Displacement (cu. in.)	220.0	329.0	182.5	182.5	140.0	140.0	152.0	140.0	140.0	140.0	140.0	140.0
Fuel System	KFI	LH FI	DME FI	DME FI	EFI	EFI	EFI	FI	FI	FI	FI	FI
Compression Ratio	7.5:1	10.4:1	11.0:1	11.0:1	10.5:1	10.5:1	10.8:1	10.5:1	9.2:1	10.5:1	9.2:1	9.2:1
BHP @ RPM (net)	355 @ 5500	345 @ 5700	236 @ 6200	236 @ 6200	155 @ 5700	150 @ 5700	170 @ 5900	146 @ 5600	200 @ 5500	146 @ 5600	200 @ 5500	200 @ 5500
Torque @ RPM (net)	384 @ 4200	369 @ 4250	225 @ 4100	225 @ 4100	155 @ 4300	155 @ 4300	167 @ 4200	151 @ 3800	238 @ 1800	151 @ 3800	238 @ 1800	238 @ 1800
Fuel Capacity (gals.)	20.3	22.7	19.6	19.6	18.0	18.0	18.0	17.4	17.4	17.4	17.4	17.4
EPA City/Hwy (mpg) — manual	13/21	12/19	17/26	17/26	20/28	20/26	18/25	19/27	20/28	19/27	20/28	20/28
EPA City/Hwy (mpg) — auto	NA	15/19	16/25	16/25	19/26	18/21	19/25	17/27	18/26	17/27	18/26	18/26

Specifications and EPA Mileage Ratings

	9000 AERO 5DR HBK	SUBARU IMPREZA FWD 4DR SDN	IMPREZA AWD 4DR SDN	IMPREZA FWD 4DR SPORT WGN	IMPREZA AWD 4DR SPORT WGN	JUSTY FWD BASE 3DR	JUSTY AWD GL 5DR	LEGACY FWD L 4DR SDN	LEGACY FWD LS 4DR SDN	LEGACY AWD L 4DR SDN	LEGACY AWD LS 4DR SDN	LEGACY AWD LSI 4DR SDN
Length (in.)	187.4	172.2	172.2	172.2	172.2	145.5	145.5	178.9	178.9	178.9	178.9	178.9
Width (in.)	69.4	67.1	67.1	67.1	67.1	60.4	60.4	66.5	66.5	66.5	66.5	66.5
Height (in.)	55.9	55.5	55.5	55.5	55.5	53.7	53.7	53.5	53.5	53.5	53.5	53.7
Curb Weight (lbs.)	3242	2325	2500	2405	2580	1845	2045	2730	2955	2970	3105	3120
Wheelbase (in.)	105.2	99.2	99.2	99.2	99.2	90.0	90.0	101.6	101.6	101.6	101.6	101.6
Track, front (in.)	59.9	57.7	57.7	57.7	57.7	52.4	52.4	57.7	57.7	57.5	57.5	57.5
Track, rear (in.)	58.7	57.1	57.1	57.1	57.1	50.8	50.8	57.3	57.3	57.3	57.3	57.3
Head Room, front (in.)	NA	39.2	39.2	39.2	39.2	38.0	38.0	38.0	36.4	38.0	36.4	36.4
Head Room, rear (in.)	NA	36.7	36.7	37.4	37.4	37.0	37.0	36.0	35.9	36.0	35.9	35.9
Shoulder Room, front (in.)	NA	52.5	52.5	52.5	52.5	50.4	51.3	54.1	54.1	54.1	54.1	54.1
Shoulder Room, rear (in.)	NA	53.3	53.3	53.3	53.3	50.7	51.0	53.7	53.7	53.7	53.7	53.7
Hip Room, front (in.)	NA	NA	NA	NA	NA	NA	NA	NA	NA	NA	NA	NA
Hip Room, rear (in.)	NA	NA	NA	NA	NA	NA	NA	NA	NA	NA	NA	NA
Leg Room, front (in.)	NA	43.1	43.1	43.1	43.1	41.5	41.5	43.1	43.1	43.1	43.1	43.1
Leg Room, rear (in.)	NA	32.5	32.5	32.4	32.4	30.2	30.2	34.8	35.0	34.8	35.0	35.0
Luggage Capacity (cu. ft.)	23.5	11.1	11.1	25.5/62.1	25.5/62.1	9.8/21.8	9.9/21.9	14.3	14.3	14.3	14.3	14.3
Engine Type	L4	H4	H4	H4	H4	L3	L3	H4	H4	H4	H4	H4
Displacement (cu. in.)	140.0	110.98	110.98	110.98	110.98	72.5	72.5	135.0	135.0	135.0	135.0	135.0
Fuel System	FI	MPFI	MPFI	MPFI	MPFI	MPFI	MPFI	MPFI	MPFI	MPFI	MPFI	MPFI
Compression Ratio	9.2:1	9.5:1	9.5:1	9.5:1	9.5:1	9.1:1	9.1:1	9.5:1	9.5:1	9.5:1	9.5:1	9.5:1
BHP @ RPM (net)	225 @ 5500	110 @ 5600	110 @ 5600	110 @ 5600	110 @ 5600	73 @ 5600	73 @ 5600	130 @ 5600	130 @ 5600	130 @ 5600	130 @ 5600	130 @ 5600
Torque @ RPM (net)	258 @ 1950	110 @ 4400	110 @ 4400	110 @ 4400	110 @ 4400	71 @ 2800	71 @ 2800	137 @ 4400	137 @ 4400	137 @ 4400	137 @ 4400	137 @ 4400
Fuel Capacity (gals.)	17.4	13.2	13.2	13.2	13.2	9.2	9.2	15.9	15.9	15.9	15.9	15.9
EPA City/Hwy (mpg) —manual	21/29	25/31	23/28	25/31	23/28	33/37	28/32	23/31	NA	21/27	NA	NA
EPA City/Hwy (mpg) —auto	18/26	24/30	22/28	24/30	22/28	NA	NA	22/29	22/29	21/27	21/27	21/27

Specifications and EPA Mileage Ratings

	LEGACY AWD SS SPT SDN	LEGACY L FWD 4DR WGN	LEGACY L AWD 4DR WGN	LEGACY AWD 4DR TRNG WGN	LOYALE 4DR WGN	SVX FWD L 2DR CPE	SVX FWD LS 2DR CPE	SVX AWD LSi 2DR CPE	SAMURAI 2DR SOFTTOP	SIDEKICK 2DR 2WD	SIDEKICK 2DR 4WD	SIDEKICK 4DR 2WD
Length (in.)	178.9	181.9	181.9	181.9	176.8	182.1	182.1	182.1	135.0	142.5	142.5	158.7
Width (in.)	66.5	66.5	66.5	66.5	65.4	69.7	69.7	69.7	60.6	64.2	64.2	64.4
Height (in.)	53.5	54.7	56.3	54.7	54.9	51.2	51.2	51.2	64.6	64.3	65.1	65.7
Curb Weight (lbs.)	3100	2825	3005	3300	2635	3375	3430	3580	2046	2253	2436	2571
Wheelbase (in.)	101.6	101.6	101.6	101.6	96.9	102.8	102.8	102.8	79.9	86.6	86.6	97.6
Track, front (in.)	57.7	57.7	57.5	57.5	55.5	59.1	59.1	59.1	51.2	54.9	54.9	54.9
Track, rear (in.)	57.3	57.1	57.1	57.1	56.1	58.3	58.3	58.3	51.6	55.1	55.1	55.1
Head Room, front (in.)	36.4	38.4	38.4	37.0	37.6	38.0	37.4	37.4	40.2	39.5	39.5	40.6
Head Room, rear (in.)	35.9	37.8	37.8	36.4	38.4	35.0	35.0	35.0	NA	39.0	39.0	40.0
Shoulder Room, front (in.)	54.1	54.1	54.1	54.1	53.5	56.1	56.1	56.1	47.6	52.5	52.5	52.5
Shoulder Room, rear (in.)	53.7	53.7	53.7	53.7	53.5	54.5	54.5	54.5	NA	50.2	50.2	51.2
Hip Room, front (in.)	NA	NA	NA	NA	NA	NA	NA	NA	NA	NA	NA	NA
Hip Room, rear (in.)	NA	NA	NA	NA	NA	NA	NA	NA	NA	NA	NA	NA
Leg Room, front (in.)	43.1	43.1	43.1	43.1	41.7	43.5	43.5	43.5	38.3	42.1	42.1	42.1
Leg Room, rear (in.)	35.0	35.6	35.6	35.6	35.2	28.5	28.5	28.5	NA	31.7	31.7	32.7
Luggage Capacity (cu. ft.)	14.3	36.2/71.0	36.2/71.0	36.2/71.0	34.5/70.3	8.2	8.2	8.2	27.8	32.9	32.9	45.0
Engine Type	H4	H4	H4	H4	H4	H6	H6	H6	L4	L4	L4	L4
Displacement (cu. in.)	135.0	135.0	135.0	135.0	108.68	202.5	202.5	202.5	79.2	97.0	97.0	97.0
Fuel System	MPFI	MPFI	MPFI	MPFI	EFI	SPFI	SPFI	SPFI	TBI	TBI	TBI	MPFI
Compression Ratio	8.0:1	9.5:1	9.5:1	8.0:1	9.5:1	10.0:1	10.0:1	10.0:1	9.5:1	8.9:1	8.9:1	9.5:1
BHP @ RPM (net)	160 @ 5600	130 @ 5600	130 @ 5600	160 @ 5600	90 @ 5200	230 @ 5400	230 @ 5400	230 @ 5400	66 @ 6000	80 @ 5400	80 @ 5400	95 @ 5600
Torque @ RPM (net)	181 @ 2800	137 @ 4400	137 @ 4400	181 @ 2800	101 @ 2800	228 @ 4400	228 @ 4400	228 @ 4400	76 @ 3500	94 @ 3000	94 @ 3000	98 @ 4000
Fuel Capacity (gals.)	15.9	15.9	15.9	15.9	15.9	18.5	18.5	18.5	10.6	11.1	11.1	14.5
EPA City/Hwy (mpg) —manual	19/25	23/31	21/27	NA	24/29	NA	NA	NA	28/29	25/27	25/27	23/26
EPA City/Hwy (mpg) —auto	18/23	22/29	21/27	18/23	22/22	17/25	17/25	17/25	NA	23/24	23/24	22/26

SUZUKI

Specifications and EPA Mileage Ratings

	SIDEKICK 4DR 4WD	SWIFT GA 3DR HB	SWIFT GT 3DR HB	SWIFT GA 4DR SDN	SWIFT GS 4DR SDN	CAMRY DX 2DR CPE	CAMRY LE 2DR CPE	CAMRY V6 LE 2DR CPE	CAMRY V6 SE 2DR CPE	CAMRY DX 4DR SDN	CAMRY LE 4DR SDN	CAMRY XLE 4DR SDN
Length (in.)	158.7	147.4	147.4	161.2	161.2	187.8	187.8	187.8	187.8	187.8	187.8	187.8
Width (in.)	64.4	62.6	62.4	62.6	62.6	69.7	69.7	69.7	69.7	69.7	69.7	69.7
Height (in.)	66.5	52.4	52.4	53.5	53.5	54.9	54.9	54.9	54.9	55.1	55.1	55.1
Curb Weight (lbs.)	2762	1781	1951	1894	1918	2910	3064	3219	3164	2932	3086	3131
Wheelbase (in.)	97.6	89.2	89.2	93.1	93.1	103.1	103.1	103.1	103.1	103.1	103.1	103.1
Track, front (in.)	54.9	53.7	53.7	53.7	53.7	61.0	61.0	61.0	61.0	61.0	61.0	61.0
Track, rear (in.)	55.1	52.8	52.8	52.8	52.8	59.0	59.0	59.0	59.0	59.0	59.0	59.0
Head Room, front (in.)	40.6	37.8	37.8	39.1	39.1	38.4	38.4	38.4	38.4	38.4	38.4	38.4
Head Room, rear (in.)	40.0	36.5	36.5	37.7	37.7	37.4	37.4	37.4	37.4	37.1	37.1	37.1
Shoulder Room, front (in.)	52.5	51.0	51.0	51.0	51.0	56.5	56.5	56.5	56.5	56.8	56.8	56.8
Shoulder Room, rear (in.)	51.2	50.6	50.5	50.4	50.4	55.1	55.1	55.1	55.1	56.1	56.1	56.1
Hip Room, front (in.)	NA	NA	NA	NA	NA	NA	NA	NA	NA	NA	NA	NA
Hip Room, rear (in.)	NA	NA	NA	NA	NA	NA	NA	NA	NA	NA	NA	NA
Leg Room, front (in.)	42.1	42.5	42.5	42.5	42.5	43.5	43.5	43.5	43.5	43.5	43.5	43.5
Leg Room, rear (in.)	32.7	29.8	29.8	32.0	32.0	33.0	33.0	33.0	33.0	35.0	35.0	35.0
Luggage Capacity (cu. ft.)	45.0	10.3	10.3	11.5	11.5	14.9	14.9	14.9	14.9	14.9	14.9	14.9
Engine Type	L4	L4	L4	L4	L4	L4	L4	V6	V6	L4	L4	L4
Displacement (cu. in.)	97.0	79.2	79.2	79.2	79.2	132.1	132.1	182.8	182.8	132.1	132.1	132.1
Fuel System	MPFI	TBI	MPFI	TBI	TBI	EFI	EFI	EFI	EFI	EFI	EFI	EFI
Compression Ratio	9.5:1	9.5:1	10.0:1	9.5:1	9.5:1	9.5:1	9.5:1	10.5:1	10.5:1	9.5:1	9.5:1	9.5:1
BHP @ RPM (net)	95 @ 5600	70 @ 6000	100 @ 6500	70 @ 6000	70 @ 6000	130 @ 5400	130 @ 5400	188 @ 5200	188 @ 5200	130 @ 5400	130 @ 5400	130 @ 5400
Torque @ RPM (net)	98 @ 4000	74 @ 3500	83 @ 5000	74 @ 3500	74 @ 3500	145 @ 4400	145 @ 4400	203 @ 4400	203 @ 4400	145 @ 4400	145 @ 4400	145 @ 4400
Fuel Capacity (gals.)	14.5	10.6	10.6	10.5	10.5	18.5	18.5	18.5	18.5	18.5	18.5	18.5
EPA City/Hwy (mpg) —manual	23/26	37/43	28/35	37/43	37/43	22/30	NA	NA	NA	22/30	NA	NA
EPA City/Hwy (mpg) —auto	22/26	29/34	NA	29/34	29/34	21/28	21/28	18/25	18/25	21/28	21/28	21/28

TOYOTA

Specifications and EPA Mileage Ratings

Specifications and EPA Mileage Ratings	CAMRY V6 LE 4DR SDN	CAMRY V6 SE 4DR SDN	CAMRY V6 XLE 4DR SDN	CAMRY DX 4DR WGN	CAMRY LE 4DR WGN	CAMRY V6 LE 4DR WGN	CELICA ST 2DR CPE	CELICA GT 2DR CPE	CELICA ST LB	CELICA GT LB	COROLLA STD 4DR SDN	COROLLA DX 4DR SDN	COROLLA LE 4DR SDN
Length (in.)	187.8	187.8	187.8	189.4	189.4	189.4	177.0	177.0	174.0	174.0	172.0	172.0	172.0
Width (in.)	69.7	69.7	69.7	69.7	69.7	69.7	68.9	68.9	68.9	68.9	66.3	66.3	66.3
Height (in.)	55.1	55.1	55.1	56.3	56.3	56.3	51.0	51.0	50.8	50.8	53.5	53.5	53.5
Curb Weight (lbs.)	3241	3186	3274	3175	3263	3406	2395	2560	2415	2580	2315	2381	2524
Wheelbase (in.)	103.1	103.1	103.1	103.1	103.1	103.1	99.9	99.9	99.9	99.9	97.0	97.0	97.0
Track, front (in.)	61.0	61.0	61.0	61.0	61.0	61.0	59.6	59.6	59.6	59.6	57.5	57.5	57.5
Track, rear (in.)	59.0	59.0	59.0	59.1	59.1	59.1	59.6	59.6	58.9	58.9	57.1	57.1	57.1
Head Room, front (in.)	38.4	38.4	38.4	39.2	39.2	39.2	38.3	38.3	38.3	38.3	38.8	38.8	38.8
Head Room, rear (in.)	37.1	37.1	37.1	38.8	38.8	38.8	34.9	34.9	34.9	34.9	37.1	37.1	37.1
Shoulder Room, front (in.)	56.8	56.8	56.8	56.8	56.8	56.8	52.4	52.4	52.4	52.4	54.1	54.1	54.1
Shoulder Room, rear (in.)	56.1	56.1	56.1	56.0	56.0	56.0	49.9	49.9	49.9	49.9	53.5	53.5	53.5
Hip Room, front (in.)	NA	NA	NA	NA	NA	NA	NA	NA	NA	NA	NA	NA	NA
Hip Room, rear (in.)	NA	NA	NA	NA	NA	NA	NA	NA	NA	NA	NA	NA	NA
Leg Room, front (in.)	43.5	43.5	43.5	43.5	43.5	43.5	43.1	43.1	43.1	43.1	42.4	42.4	42.4
Leg Room, rear (in.)	35.0	35.0	35.0	34.7	34.7	34.7	26.6	26.6	26.6	26.6	33.0	33.0	33.0
Luggage Capacity (cu. ft.)	14.9	14.9	14.9	40.5	40.5	40.5	10.6	10.6	16.2	16.2	12.7	12.7	12.7
Engine Type	V6	V6	V6	L4	L4	V6	L4	L4	L4	L4	L4	L4	L4
Displacement (cu. in.)	182.8	182.8	182.8	132.1	132.1	182.8	107.5	132.1	107.5	132.1	96.8	107.5	107.5
Fuel System	EFI	EFI	EFI	EFI	EFI	EFI	EFI	EFI	EFI	EFI	EFI	EFI	EFI
Compression Ratio	10.5:1	10.5:1	10.5:1	9.5:1	9.5:1	10.5:1	9.5:1	9.5:1	9.5:1	9.5:1	9.5:1	9.5:1	9.5:1
BHP @ RPM (net)	188 @ 5200	188 @ 5200	188 @ 5200	130 @ 5400	130 @ 5400	188 @ 5200	110 @ 5600	135 @ 5400	110 @ 5600	135 @ 5400	105 @ 5800	115 @ 5600	115 @ 5600
Torque @ RPM (net)	203 @ 4400	203 @ 4400	203 @ 4400	145 @ 4400	145 @ 4400	203 @ 4400	115 @ 2800	145 @ 4400	115 @ 2800	145 @ 4400	100 @ 4800	115 @ 2800	115 @ 2800
Fuel Capacity (gals.)	18.5	18.5	18.5	18.5	18.5	18.5	15.9	15.9	15.9	15.9	13.2	13.2	13.2
EPA City/Hwy (mpg) —manual	NA	NA	NA	21/28	21/28	NA	27/34	23/29	27/34	23/29	27/34	27/33	27/33
EPA City/Hwy (mpg) —auto	18/25	18/25	18/25	21/28	21/28	18/25	26/32	23/30	26/32	23/30	26/29	26/33	26/33

Specifications and EPA Mileage Ratings	COROLLA DX 5DR WGN	LAND CRUISER 4DR WGN	MR2 2DR CPE	MR2 TURBO 2DR CPE	PASEO 2DR CPE	PREVIA DX VAN	PREVIA LE VAN	PREVIA DX AWD VAN	PREVIA LE AWD VAN	SUPRA BASE 2DR CPE	SUPRA TURBO 2DR CPE	TERCEL STD 2DR SDN	TERCEL DX 2DR SDN
Length (in.)	172.0	188.2	164.2	164.2	163.2	187.0	187.0	187.0	187.0	177.8	177.8	161.8	161.8
Width (in.)	66.0	76.0	66.9	66.9	65.2	70.8	70.8	70.8	70.8	71.3	71.3	64.8	64.8
Height (in.)	55.3	73.2	48.6	48.6	50.2	68.7	68.7	69.1	69.1	49.8	49.8	53.2	53.2
Curb Weight (lbs.)	2403	4762	2657	2885	2070	3610	3730	3830	3950	3215	3415	1950	1975
Wheelbase (in.)	97.0	112.2	94.5	94.5	93.7	112.8	112.8	112.8	112.8	100.4	100.4	93.7	93.7
Track, front (in.)	57.5	62.8	57.9	57.9	55.3	61.6	61.6	61.6	61.6	59.8	59.8	55.1	55.1
Track, rear (in.)	57.1	63.0	57.1	57.1	54.9	61.2	61.2	61.2	61.2	60.0	60.0	56.3	56.3
Head Room, front (in.)	38.8	40.7	37.5	37.5	37.7	39.4	39.4	39.4	39.4	37.5	37.5	38.7	38.7
Head Room, rear (in.)	39.7	36.5	NA	NA	32.0	37.8	37.8	37.8	37.8	32.9	32.9	36.7	36.7
Shoulder Room, front (in.)	54.1	58.7	54.0	54.0	53.6	61.1	61.1	61.1	61.1	54.2	54.2	53.0	53.0
Shoulder Room, rear (in.)	53.5	59.5	NA	NA	52.4	60.6	60.6	60.6	60.6	43.8	43.8	52.4	52.4
Hip Room, front (in.)	NA	NA	NA	NA	NA	56.9	56.9	56.9	56.9	NA	NA	NA	NA
Hip Room, rear (in.)	NA	NA	NA	NA	NA	57.4	57.4	57.4	57.4	NA	NA	NA	NA
Leg Room, front (in.)	42.4	42.2	43.4	43.4	41.1	40.1	40.1	40.1	40.1	44.0	44.0	41.2	41.2
Leg Room, rear (in.)	33.0	28.6	NA	NA	30.0	36.3	36.3	36.3	36.3	23.8	23.8	31.9	31.9
Luggage Capacity (cu. ft.)	31.4	75.0/91.1	6.72	6.72	7.7	33.1/157.8	33.1/157.8	33.1/157.8	33.1/157.8	10.1	10.1	10.7	10.7
Engine Type	L4	L6	L4	L4	L4	L4	L4	L4	L4	L6	L6	L4	L4
Displacement (cu. in.)	107.5	273.3	132.1	122.0	91.4	148.8	148.8	148.8	148.8	182.9	182.9	88.9	88.9
Fuel System	EFI	EFI	EFI	EFI	EFI	EFI	EFI	EFI	EFI	SEFI	SEFI	EFI	EFI
Compression Ratio	9.5:1	9.0:1	9.5:1	9.5:1	9.4:1	9.0:1	9.0:1	9.0:1	9.0:1	10.0:1	8.5:1	9.3:1	9.3:1
BHP @ RPM (net)	115 @ 5600	212 @ 4600	135 @ 5400	200 @ 6000	100 @ 6400	138 @ 5000	138 @ 5000	138 @ 5000	138 @ 5000	220 @ 5800	320 @ 5600	82 @ 5200	82 @ 5200
Torque @ RPM (net)	115 @ 2800	275 @ 3200	145 @ 4400	200 @ 3200	91 @ 3200	154 @ 4000	154 @ 4000	154 @ 4000	154 @ 4000	210 @ 4800	315 @ 4000	89 @ 4400	89 @ 4400
Fuel Capacity (gals.)	13.2	25.1	14.3	14.3	11.9	19.9	19.9	19.9	19.9	18.2	18.2	11.9	11.9
EPA City/Hwy (mpg) —manual	27/33	NA	22/29	20/27	28/34	NA	NA	NA	NA	18/23	17/23	32/36	28/34
EPA City/Hwy (mpg) —auto	26/33	12/15	21/28	NA	26/32	17/22	17/22	17/21	17/21	18/24	19/23	NA	26/29

Specifications and EPA Mileage Ratings

	TERCEL DX 4DR SDN	4RUNNER SRS V6 4DR 2WD	4RUNNER SRS 4DR 4WD	4RUNNER SRS V6 4DR 4WD	2WD TRUCK STD REG CAB	2WD TRUCK DX REG CAB	2WD TRUCK DX XTRACAB	2WD TRUCK V6 DX XTRACAB	2WD TRUCK V6 SRS XTRACAB	4WD TRUCK DX REG CAB	4WD TRUCK DX XTRACAB	4WD TRUCK V6 DX REG CAB	4WD TRUCK V6 DX XTRACAB
Length (in.)	161.8	176.6	176.6	176.6	174.4	174.4	193.1	193.1	193.1	174.6	193.1	174.6	193.1
Width (in.)	64.8	66.5	66.5	66.5	66.5	66.5	66.5	66.5	66.5	66.5	66.5	66.5	66.5
Height (in.)	53.2	66.1	66.1	66.1	60.8	60.8	61.0	61.0	61.0	60.8	61.0	67.1	67.3
Curb Weight (lbs.)	2005	4105	3825	4105	2690	2730	2970	3095	3120	3585	3540	3785	3775
Wheelbase (in.)	93.7	103.3	103.3	103.3	103.0	103.0	121.9	121.9	121.9	103.0	121.9	103.0	121.9
Track, front (in.)	55.1	56.3	56.3	56.3	53.3	53.3	53.9	53.9	53.9	56.3	56.3	56.3	56.3
Track, rear (in.)	56.3	56.1	56.1	56.1	53.9	53.9	54.3	54.3	54.3	56.1	56.1	56.1	56.1
Head Room, front (in.)	38.2	38.7	38.7	38.7	38.3	38.3	38.6	38.6	38.6	38.3	38.6	38.3	38.6
Head Room, rear (in.)	36.2	38.3	38.3	38.3	NA	NA	34.7	34.7	34.7	NA	34.7	NA	34.7
Shoulder Room, front (in.)	53.0	53.9	53.9	53.9	55.4	54.8	54.8	54.8	53.9	54.8	53.9	54.8	53.9
Shoulder Room, rear (in.)	52.2	53.9	53.9	53.9	NA	NA	55.7	55.7	55.7	NA	55.7	NA	55.7
Hip Room, front (in.)	NA	NA	NA	NA	54.5	54.3	54.5	55.7	54.1	54.3	54.1	54.3	54.1
Hip Room, rear (in.)	NA	NA	NA	NA	41.5	NA	53.2	53.2	53.4	NA	53.4	NA	53.4
Leg Room, front (in.)	41.2	41.5	41.5	41.5	41.5	41.5	43.7	43.7	43.7	41.5	43.7	41.5	43.7
Leg Room, rear (in.)	31.9	31.6	31.6	31.6	NA	NA	NA	NA	NA	NA	NA	NA	NA
Luggage Capacity (cu. ft.)	10.7	43.5/78.3	43.5/78.3	43.5/78.3	L4	L4	L4	NA	NA	L4	L4	NA	NA
Engine Type	L4	V6	L4	V6	L4	L4	L4	V6	V6	L4	L4	V6	V6
Displacement (cu. in.)	88.9	180.6	144.4	180.6	144.4	144.4	144.4	180.6	180.6	144.4	144.4	180.6	180.6
Fuel System	EFI	EFI	EFI	EFI	EFI	EFI	EFI	EFI	EFI	EFI	EFI	EFI	EFI
Compression Ratio	9.3:1	9.0:1	9.3:1	9.0:1	9.3:1	9.3:1	9.3:1	9.0:1	9.0:1	9.3:1	9.3:1	9.0:1	9.0:1
BHP @ RPM (net)	82 @ 5200	150 @ 4800	116 @ 4800	150 @ 4800	116 @ 4800	116 @ 4800	116 @ 4800	150 @ 4800	150 @ 4800	116 @ 4800	116 @ 4800	150 @ 4800	150 @ 4800
Torque @ RPM (net)	89 @ 4400	NA	140 @ 2800	NA	140 @ 2800	140 @ 2800	140 @ 2800	180 @ 3400	180 @ 3400	140 @ 2800	140 @ 2800	180 @ 3400	180 @ 3400
Fuel Capacity (gals.)	11.9	17.2	17.2	17.2	17.2	17.2	19.3	19.3	19.3	17.2	19.3	17.2	19.3
EPA City/Hwy (mpg) —manual	28/34	NA	19/22	15/18	23/28	23/28	23/28	16/21	16/21	19/22	19/22	15/18	15/18
EPA City/Hwy (mpg) —auto	26/29	17/21	NA	14/16	NA	22/25	22/25	18/23	18/23	18/19	NA	NA	13/17

Specifications and EPA Mileage Ratings	JETTA III GLX 4DR SDN	JETTA III GLS 4 DR SDN	JETTA III GL 4DR SDN	GOLF III 4DR	GOLF III 2DR	CORRADO SLC 2DR CPE	1-TON TRUCK DX 2WD V6	T100 TRUCK SR5 4WD V6	T100 TRUCK DX 4WD V6	T100 TRUCK SR5 2WD V6	T100 TRUCK DX 2WD V6	4WD TRUCK V6 SR5 XTRACAB
Length (in.)	173.4	173.4	173.4	160.5	160.5	159.4	209.1	209.1	209.1	209.1	209.1	193.1
Width (in.)	66.7	66.7	66.7	66.7	66.7	66.5	75.2	75.2	75.2	75.2	75.2	66.5
Height (in.)	56.2	56.1	56.1	56.2	56.2	51.9	66.7	70.1	70.1	66.7	66.7	67.3
Curb Weight (lbs.)	2915	2647	2647	2577	2511	2808	3490	3910	3875	3450	3400	3815
Wheelbase (in.)	97.4	97.4	97.4	97.4	97.4	97.2	121.8	121.8	121.8	121.8	121.8	121.9
Track, front (in.)	57.1	57.6	57.6	57.6	57.6	57.2	61.8	63.6	63.6	61.6	61.6	56.3
Track, rear (in.)	56.0	56.9	56.9	56.9	56.9	56.4	64.0	63.7	63.7	63.7	63.7	56.1
Head Room, front (in.)	37.5	39.2	39.2	39.2	39.2	37.0	39.6	39.6	39.6	39.6	39.6	38.6
Head Room, rear (in.)	37.3	37.3	37.3	37.4	37.4	35.0	NA	NA	NA	NA	NA	34.7
Shoulder Room, front (in.)	53.8	53.8	53.8	53.8	54.0	53.8	62.4	62.4	62.4	62.4	62.4	54.8
Shoulder Room, rear (in.)	52.8	52.8	52.8	52.8	54.6	50.4	NA	NA	NA	NA	NA	55.7
Hip Room, front (in.)	53.2	53.2	53.2	53.2	52.8	52.8	NA	NA	NA	NA	NA	54.5
Hip Room, rear (in.)	52.3	52.3	52.3	52.3	51.9	44.5	NA	NA	NA	NA	NA	53.4
Leg Room, front (in.)	42.3	42.3	42.3	42.3	42.3	41.7	42.4	42.4	42.4	42.4	42.4	43.7
Leg Room, rear (in.)	31.5	31.5	31.5	31.5	31.5	31.2	NA	NA	NA	NA	NA	NA
Luggage Capacity (cu. ft.)	15.0	15.0	15.0	16.9	17.5	15.3	NA	NA	NA	NA	NA	NA
Engine Type	L6	L4	L4	L4	L4	L6	V6	V6	V6	V6	V6	V6
Displacement (cu. in.)	170.0	121.0	121.0	121.0	121.0	170.0	180.6	180.6	180.6	180.6	180.6	180.6
Fuel System	SPFI	SPFI	SPFI	SPFI	SPFI	SPFI	EFI	EFI	EFI	EFI	EFI	EFI
Compression Ratio	10.0:1	10.0:1	10.0:1	10.0:1	10.0:1	10.0:1	9.0:1	9.0:1	9.0:1	9.0:1	9.0:1	9.0:1
BHP @ RPM (net)	172 @ 5800	115 @ 5400	115 @ 5400	115 @ 5400	115 @ 5400	178 @ 5800	150 @ 4800	150 @ 4800	150 @ 4800	150 @ 4800	150 @ 4800	150 @ 4800
Torque @ RPM (net)	177 @ 4200	122 @ 3200	122 @ 3200	122 @ 3200	122 @ 3200	177 @ 4200	180 @ 3400	180 @ 3400	180 @ 3400	180 @ 3400	180 @ 3400	180 @ 3400
Fuel Capacity (gals.)	14.5	14.5	14.5	14.5	14.5	18.5	24.3	24.3	24.3	24.3	24.3	19.3
EPA City/Hwy (mpg) —manual	18/25	23/31	23/31	24/31	24/31	18/24	16/21	15/18	15/18	16/21	16/21	15/18
EPA City/Hwy (mpg) —auto	17/25	21/27	21/27	21/28	21/28	18/25	16/20	17/17	17/17	16/20	16/20	13/17

VOLKSWAGEN

Specifications and EPA Mileage Ratings	PASSAT GLX 4DR SDN	PASSAT GLX 4DR WGN	850 4DR SDN LEVEL I	850 4DR SDN LEVEL II	850 4DR WGN LEVEL II	850 TURBO 4DR SDN	850 TURBO 4DR WGN	940 4DR SDN LEVEL I	940 4DR WGN LEVEL I	940 4DR SDN LEVEL II	940 4DR WGN LEVEL II	960 4DR SDN LEVEL II
Length (in.)	180.0	179.9	183.5	183.5	185.4	183.5	185.4	191.7	189.3	191.7	189.3	191.7
Width (in.)	67.1	67.1	69.3	69.3	69.3	69.3	69.3	69.3	69.3	69.3	69.3	69.3
Height (in.)	56.2	58.7	55.7	55.7	55.7	55.7	55.7	55.5	56.5	55.5	56.5	55.5
Curb Weight (lbs.)	3152	3197	3180	3180	3300	3280	3400	3205	3280	3260	3340	3490
Wheelbase (in.)	103.3	103.3	104.9	104.9	104.9	104.9	104.9	109.1	109.1	109.1	109.1	109.1
Track, front (in.)	58.4	58.4	59.8	59.8	59.8	59.8	59.8	57.5	57.9	57.5	57.9	57.5
Track, rear (in.)	56.2	56.2	57.9	57.9	57.9	57.9	57.9	57.5	57.5	57.5	57.5	57.5
Head Room, front (in.)	37.6	38.0	39.1	38.0	38.0	38.0	38.0	38.6	38.6	38.6	38.6	38.6
Head Room, rear (in.)	37.4	39.0	37.8	37.3	37.3	37.3	37.3	37.1	37.6	37.1	37.6	37.1
Shoulder Room, front (in.)	55.2	55.2	57.1	57.1	57.1	57.1	57.1	56.4	56.4	56.4	56.4	56.4
Shoulder Room, rear (in.)	53.9	53.9	56.3	56.3	56.3	56.3	56.3	56.4	56.4	56.4	56.4	56.4
Hip Room, front (in.)	52.8	52.8	55.2	55.2	55.2	55.2	55.2	54.7	54.7	54.7	54.7	54.7
Hip Room, rear (in.)	53.9	53.9	55.2	55.2	55.2	55.2	55.2	54.7	54.7	54.7	54.7	54.7
Leg Room, front (in.)	43.6	43.6	41.4	41.4	41.4	41.4	41.4	41.0	41.0	41.0	41.0	41.0
Leg Room, rear (in.)	35.3	35.3	32.3	32.3	35.2	32.3	35.2	34.7	34.7	34.7	34.7	34.7
Luggage Capacity (cu. ft.)	14.4	34.3	14.7	14.7	37.1/67.0	14.7	37.1/67.0	16.6	39.3/74.9	16.6	39.3/74.9	16.6
Engine Type	L6	L6	L5	L5	L5	L5	L5	L4	L4	L4	L4	L6
Displacement (cu. in.)	170.0	170.0	148.6	148.6	148.6	141.5	141.5	141.3	141.3	141.3	141.3	178.3
Fuel System	SPFI	SPFI	FI	FI	FI	FI	FI	FI	FI	FI	FI	FI
Compression Ratio	10.0:1	10.0:1	10.5:1	10.5:1	10.5:1	8.5:1	8.5:1	9.8:1	9.8:1	8.7:1	8.7:1	10.7:1
BHP @ RPM (net)	172 @ 5800	172 @ 5800	168 @ 6200	168 @ 6200	168 @ 6200	222 @ 5200	222 @ 5200	114 @ 5400	114 @ 5400	162 @ 4800	162 @ 4800	201 @ 6000
Torque @ RPM (net)	177 @ 4200	177 @ 4200	162 @ 3300	162 @ 3300	162 @ 3300	221 @ 2100	221 @ 2100	136 @ 2150	136 @ 2150	195 @ 3450	195 @ 3450	197 @ 4300
Fuel Capacity (gals.)	18.5	18.5	19.3	19.3	19.3	19.3	19.3	19.8	19.8	19.8	19.8	21.8
EPA City/Hwy (mpg) —manual	18/25	18/25	20/28	20/28	20/28	NA	NA	NA	NA	NA	NA	NA
EPA City/Hwy (mpg) —auto	18/25	18/25	20/27	20/27	20/27	19/26	19/26	19/27	19/27	19/24	19/24	17/25

VOLVO

Specifications and EPA Mileage Ratings	960 4DR SDN LEVEL II	960 4DR WGN LEVEL II
Length (in.)	191.7	189.3
Width (in.)	69.3	69.3
Height (in.)	55.5	56.5
Curb Weight (lbs.)	3490	3460
Wheelbase (in.)	109.1	109.1
Track, front (in.)	57.9	57.9
Track, rear (in.)	57.5	57.5
Head Room, front (in.)	38.6	38.6
Head Room, rear (in.)	37.1	37.6
Shoulder Room, front (in.)	56.4	56.4
Shoulder Room, rear (in.)	56.4	56.4
Hip Room, front (in.)	54.7	54.7
Hip Room, rear (in.)	54.7	54.7
Leg Room, front (in.)	41.0	41.0
Leg Room, rear (in.)	34.7	34.7
Luggage Capacity (cu. ft.)	16.6	39.3/74.9
Engine Type	L6	L6
Displacement (cu. in.)	178.3	178.3
Fuel System	FI	FI
Compression Ratio	10.7:1	10.7:1
BHP @ RPM (net)	201 @ 6000	201 @ 6000
Torque @ RPM (net)	197 @ 4300	197 @ 4300
Fuel Capacity (gals.)	21.8	19.8
EPA City/Hwy (mpg) —manual	NA	NA
EPA City/Hwy (mpg) —auto	17/25	17/25

These are programs offered by the manufacturers to increase the sales of slow-selling models or to reduce excess inventories. While the manufacturer's rebates are passed directly on to the buyer, dealer incentives are passed on only to the dealer—who may or may not elect to pass the savings on to the customer.

The following incentives and rebates were in effect at time of publication. Please note, however, that these programs often change frequently.

For updated information regarding Dealer Incentives and Manufacturer's Rebates, call Nationwide Auto Brokers, Inc. at **313-559-6661**.

Dealer Incentives
Manufacturer Rebates

	DEALER INCENTIVE ($)	MFG'S REBATE ($)
AUDI		
90 (1993)	1500	
100 (1993)	1750	
COLT		
Colt 2-Dr		300
Colt 4-Dr		500
Colt Vista		300
GEO		
Metro		300
HYUNDAI		
Elantra		500
Excel		250
Scoupe		250
Sonata		1000
ISUZU		
Pickup	400-1100	
Rodeo 4WD	750	
Trooper	1000	
MAZDA		
Base Pickup	500	
Other Pickups	200	
Protege		1000
MITSUBISHI		
Diamante		1000-1200
Eclipse		700
Expo/Expo LRV	500	
Mirage	250	500
Pickup		800-1200
NISSAN		
Maxima GXE	1000	
Pickup	500-1000	
Pathfinder	500	
Sentra	400	
SUBARU		
Justy (1993)		1000
Legacy (1993)	2500-3000	
TOYOTA		
Corolla w/o Value Pkg	400	
T100 Pickup	1500-1900	
Base Pickup	600-1000	
Other Pickups	200-600	
Tercel	300-700	

Buying your next New Car

Every new car buyer has but one thought in mind — to save money by getting a "good deal". Your goal should be to pay 2-4% over the dealer cost, not the 10-12% the dealer wants you to pay. Use the following guide to help you plan your new car purchases:

Step 1 Choose the make, model and accessories you want.

Step 2 Visit a local dealership to test drive the model you intend to buy. Pay special attention to all-around visibility, convenience of controls, seating comfort, steering response, handling acceleration and braking.

Step 3 Once you've decided on a particular model, check with your insurance company to make sure the cost of insuring the vehicle falls within your budget.

Step 4 Contact your bank or credit union to obtain loan-rate information. Later on, you can compare their arrangement with the dealer's financing plan.

Step 5 Use the information in this book to determine the dealer's actual cost. To do this:

—total the Dealer column costs for the model and accessories you want

—add the destination charge and advertising fee to this amount

—add to the dealer's cost what you think is a reasonable dealer profit. (On most Imports, a reasonable amount is $300-$800 – this excludes "hot selling models" or very expensive cars which will command a higher dealer profit) *This sum represents the dealer's cost.*

Step 6 Bargain for the best price – visit several dealerships. The dealer who comes closest to your "target price" should get your business. Be sure that the dealer's price quote will be your final cost. Beware of dealer charges! When you buy a car, you should be buying the car – not the extras. Don't be coerced into buying items such as rustproofing, undercoating, extended warranties, etc., unless you really want them.

Step 7 Deduct any manufacturer's rebates/dealer incentives from your final cost.

Step 8 If your present car will be used as a "trade-in" now is the time to deduct the dealer's appraised value. (It's often better to sell your "trade-in" privately. You'll get a better price than the wholesale price a dealer will offer you).

Step 9 Add applicable state and/or local taxes.

Edmund's STEP-BY-STEP COSTING FORM

MAKE: _____

MODEL: _____

BODY STYLE: _____

EXTERIOR COLOR: _____

INTERIOR COLOR: _____

TOP COLOR (IF APPL.) _____

ITEMS	DEALER COST	LIST PRICE	BEST DEAL
Basic Model Price Only			
Optional Equipment			
1.			
2.			
3.			
4.			
5.			
6.			
7.			
8.			
9.			
10.			
11.			
12.			
13.			
14.			
15.			
16.			
17.			
18.			
19.			
20.			
Dealer Advertising Amount			
Dealer Preparation Amount			
Initial Gas & Oil			
Freight Amount (to your area)			
TOTAL COST —*Excluding Local Sales Tax, Registration & Inspection Fees*			

Edmund's STEP-BY-STEP COSTING FORM

MAKE: _____   EXTERIOR COLOR: _____

MODEL: _____   INTERIOR COLOR: _____

BODY STYLE: _____   TOP COLOR (IF APPL.) _____

ITEMS	DEALER COST	LIST PRICE	BEST DEAL
Basic Model Price Only			
Optional Equipment			
1.			
2.			
3.			
4.			
5.			
6.			
7.			
8.			
9.			
10.			
11.			
12.			
13.			
14.			
15.			
16.			
17.			
18.			
19.			
20.			
Dealer Advertising Amount			
Dealer Preparation Amount			
Initial Gas & Oil			
Freight Amount (to your area)			
TOTAL COST —*Excluding Local Sales Tax, Registration & Inspection Fees*			

KEEPING YOUR CAR BEAUTIFUL

PROPER WASHING AND WAXING TECHNIQUES

Frequent washing and waxing of your car can keep the finish looking like new and also instills a sense of pride in you. You look and feel better when you're driving a shiny car.

Washing your car yourself weekly is also great preventative maintenance. It allows you to get up close and personal with your car. At such close range it is easy to spot any nicks in the paint, an insect-clogged radiator, or uneven tire wear.

There are three methods of washing your car — at home, a coin-operated car wash and an automatic car wash.

Washing your car in your driveway looks to be the cheapest. But in the terms of water usage, it might be the most expensive.

According to the car wash industry, the typical driveway car wash uses from 90 to 150 gallons of water. An automatic car wash uses up to 32 gallons and the coin-operated wash is the most water efficient at 16 gallons.

WASHING A CAR AT HOME

Washing your car in your driveway on a Saturday afternoon is as American as mom, baseball and apple pie. Here's how to do it right.

First off, always use a nozzle that shuts off when the trigger is released. This feature can save more than 100 gallons of precious water. In addition, these nozzles also boost water pressure to enhance the cleaning action.

Always use a soap product specifically designed for washing cars. These products soften hard water to reduce water spotting and will not strip off wax like household cleaners.

Park the vehicle in the shade, again to reduce water spotting. Next, wet the entire surface with plain water, going over the lower body panels twice. This rinses away the loose surface dirt and grime and softens any remaining debris. Make sure to spray under the wheel wells to knock down any accumulated dirt.

Next, with your bucket of special car soap solution, wash from the top of the car and work down using a circular motion. Rinse the washing cloth frequently to flush out any grime and grit that could scratch the paint.

When the entire car has been soaped up, immediately rinse with plenty of water. Do not allow the soap to dry on the car.

After the car has been thoroughly rinsed, use a chamois to wipe off and dry the exterior. A terrycloth towel, or old cotton T-shirt also works well. For either washing, drying or waxing cloths, do not use cloths with synthetic materials that contain abrasive fibers that can scratch the paint.

Any road tar or insects that survived the car washing process can easily be removed by spraying WD-40 on the area. Remember to wash any area that has been sprayed with WD-40 as it tends to attract dust and dirt.

USING A COIN-OPERATED CAR WASH

A coin-operated car wash can be the best "green" car wash, using the least amount of water when compared to washing a car at home or at an automatic car wash. A facility that recycles its water will save even more precious water.

The best coin-op washes have a brush and spray wand at every stall. With the spray wand wet the car's surface with plain water, going over the lower body panels twice. Next, select the brush and the soap setting and use a circular motion to wash every section of the exterior. Before using the brush, run your hand over the bristles to make sure it is free of any abrasive grit that could scratch the finish.

Then, go back to the wand, select rinse and rinse all the soap off the car. Using a coin-op car wash can be a race against time, however, it is false economy to skimp on a few quarters if the time runs out and soap still remains on the car.

After rinsing you can opt for the wax setting. The wax used by coin-op facilities is a fine liquid and offers some protection, but not the level of a paste or creamy liquid wax that is applied by hand.

After the car is completely rinsed, dry it with a chamois or a cotton terrycloth towel or old T-shirt.

Some final coin-op tips: If there is not someone waiting behind you, dry the car in the shade of the stall to prevent water spotting. And if you have a choice of stalls, always choice the stall closest the pump room, which will have more pressure.

USING AN AUTOMATIC CAR WASH

You don't have to touch anything to have your car washed at an automatic car wash. It costs more, but for many it is worth it.

What you should do is make sure the facility has the latest "brushless" systems that are gentle on a car's finish. Also make sure your vehicle's wheels are not too wide for the car wash track. Check if any radio or cellular telephone antennas need to be removed or lowered.

Automatic car washes are ideal to use when it's too cold or wet to wash a car by hand, but you want to remove any winter slush or road salt.

Many automatic car wash facilities have special rates for customers that have their vehicles washed on a weekly schedule.

WAXING A CAR

You'll know it is time to wax your car when during your weekly car wash, or when it rains, water droplets no longer bead up.

The beading up test is the best indicator of when it is time to apply wax again. Depending on the type and brand of wax, if the car is kept in the garage and its usage, the time to wax could range from three months to one year.

Most late-model cars and nearly all new cars have a clear-coat paint finish. With a clear coat, a color coat is painted and is then sealed by a clear coat of acrylic resin, polyurethane or powder paint.

The clear coat adds a high gloss and protects the color coat, making for a highly durable and bright finish.

However, a clear-coat finish still needs a periodic waxing to protect the finish and remove dulling deposits. Since an older-style wax with abrasives could scratch a clear-coat finish, use only waxes with labels that clearly state they are recommended for a clear-coat finish.

The first step in waxing a car is to prepare the surface. Do this by a thorough washing of the exterior, including removing any road tar or insects. Again, WD-40 works great on tar and bugs.

Next use a damp, cotton cloth to apply the wax. Work on a small, two-square-foot area at one time. Apply the wax lightly in a circular motion and cover the working area. When it dries to a haze, or turns powdery, get a second clear, soft, cotton cloth and buff the area to a shine. Frequently turn the cloth over to prevent wax build-up.

A creamy liquid wax is the easiest to apply, but generally is not as durable as a paste wax. With either type of wax, applying more than one coat of wax is a waste of energy. Car wax does not build up layer by layer.

FINAL TOUCHES

A car wash and wax job is not complete until the windows have been cleaned inside and out with glass cleaner, the chrome brightened up with chrome cleaner and the tires and rubber trim treated with a rubber, vinyl, leather treatment like Armor All.

Such vinyl and leather protective sprays also work well on the interior components like the seats, dash and dashboard. But avoid getting them on the glasswork, as the silicone in some products can damage the window tint film. It's easy enough apply the solution on a clean cloth and then wipe the interior pieces near any glass.

For cloth interiors, spraying a treatment like Scotchgard can protect the fabric and make it easier to clean off any future accidents.

Carpets can be treated like the carpets in your home. Vacuum regularly and use a carpet shampoo when more heavy duty cleaning and spot removal is needed. Rubber or fabric sisal or coco mats can protect the carpets from wearing through.

Any exterior nicks or scratches in the paint could be refinished with touch-up paint to prevent rust from occurring.

Touch-up paint, available in your vehicle's exact factory color, is available at auto parts stores and from new car dealers. Following the simple instructions on the package will not insure a perfect match. The difference in color often is caused by the natural fading your original paint job has done throughout the years.

AUTO DETAILING

Spoil your car. Don't just wash it, have it "detailed."

Detailing—sort of a beauty spa for cars—is catching on throughout the nation. Steve's Detail, Ming, Beverly Hills Detailing and Tidy Car are among the national franchises that the growing industry has spawned. In addition, there are independent detailers that work out of small shops, home garages or from mobile units.

However, compared to a bucket of soapy water and a Saturday afternoon, spoiling your car does not come cheap. A complete auto detail—interior, exterior, trunk and engine compartment—can cost $100 and up.

Surprisingly, even at triple-digit prices, many motorists are opting for the super cleaning and polishing of detailing.

The growth of detailing has paralleled the escalating price of new cars. Making your old car "like new" is much cheaper than buying a new car.

While the franchises and independents all claim to have a superior technique, all detailing firms do basically the same services in a complete job:

- Hand wash exterior.
- Vacuum and shampoo interior and trunk.
- Apply leather-vinyl treatment to interior.
- Remove any oxidized paint.
- Wax and-or buff exterior.
- Polish chrome and wheels.
- Pressure clean engine compartment.
- Clean and apply dressing on tires.
- Clean windows inside and out.

Other optional services offered at most detail shops include undercoating, pinstriping, installing vinyl moldings, hand car washes and tinting windows.

AUTO BODY WORK AND PAINTING

If you have a unibody car that has been damaged in an accident, have it repaired only by a repair shop that has a unibody frame machine.

With the emphasis on maximum fuel economy, auto engineers lightened vehicles by adopting "frameless" unibody construction. With unibody construction the body panels serve to locate and support major components, including the suspension, engine and transmission.

"This industry is changing so fast, if you don't keep up with it, it'll just leave you behind," said Don Wood, an instructor for the Inter-Industry Conference on Auto Collision Repair. "I don't like calling them bodymen any more, they're technicians."

Wood said 80 percent of the cars on the road and in body shops today are unibodies. "It's going to be 100 percent pretty soon," he said.

Damage to a car with a separate frame is often limited to cosmetic body work that would not affect the safety or strength of the vehicle. With a unibody, body damage often affects the strength and location of key suspension components.

The non-profit repair conference, called I-Car, was formed in 1979 for the purpose of developing proper techniques and training materials on auto collision repairs. Member groups include auto insurance firms, dismantlers, toolmakers and automakers including Ford Motor Co., General Motors Corp. and Toyota Motor Sales.

In nationwide courses, I-Car certifies auto body workers who have graduated from the training.

The curriculum includes learning the proper setup of a frame machine that literally pulls the damaged vehicle into proper position. The unit uses factory alignment points to bring the vehicle back into specifications. A frame machine, said Wood, could cost up to $40,000. "A lot of small shops don't have the equipment," he said. "A lot of small shops send out their frame work."

In addition to body shop personnel, Wood said insurance adjusters also attend the I-Car classes.

"They've got to know how to repair these cars when they're writing these estimates," he said.

Paint techniques and equipment have also gone through massive changes. The changes have been partly due to new advances in painting and also new emission regulations for the auto painting industry.

With auto painting, you get what you pay for. A better paint job costs more money. The difference between a $99.95 paint job and a $2,500 one is preparation, better materials and much higher quality standards.

If you want a factory-like paint job, seek out a paint shop with a heated "downdraft" paint booth.

According to Wood, factory finishes are applied to empty body shells at approximately 278 degrees, impossible to duplicate outside of the factory because a roadworthy car's components including tires, interior and electronics, cannot withstand such high temperatures.

However, with a $50,000 heated booth, the car is painted and then the temperature is raised up to 120 degrees. The high temperature allows the paint to "reflow" and smooth out, resulting in a smoother finish. In addition, normal drying time is cut from four hours to just one hour.

"The faster you get the car to dry, the less dirt you have in it," said Wood.

The downdraft booth also eliminates much of the dirt and impurities by managing the air flow in the booth to bypass the freshly painted vehicle.

Wood said a downdraft booth also lends itself well to new emission standards that seriously limit the volume of contaminates produced in the painting process. New low-volume spray guns also reduce auto painting emissions by putting more paint on the vehicle with less overspray.

Excerpt from the book The Ultimate Owner's Manual, *copyright ©1991 by Edmund Publications Corporation. The book is available for $8.95 plus $3.00 shipping/handling, from Edmund's Publication, 300 N. Sepulveda Blvd., Suite 2050, El Segundo, CA 90245*

Edmund's CLASSIFIED ADS

To Place a Classified Ad

Standard Rate:
  $5.00 per word.
  20 word minimum.
Bold Face Type:
  add $1.00 per word.
Borders:
  $25.00 per column inch.
Classified Display:
  $125 per column inch

Counting Words: Two initials, abbreviations, numerals and symbols are counted as one word. Telephone number including area code and zip codes are one word. (Zip code must appear in every ad with an address). Multiple name cities are counted as one word. Normal punctuation is no charge.

Payment must be received with copy. Check, Money Order, MasterCard or Visa accepted.
Payment:
❑ Check or Money Order
❑ Visa
❑ MasterCard
❑ P.O. No._____

Credit Card # _____ Expires ____

Cardholder Name: ____

Signature ____

Call 407-767-0557 or fax 407-767-6583 or mail to: P.O. Box 1139, Longwood, FL 32752

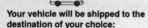

Edmund's

To help us improve the information content of our books,
please complete this questionnaire and mail to:

Edmund Publications Corporation
300 N. Sepulveda Blvd., Suite 2050
El Segundo, Ca 90245

1. **Where did you purchase this Edmund's Book?**
   ❏ BOOKSTORE   ❏ NEWSSTAND   ❏ OTHER

2. **How many times have you purchased editions of Edmund's USED CAR PRICES books?**
   ❏ ONCE   ❏ TWICE   ❏ THREE TIMES   ❏ FOUR TIMES OR MORE

3. **What is your vehicle preference?**
   CHECK ONE: ❏ AMERICAN   ❏ IMPORT
   CHECK ONE OR MORE: ❏ CAR   ❏ VAN   ❏ TRUCK   ❏ SPORTS UTILITY

4. **What is your budget/price for buying a new vehicle?**
   ❏ UNDER $10,000   ❏ $10 - 15,000   ❏ $15 - 20,000   ❏ $20 - 30,000
   ❏ $30 -40,000   ❏ $40,00 AND UP

5. **Which Edmund's NEW VEHICLE PRICE GUIDES have you purchased in the past?**
   ❏ AMERICAN CARS   ❏ IMPORTS   ❏ VAN, PICKUP, SPORTS UTILITY   ❏ ECONOMY

6. **Would you like to use a computerized version of Edmund's Price Guides?**
   ❏ NO   YES FOR: ❏ IBM PC   ❏ WINDOWS   ❏ MACINTOSH

ANY COMMENTS: _____

_____

_____

To be advised directly of special offers from Edmund's, please complete the following. Thank you.

NAME _____

ADDRESS _____

CITY, STATE, ZIP _____

TELEPHONE _____
                                                    12703

Edmund's SINGLE COPIES / ORDER FORM

Please send me:

❑ **USED CAR PRICES** *(includes S&H)* ....$ 8.25

❑ **NEW CAR PRICES** *(includes S&H)*...$ 7.25

❑ **VAN, PICKUP, SPORT UTILITY BUYER'S GUIDE** *(includes S&H)*....$ 7.25

❑ **IMPORT CAR PRICES** *((includes S&H)* ....$ 7.25

❑ **ECONOMY CAR BUYING GUIDE** *(includes S&H)*...........................$ 8.25

Name _____

Address _____

City, State, Zip _____

Phone _____

I2703

PAYMENT: ❑ MASTERCARD ❑ VISA ❑ CHECK or MONEY ORDER $_____

Make check or money order payable to:

Edmund Publications Corporation, *P.O. Box 338, Shrub Oak, NY 10588*

For more information or to order by phone, call (914) 962-6297

Credit Card # _____   Exp. Date: _____

CardHolder Name _____   Signature _____

Prices above are for shipping within the U.S. and Canada only. Other countries please add $5.00 to the cover price per book (via air mail) and $2.00 to the cover price per book (surface mail). Please pay through an American Bank or with American currency. Rates subject to change without notice.

Edmund's SUBSCRIPTIONS / ORDER FORM

Please send me a one-year subscription for:

☐ **USED CAR PRICES** *(includes bulk rate shipping/handling)* .... **$ 29.75**
CANADA $37.25/FOREIGN COUNTRIES $53.75 *(includes air mail shipping/handling)*
now 6 issues instead of 4

☐ **NEW CAR PRICES** *(includes bulk rate shipping/handling)* .... **$ 15.00**
CANADA $18.75/FOREIGN COUNTRIES $27.00 *(includes air mail shipping/handling)*
3 issues per year

☐ **VAN, PICKUP, SPORTS UTILITY** *(includes bulk rate shipping/handling)* .... **$ 15.00**
CANADA $18.75/FOREIGN COUNTRIES $27.00 *(includes air mail shipping/handling)*
3 issues per year

☐ **IMPORT CAR PRICES** *(includes bulk rate shipping/handling)* .... **$ 15.00**
CANADA $18.75/FOREIGN COUNTRIES $27.00 *(includes air mail shipping/handling)*
3 issues per year

☐ **NEW VEHICLE PRICES** *(includes bulk rate shipping/handling)* .... **$ 55.00**
CANADA $68.75/FOREIGN COUNTRIES $99.00 *(includes air mail shipping/handling)*
- includes the complete automotive market of new vehicles - 11books:

- 3 NEW CAR PRICES (Domestic)
- 3 IMPORT CAR PRICES
- 3 VAN, PICKUP, SPORT UTILITY
- 2 ECONOMY CAR BUYING GUIDE

☐ **NEW & USED CAR PRICES** *(includes bulk rate shipping/handling)* .... **$ 59.75**
CANADA $74.75/FOREIGN COUNTRIES $107.75 *(includes air mail shipping/handling)*
12 books:

- 6 USED CAR PRICES
- 3 NEW CAR PRICES (Domestic)
- 3 IMPORT CAR PRICES

☐ **PREMIUM SUBSCRIPTION** *(includes bulk rate shipping/handling)* .... **$ 84.75**
CANADA $106.00/FOREIGN COUNTRIES $152.75 *(includes air mail shipping/handling)*
- includes all of the above - 17 books:

- 6 USED CAR PRICES
- 3 NEW CAR PRICES (Domestic)
- 3 IMPORT CAR PRICES
- 3 VAN, PICKUP, SPORT UTILITY
- 2 ECONOMY CAR BUYING GUIDE

Name _____

Address _____ Phone _____

City, State, Zip _____

PAYMENT: ☐ MASTERCARD   ☐ VISA   ☐ CHECK or MONEY ORDER —AMOUNT $_____
Make check or money order payable to: **Edmund Publications Corporation,**
P. O. Box 338, Shrub Oak, NY 10588   *Rates subject to change without notice.*

Credit Card # _____   Exp. Date: _____

Cardholder Name: _____   Signature: _____

12703

Edmund's

SCHEDULED RELEASE DATES FOR 1993/94*

VOL. 27/28		RELEASE DATE	COVER DATE
U2801	USED CAR PRICES	JAN 94	MAR 94
N2801	NEW CAR PRICES [Domestic]	FEB 94	JUN 94
S2801	VAN, PICKUP, SPORT UTILITY BUYER'S GUIDE	FEB 94	JUN 94
I2801	IMPORT CAR PRICES	MAR 94	JUL 94
E2801	ECONOMY CAR BUYER'S GUIDE	FEB 94	JUN 94
U2802	USED CAR PRICES	MAR 94	MAY 94
N2802	NEW CAR PRICES [Domestic]	MAY 94	NOV 94
S2802	VAN, PICKUP, SPORT UTILITY BUYER'S GUIDE	MAY 94	NOV 94
U2803	USED CAR PRICES	MAY 94	JUL 94
I2802	IMPORT CAR PRICES	JUN 94	DEC 94
E2802	ECONOMY CAR BUYER'S GUIDE	JUN 94	OCT 94
U2804	USED CAR PRICES	JUL 94	SEP 94
U2805	USED CAR PRICES	SEP 94	NOV 94
N2803	NEW CAR PRICES [Domestic]	NOV 94	FEB 95
S2803	VAN, PICKUP, SPORT UTILITY BUYER'S GUIDE	NOV 94	FEB 95
U2806	USED CAR PRICES	NOV 94	JAN 95
I2803	IMPORT CAR PRICES	DEC 94	APR 95

*Subject to Change